Lecture Notes in Computer Science 3145

Commenced Publication in 1973
Founding and Former Series Editors:
Gerhard Goos, Juris Hartmanis, and Jan van Leeuwen

Phil Trinder   Greg Michaelson
Ricardo Peña (Eds.)

Implementation of Functional Languages

15th International Workshop, IFL 2003
Edinburgh, UK, September 8-11, 2003
Revised Papers

 Springer

Volume Editors

Phil Trinder
Greg Michaelson
Heriot-Watt University
School of Mathematical and Computer Sciences
Riccarton, EH14 4AS, UK
E-mail: {trinder, greg}@macs.hw.ac.uk

Ricardo Peña
Universidad Complutense de Madrid
Facultad de Informática
Departamento Sistemas Informáticos y Programación
C/ Juan del Rosal, 8, 28040 Madrid, Spain
E-mail: ricardo@sip.ucm.es

Library of Congress Control Number: 2004114139

CR Subject Classification (1998): D.3, D.1.1, F.3

ISSN 0302-9743
ISBN 3-540-23727-5 Springer Berlin Heidelberg New York

Springer is a part of Springer Science+Business Media

springeronline.com

© Springer-Verlag Berlin Heidelberg 2004
Printed in Germany

Typesetting: Camera-ready by author, data conversion by Olgun Computergrafik
Printed on acid-free paper   SPIN: 11342205   06/3142   5 4 3 2 1 0

Preface

Functional programming has a long history, reaching back through early realizations in languages like LISP to foundational theories of computing, in particular λ-calculus and recursive function theory. In turn, functional programming has had wide influence in computing, both through developments within the discipline, such as formal semantics, polymorphic type checking, lazy evaluation and structural proof, and as a practical embodiment of formalized approaches, such as specification, transformation and partial application.

One of the engaging features of functional programming is precisely the crossover between theory and practice. In particular, it is regarded as essential that all aspects of functional programming are appropriately formalized, especially the specification and implementation of functional languages. Thus, specialist functional programming events like the International Workshop on the Implementation of Functional Languages (IFL) attract contributions where strong use is made of syntactic, semantic and meta-mathematical formalisms to motivate, justify and underpin very practical software systems.

IFL grew out of smaller workshops aimed at practitioners wrestling with the nuts and bolts of making concrete implementations of highly abstract languages. Functional programming has always been bedeviled by an unwarranted reputation for slow and inefficient implementations. IFL is one venue where such problems are tackled head on, always using formal techniques to justify practical implementations.

The 15th International Workshop on the Implementation of Functional Languages (IFL 2003) was held in Edinburgh, Scotland from the 8th to the 11th of September, 2003. Forty-two people attended the workshop, with participants from Australia, Germany, The Netherlands, Hungary, Ireland, Russia, Spain, Sweden and the USA, as well as from the UK.

There were 32 presentations at IFL 2003, in streams on testing, compilation and implementation, applications, language constructs and programming, types and program analysis, concurrency and parallelism, and language interfacing. Twenty-eight papers were submitted for the draft proceedings. After refereeing, 12 papers were selected for publication in these proceedings, an acceptance rate of 42%.

The Programme Committee was pleased to award the 2nd Peter Landin Prize for the best IFL paper to Pedro Vasconcelos, first author of *Inferring Costs for Recursive, Polymorphic and Higher-Order Functional Programs*[1].

The 16th International Workshop on the Implementation and Application of Functional Languages will be held in Lübeck, Germany in September 2004. For further details, please see: http://www.isp.uni-luebeck.de/ifl04/index.htm .

---

[1] Co-author Kevin Hammond honorably declined to share the prize as he was associated with its establishment.

Acknowledgments

IFL 2003 was organized by the Department of Computer Science, School of Mathematical and Computer Sciences, Heriot-Watt University.

We would like to thank June Maxwell and Christine Mackenzie for their most able workshop administration and financial arrangements. We would also like to thank Andre Rauber Du Bois for wrangling the WWW site, and Abyd Al Zain and Jann Nystrom for workshop gophering.

We are pleased to acknowledge the sponsorship of the British Computer Society Formal Aspects of Computing Special Interest Group.

May 2004   Phil Trinder, Greg Michaelson and Ricardo Peña

Programme Committee

Thomas Arts	IT-University in Gothenburg, Sweden
Clemens Grelck	University of Lübeck, Germany
Stephen Gilmore	University of Edinburgh, UK
Kevin Hammond	University of St Andrews, UK
Frank Huch	Christian Albrechts University of Kiel, Germany
Barry Jay	University of Technology, Sydney, Australia
Greg Michaelson (Chair)	Heriot-Watt University, UK
Yolanda Ortega Mallen	Universidad Complutense de Madrid, Spain
Ricardo Peña	Universidad Complutense de Madrid, Spain
Simon Peyton Jones	Microsoft Research, UK
Rinus Plasmeijer	University of Nijmegen, The Netherlands
Jocelyn Serot	Blaise Pascal University, France
Phil Trinder (Chair)	Heriot-Watt University, UK
David S. Wise	Indiana University, USA

Referees

Abdallah Al Zain	Ralf Laemmel	Clara Segura
Artem Alimarine	Hans-Wolfgang Loidl	Sjaak Smetsers
Bernd Braßel	Rita Loogen	Jonathan Sobel
Olaf Chitil	Jan Henry Nystrom	Don Syme
Koen Claessen	Enno Ohlebusch	John van Groningen
Walter Dosch	Lars Pareto	Arjen van Weelden
Andre Rauber Du Bois	Robert Pointon	Pedro Vasconcelos
David de Frutos Escrig	Fernando Rubio	
Michael Hanus	Sven-Bodo Scholz	

Sponsors

Table of Contents

Implementation of Functional Languages

I   Language Constructs and Programming

Lazy Assertions... 1
    Olaf Chitil, Dan McNeill, and Colin Runciman

Interfacing Haskell with Object-Oriented Languages.................. 20
    André T.H. Pang and Manuel M.T. Chakravarty

A Functional Shell That Dynamically Combines Compiled Code........ 36
    Arjen van Weelden and Rinus Plasmeijer

II   Static Analysis and Types

Polymorphic Type Reconstruction Using Type Equations.............. 53
    Venkatesh Choppella

Correctness of Non-determinism Analyses
in a Parallel-Functional Language.................................. 69
    Clara Segura and Ricardo Peña

Inferring Cost Equations for Recursive, Polymorphic
and Higher-Order Functional Programs............................. 86
    Pedro B. Vasconcelos and Kevin Hammond

III   Paralelism

Dynamic Chunking in Eden.. 102
    Jost Berthold

With-Loop Scalarization – Merging Nested Array Operations.......... 118
    Clemens Grelck, Sven-Bodo Scholz, and Kai Trojahner

Building an Interface Between Eden and Maple:
A Way of Parallelizing Computer Algebra Algorithms 135
    Rafael Martínez and Ricardo Peña

Generic Graphical User Interfaces................................. 152
    Peter Achten, Marko van Eekelen, and Rinus Plasmeijer

Polytypic Programming in Haskell 168
    Ulf Norell and Patrik Jansson

Author Index 185

Lazy Assertions

Olaf Chitil, Dan McNeill, and Colin Runciman

Department of Computer Science, The University of York, UK

Abstract. Assertions test expected properties of run-time values without disrupting the normal working of a program. So in a lazy functional language assertions should be lazy – not forcing evaluation, but only examining what is evaluated by other parts of the program. We explore the subtle semantics of lazy assertions and describe sequential and concurrent variants of a method for checking lazy assertions. All variants are implemented in Haskell.

1 Introduction

A programmer writing a section of code often has in mind certain assumptions or intentions about the values involved. Some of these assumptions or intentions are expressed in a way that can be verified by a compiler, for example as part of a type system. Those beyond the expressive power of static types could perhaps be proved separately as theorems, but such a demanding approach is rarely taken. Instead of leaving key properties unexpressed and unchecked, a useful and comparatively simple option is to express them as *assertions* – boolean-valued expressions that the programmer assumes or intends will always be true. Assertions are checked at run-time as they are encountered, and any failures are reported. If no assertion fails, the program runs just as it would normally, apart from the extra time and space needed for checking.

The usefulness of assertions in conventional state-based programming has long been recognised, and many imperative programming systems include some support for them. In these systems, each assertion is attached to a *program point*; whenever control reaches that point the corresponding assertion is immediately evaluated to a boolean result. Important special cases of program points with assertions include points of entry to, or return from, a procedure.

In a functional language, the basic units of programs are expressions rather than commands. The commonest form of expression is a function application. So our first thought might be that an assertion in a functional language can simply be attached to an expression: an assertion about arguments (or 'inputs') alone can be checked before the expression is evaluated and an assertion involving the result (or 'output') can be checked afterwards. But in a lazy language this view is at odds with the need to preserve normal semantics. Arguments may be unevaluated when the expression is entered, and may remain unevaluated or only partially evaluated even after the expression has been reduced to a result. The result itself may only be evaluated to *weak head-normal form*. So neither arguments nor result can safely be the subjects of an arbitrary boolean assertion that could demand their evaluation in full.

P. Trinder, G. Michaelson, and R. Peña (Eds.): IFL 2003, LNCS 3145, pp. 1–19, 2004.

How can assertions be introduced in a lazy functional language? How can we satisfy our eagerness to evaluate assertions, so that failures can be caught as soon as possible, without compromising the lazy evaluation order of the underlying program to which assertions have been added? We aim to support assertions by a small but sufficient library defined in the programming language itself. This approach avoids the need to modify compilers or run-time systems and gives the programmer a straightforward and familiar way of using a new facility. Specifically, we shall be programming in Haskell[3].

The rest of the paper is organised as follows. Section 2 uses two examples to illustrate the problem with eager assertions in a lazy language. Section 3 outlines and illustrates the contrasting nature of lazy assertions. Section 4 first outlines an implementation of lazy assertions that postpones their evaluation until the underlying program is finished; it then goes on to describe alternative implementations in which each assertion is evaluated by a concurrent thread. Section 5 uncovers a residual problem of sequential demand within assertions. Section 6 gives a brief account of our early experience using lazy assertions in application programs. Section 7 discusses related work. Section 8 concludes and suggests future work.

2   Eager Assertions Must Be True

A library provided with the Glasgow Haskell compiler[1] already includes a function `assert :: Bool -> a -> a`. It is so defined that `assert True x = x` but an application of `assert False` causes execution to halt with a suitable error message. An application of `assert` always expresses an *eager* assertion because it is a strict function: evaluation is driven by the need to reduce the boolean argument, and no other computation takes place until the value `True` is obtained.

Example: Sets as Ordered Trees

Consider the following datatype.

```
data Ord a => Set a  = Empty
                     | Union (Set a) a (Set a)
```

Functions defined over sets include `with` and `elem`, where s `with` x represents $s \cup \{x\}$ and x `elem` s represents the membership test $x \in s$.

```
with :: Ord a => Set a -> a -> Set a
Empty           'with' x = Union Empty x Empty
(Union s1 y s2) 'with' x = case compare x y of
                    LT -> Union (s1 'with' x) y s2
                    EQ -> Union s1 y s2
                    GT -> Union s1 y (s2 'with' x)
```

---

[1] http://www.haskell.org/ghc

```
elem :: Ord a => a -> Set a -> Bool
x 'elem' Empty           = False
x 'elem' (Union s1 y s2) = case compare x y of
                             LT -> x 'elem' s1
                             EQ -> True
                             GT -> x 'elem' s2
```

The `Ord a` qualification in the definition of `Set` and in the signatures for `with` and `elem` only says that comparison operators are defined for the type `a`. It does *not* guarantee that `Set a` values are strictly ordered trees, which is what the programmer intends. To assert this property, we could define the following predicate.

```
strictlyOrdered :: Ord a => Set a -> Bool
strictlyOrdered = soBetween Nothing Nothing
    where
    soBetween _ _ Empty           = True
    soBetween lo hi (Union s1 x s2) = between lo hi x &&
                                      soBetween lo (Just x) s1 &&
                                      soBetween (Just x) hi s2
    between lo hi x = maybe True (< x) lo && maybe True (> x) hi
```

Something else the programmer intends is a connection between `with` and `elem`. It can be expressed by asserting `x 'elem' (s 'with' x)`. Combining this property with the ordering assertion we might define:

```
s 'checkedWith' x = assert post s'
                where
                s'   = assert pre s 'with' x
                pre  = strictlyOrdered s
                post = strictlyOrdered s' && x 'elem' s'
```

Observations. The eager assertions in `checkedWith` may 'run ahead' of evaluation actually required by the underlying program, forcing fuller evaluation of tree structures and elements. The strict-ordering test is a conjunction of two comparisons for *every* internal node of a tree, forcing the entire tree to be evaluated (unless the test fails). Even the check involving `elem` forces the path from the root to `x`.

Does this matter? Surely some extra evaluation is inevitable when non-trivial assertions are introduced? It does matter. If assertion-checking forces evaluation it could degenerate into a pre-emptive, non-terminating and unproductive process. What if, for example, a computation involves the set of all integers, represented as in Figure 1? Functions such as `elem` and `with` still produce useful results. But `checkedWith` eagerly carries the whole computation away on an infinite side-track!

Even where eager assertions terminate they may consume time or space out of proportion with normal computation. Also, assertions are often checked in the

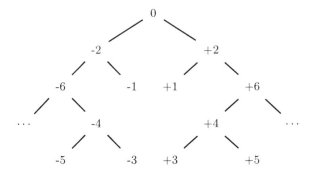

Fig. 1. A tree representation of the infinite set of integers. Each integer i occurs at a depth no greater than $2\log_2(\mathrm{abs}(i)+1)$. Differences between adjacent elements on leftmost and rightmost paths are successive powers of two.

hope of shedding light on a program failure; it could be distracting to report a failed assertion about values that are irrelevant as they were never needed by the failing program.

3   Lazy Assertions Must Not Be False

So assertions should only examine those parts of their subject data structures that are in any case demanded by the underlying program. Lazy assertions should make a (provisional) assumption of validity about other data not (yet) evaluated. Computation of the underlying program should proceed not only if an assertion reduces to `True`, but also if it cannot (yet) be reduced to a value at all; the only constraint is that an assertion must never reduce to `False`.

If we are to guard data structures that are the subjects of assertions from over-evaluation, we cannot continue to allow arbitrary boolean expressions involving these structures. We need to separate the *predicate* of the assertion from the *subject* to which it is applied. An implementation of assertions should combine the two using only a special evaluation-safe form of application. So the type of `assert` becomes

```
assert :: (a -> Bool) -> a -> a
```

where `assert p` acts as a lazy partial identity.

Example Revisited

If we had an implementation of this lazy `assert`, how would it alter the ordered-tree example? In view of the revised type of `assert`, the definition of `checkedWith` must be altered slightly, making `pre` and `post` predicates rather than booleans.

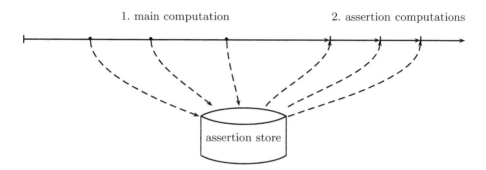

Fig. 2. Delayed Assertions in Time.

```
s 'checkedWith' x = assert post (assert pre s 'with' x)
                    where
                    pre  = strictlyOrdered
                    post = \s' -> strictlyOrdered s' && x 'elem' s'
```

Now the computation of a `checkedWith` application proceeds more like a normal application of `with`. Even if infinite sets are involved, the corresponding assertions are only partially computed, up to the limits imposed by the finite needed parts of these sets.

4   Implementation

Having established the benefits of lazy assertions we now turn to the question of how they can be implemented in Haskell. We develop an assertion library in steps: we start with a simple version, criticise it, and then refine it to the next version.

4.1   Delayed Assertions

We have to ensure that the evaluation of the assertions cannot disturb the evaluation of the underlying program. A very simple idea for achieving this is to evaluate all assertions *after* termination of the main computation.

Figure 2 illustrates the idea. The main computation only evaluates the underlying program and collects all assertions in a global store. After termination of the main computation assertions are taken from the store and evaluated one after the other.

We are certain that lazy assertions cannot be implemented within pure Haskell 98. In particular we need the function `unsafePerformIO :: IO a -> a` to perform actions of the IO monad without giving `assert` a monadic type. We aim to minimise the use of language extensions and restrict ourselves to extensions supported by most Haskell systems. Our implementation is far more concise and potentially portable than any modification of a compiler or run-time system could be.

Which extensions do we need for delayed assertions? Extended exceptions enable a program to catch all erroneous behaviour of a subcomputation. They ensure that all assertions are evaluated, even if the main computation or any other assertion evaluated earlier fails. A mutable variable of type `IORef` implements the global assertion store. Finally `unsafePerformIO :: IO a -> a` enables us to implement `assert` using exceptions and mutable variables [7].

Properties of the Implementation. This simple implementation does not prevent an assertion from evaluating a test argument further than the main computation did. Because assertion checking is delayed, over-evaluation cannot disturb the main computation, but it can cause run-time errors or non-termination in the evaluation of an assertion (see Section 2).

4.2   Avoiding Over-Evaluating

To avoid over-evaluation do we need any non-portable "function" for testing if an expression is evaluated? No, exceptions and the function `unsafePerformIO` are enough. We can borrow and extend a technique from the Haskell Object Observation Debugger (HOOD) [4]. We arrange that as evaluation of the underlying program demands the value of an expression wrapped with an assertion, the main computation makes a copy of the value. Thus the copy comprises exactly those parts of the value that were demanded by the evaluation of the underlying program.

We introduce two new functions, `demand` and `listen`. The function `demand` is wrapped around the value that is consumed by the main computation. The function returns that value and, whenever a part of the value is demanded, the function also adds the demanded part to the copy. The assertion uses the result of the function `listen`. The function `listen` simply returns the copy; because `listen` is only evaluated after the main computation has terminated, `listen` returns those parts of the value that were demanded by the main computation. If the result of `listen` is evaluated further, then it raises an exception. For every part of a value there is a `demand`/`listen` pair that communicates via an `IORef`. The value of the `IORef` is `Unblocked v` to pass a value v (weak head normal form) or `Blocked` to indicate that the value was not (yet) demanded. The implementation of `demand` is specific for every type. Hence we introduce a class `Assert` and the type of `assert` becomes `Assert a => String -> (a -> Bool) -> a -> a`. Appendix A gives the details of the implementation.

Properties of the Implementation. An assertion can use exactly those parts of values that are evaluated by the main computation, no less, no more. However, if an assertion fails, the programmer is informed rather late; because of the problem actually detected by the assertion, the main computation may have run into a run-time error or worse a loop. The computation is then also likely to produce a long, fortunately ordered, list of failed assertions. A programmer wants to know about a failed assertion before the main computation uses the faulty value!

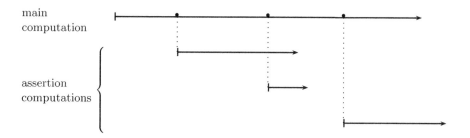

Fig. 3. Concurrent Assertions in Time.

4.3   Concurrent Assertions

How can we evaluate assertions as eagerly as possible yet still only using data that is demanded by the main computation? Rather than delaying assertion checking to the end, we can evaluate each assertion in a separate thread concurrently to the main computation. We require a further extension of Haskell 98: Concurrent Haskell [7].

Figure 3 illustrates the idea. Each evaluation of `assert` in the main computation starts a new thread for evaluating the assertion itself. As before, the value tested by an assertion is copied as it is demanded by the main computation and the copy is used by the assertion. Replacing the `IOVar` shared by a `demand/listen` pair by an `MVar` synchronises the assertion thread with the demand of the main computation. The assertion thread has to wait when it tries to evaluate parts of the copy that do not (yet) exist.

Properties of the Implementation. Concurrency ensures that even if the main computation runs into an infinite loop, a failed assertion will be reported. In general failed assertions may be reported earlier. However, there is no guarantee, because the scheduler is free to evaluate assertions at any time. They may – and in practice often are – evaluated after the main computation has terminated.

4.4   Priority of Assertions

To solve the problem we need to give assertion threads priority over the main computation. Unfortunately Concurrent Haskell does not provide threads with different priorities. However, coroutining enables us to give priority to assertions. We explicitly pass control between each assertion thread and the main thread. When an assertion demands a part of a value that has not yet been demanded by the main computation, the assertion thread is blocked and control is passed to the main thread. Whenever the main thread demands another part of the tested value and an assertion thread is waiting for that value, the main thread is blocked and control is passed to the assertion thread. Thus the assertion always gets a new part of the value for testing *before* it is used by the main computation. Figure 4 illustrates the idea and Appendix B gives the details of the implementation which uses semaphores to pass control.

main
computation

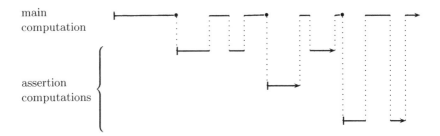

assertion
computations

Fig. 4. Concurrent Assertions with Priority in Time.

Properties of the Implementation. Coroutining ensures that a failed assertion is reported before the main computation uses the faulty value. Furthermore, the implementation does not hold onto all data needed by assertions until the end of the computation, because assertions are evaluated as early as possible without over-evaluation. However, assertions that cannot be fully evaluated are still live until the end of the whole computation.

4.5   Garbage Collecting Stuck Assertions

When a tested value is no longer reachable from the main computation thread, it will no longer be demanded by the main computation and hence the assertion thread is permanently stuck. We extend the coroutining implementation with finalisers [8] that kill an assertion thread when its value is no longer reachable from the main computation thread.

Properties of the Implementation. This implementation reduces the requirements for space and threads.

4.6   Conclusions

During development we identified the following important properties of a lazy assertion library.

- Evaluation of assertions does not influence the main computation.
- Assertions do not evaluate values further than the main computation does.
- A failed assertion is reported before the main computation uses the faulty value.
- The requirements for space and threads are minimised.

For each property we developed a new implementation. Unfortunately we find that the implementations using coroutining violate the first property. Suppose we define `assertFun` as follows to assert a relation between the argument and result of a function.

```
assertFun :: (Assert a, Assert b)
          => String -> (a->b->Bool) -> (a->b) -> (a->b)
assertFun n p f i = o'
  where
  (i',o') = assert n (uncurry p) (i,f i')
```

This cyclic definition works fine with all but the coroutining implementations of `assert`. With coroutining a deadlock occurs because the assertion thread waits for the input `i'` of the function which has to be produced by the assertion thread itself.

We conclude that the concurrent implementation without priorities is the most useful implementation we have. We have to aim for a concurrent implementation with priorities and garbage collection of stuck assertions that controls threads less restrictively than coroutining.

5   Sequential Semantics Causes Stuck Assertions

We noted in Section 3 that lazy assertions must not be `False`. Computation of the underlying program should proceed not only if an assertion reduces to `True`, but also if computation of the assertion is *stuck*, that is the assertion cannot (yet) be reduced to a value at all. Consequently our implementations do not distinguish between assertions that reduce to `True` and assertions that are stuck.

Evaluation order can often be disregarded when considering the correctness of lazy functional programs. Lazy evaluation does, however, specify a mostly sequential semantics. The semantics of logical connectives such as (`&&`) are not symmetric. When the order in which an assertion demands components of a data structure does not agree with the order in which the main computation demands the components of that data structure, the assertion can get stuck.

Example Revisited Again

Consider evaluation of the following expression:

```
5 'elem' (assert "ordered" strictlyOrdered
   (Union (Union Empty 2 Empty) 3 (Union Empty 1 Empty)))
```

The given set is not strictly ordered, but no assertion fails! This is because only the part

```
Union _ 3 (Union _ 1 Empty)
```

of the set is ever demanded by the computation (_ indicates an undemanded expression). The computation of the function `strictlyOrdered` traverses the tree representation of the set in preorder. Hence it gets stuck on the unevaluated left subtree of the root `Union` constructor. Consequently it never makes the comparison 3 < 1 which would immediately make the assertion fail.

Detecting the Problem. It would help to list at the end of all computation all assertions that are stuck. It is easy to extend our implementations to do this.

A Solution? We could avoid sequentiality in the assertion by creating a separate assertion for each atomic test. In the following definition the sequential (&&)s have been replaced by `asserts` that do not actually check any property of their last arguments but start separate assertions. This assertion is as eager as possible, because each `between` comparison is separate.

```
assertStrictlyOrdered :: Ord a => String -> Set a -> Set a
assertStrictlyOrdered n = assert n (soBetween Nothing Nothing)
  where
  soBetween _ _ Empty            = True
  soBetween lo hi (Union s1 x s2) =
    assert n (const (soBetween lo (Just x) s1)) $
    assert n (const (soBetween (Just x) hi s2)) $
    between lo hi x
  between lo hi x = maybe True (< x) lo && maybe True (> x) hi
```

These assertions within assertions work with all implementations except for the coroutining ones. Again coroutining leads to a deadlock.

Using assertions within assertions is a trick that should not be our final answer to the problem of stuck sequential assertions. An alternative implementation might use a new type that replaces `Bool` and provides a parallel logical conjunction.

6   Larger Applications

As yet we have only tried out lazy assertions in a few programs of modest size. We note briefly some of our experience with two of these programs.

Clausify

The `clausify` program puts propositions represented using the type

```
data Prop = Sym Char    | Neg Prop
          | Dis Prop Prop | Con Prop Prop
          | Imp Prop Prop | Eqv Prop Prop
```

into clausal form, by a composition of several stages. We found it convenient to write assertions using an auxiliary function

```
propHas :: (Prop -> Bool) -> Prop -> Bool
```

defined so that `propHas t p` applies test `t` both to `p` itself and to all `Prop`s that `p` contains. We also find a use for implication lifted to predicate level

```
implies :: (a -> Bool) -> (a -> Bool) -> (a -> Bool).
```

After successive stages, the following assertions should hold, cumulatively:

1. `propHas (\p -> not (isImp p || isEqv p))`
   Imp and Eqv are eliminated.
2. `propHas (isNeg 'implies' (\(Neg q) -> isSym q))`
   In addition, `Neg (Sym _)` is the only permitted form of negation.
3. `propHas (isDis 'implies' \(Dis p q) -> not (isCon p || isCon q))`
   Further, no `Con` occurs within a `Dis`.

If a fault is introduced into any of these stages, so that it fails to normalise a proposition as it should, the result is typically a pattern-matching failure in a later stage. We found that lazy assertion checking often reports the failure in the earlier stage, but sometimes inconclusively reports the relevant assertion as stuck. To minimise stuckness one has to think carefully about evaluation order in assertions.

Pasta

Further issues arose when we introduced lazy assertions in **pasta**, an interpreter for a small imperative language with dynamic data structures. Our goal was to assert a data invariant for a moderately complex data structure representing the environment and store:

```
data EnvStore = ES {sig   :: Signature,
                    ops   :: [Operation],
                    scope :: [Name],
                    stack :: [Value],
                    heap  :: [StructVal]}
```

To make assertions over `EnvStore` values would seem to require an `Assert` instance for `EnvStore`. But because of the various component types (and *their* component types etc.) this would mean a fair bit of work in several different modules. As the invariant properties relate only the scope, stack and heap, we avoid much of this work by embedding the invariant assertion in a smart constructor like this:

```
es si o sc st h = ES si o sc' st' h'
  where
  (sc',st',h') = assert "ES invariant" dataInv (sc,st,h)
```

The details of `dataInv` are not important here. The most surprising result was that *none* of the `dataInv` assertions was ever fully evaluated! The explanation is that the interpreter uses `EnvStore` values in a single-threaded way, and each state change only involves accessing a small part of the relevant `EnvStore`. Since lazy assertions only check the parts actually used by the program, they never get to check a complete `EnvStore` structure. The contrast with an eager data invariant is striking.

7   Related Work

The work reported in this paper started as a BSc project. The second author's dissertation [5] describes experiments with an earlier version of concurrent assertions.

In Section 4 we adapted a technique first used in HOOD [4]. HOOD defines a class of types for which an `observe` function is defined. Programmers annotate expressions whose values they wish to observe by applying `observe` *label* to them, where *label* is a descriptive string. These applicative annotations act as identities with a useful side-effect: each value to which an annotated expression reduces – *so far as it is demanded by lazy evaluation* – is recorded, fragment by fragment as it is evaluated, under the appropriate label. The similarity of `observe` and `assert` is clear, but an important difference is that whereas `observe` records a sequence of labelled fragments for subsequent inspection or separate processing, `assert` reassembles them for further computation within the same Haskell program. A HOOD programmer can evaluate by inspection any assumptions or intentions they may have about recorded values, but this inspection is a laborious and error-prone alternative to machine evaluation of predicates.

HOOD does not require threads or non-trivial delayed computations. A fragment of a value is recorded just when it is demanded. It would be nice if the implementation of assertions could be that simple. However, an assertion usually relates several fragments of a value, for example, it may compare two numbers in a tree. The assertion can only be checked when the last of the two numbers becomes available, no matter in which order they are demanded by the main computation. Additionally, the demands of the assertion predicate can only be determined by applying it to an argument.

Another well-established Haskell library for checking properties of functional programs is QuickCheck [1]. Properties are defined as boolean-valued functions, as in the example:

```
prop_ElemWith :: Set Int -> Int -> Bool
prop_ElemWith s x = x 'elem' (s 'with' x) == True
```

Evaluating `quickCheck prop_ElemWith` checks the property using a test suite of *pseudo-randomly generated* sets and elements as the values of `s` and `x`. The test-value generators are type-determined and they can be customised by programmers. QuickCheck reports statistics of successful tests and details of any failing case discovered. This sort of testing nicely complements assertions. QuickCheck properties are not limited to expressions that fit the context of a particular program point, and a separate testing process imposes no overhead when an application is run. But assertions have the advantage of testing values that actually occur in a program of interest, and provide a continuing safeguard against undetected errors.

Möller [6] offers a different perspective on the role of assertions in a functional language. The motivating context for his work is transformational program development; assertions carry parts of the specification and are subject to refinement. He assumes strict semantics, however, and does not consider the problem of assertions in a lazy language.

8   Conclusions and Future Work

Assertions, first used in call-by-value procedural languages, can also be useful in a call-by-need functional language; but they should be constrained appropriately. The key requirement is that assertion-checking never forces evaluation beyond the needs of the underlying program.

We have shown how appropriately lazy assertions can be supported by a high-level library. Our account has been based on experimental prototypes developed using the Glasgow Haskell Compiler, and these prototypes do rely on some of the language extensions this compiler supports. We would prefer to have a more portable library.

It would be easy to extend the reports from a failed assertion to include the evaluated part of its subject value. To allow the causes of assertion failures to be traced, we may eventually support the use of assertions in connection with Hat [9, 2].

We do need more experience with the use of lazy assertions in larger applications. So far we have found that expressing assertions in the functional language itself is a pleasant task, but it might be useful to include a few standard combinators in the library, especially for making assertions about functional (and perhaps monadic) values. Programming lazy assertions to fail as eagerly as possible can be tricky, and it is not yet clear whether suitable abstractions such as concurrent logical operators will help. We also need to explore further the effect of assertions on the time and space performance of a program, particularly as the copying of values can cause a loss of sharing. Pragmatics are not easily hidden by abstraction!

Acknowledgements

Thanks to Dean Herington, Claus Reinke and Simon Peyton Jones for their contributions to a discussion on the Haskell mailing list about how to achieve data-driven concurrency.

References

1. K. Claessen and R. J. M. Hughes. QuickCheck: a lightweight tool for random testing of Haskell programs. In *Proc. 5th Intl. ACM Conference on Functional Programming*, pages 268–279. ACM Press, 2000.
2. K. Claessen, C. Runciman, O. Chitil, J. Hughes, and M. Wallace. Testing and tracing lazy functional programs using QuickCheck and Hat. In *Lecture notes of the 4th Intl. Summer School in Advanced Functional Programming*. 40pp, to appear in Springer LNCS, 2002.
3. S. L. Peyton Jones (Ed.). Haskell 98: a non-strict, purely functional language. *Journal of Functional Programming*, 13(1):special issue, 2003.
4. A. Gill. Debugging Haskell by observing intermediate datastructures. *Electronic Notes in Theoretical Computer Science*, 41(1), 2001. (Proc. 2000 ACM SIGPLAN Haskell Workshop).

5. D. McNeill. Concurrent data-driven assertions in a lazy functional language. Technical report, BSc Project Dissertation, Department of Computer Science, University of York, 2003.
6. B. Möller. Applicative assertions. In J. L. A. van de Snepscheut, editor, *Mathematics of Program Construction*, pages 348–362. Springer LNCS 375, 1989.
7. S. L. Peyton Jones. Tackling the awkward squad: monadic input/output, concurrency, exceptions and foreign-language calls in haskell. In C. A. R. Hoare, M. Broy, and R. Steinbruggen, editors, *Engineering theories of software construction*, pages 47–96. IOS Press, 2001.
8. Simon L. Peyton Jones, Simon Marlow, and Conal Elliott. Stretching the storage manager: Weak pointers and stable names in haskell. In *Implementation of Functional Languages, 11th International Workshop, IFL'99*, volume 1868 of *LNCS 1868*, pages 37–58, 2000.
9. M. Wallace, O. Chitil, T. Brehm, and C. Runciman. Multiple-view tracing for Haskell: a new Hat. In *ACM Workshop on Haskell*, 2001.

A   Sequential Implementation: Delayed Assertions Avoiding Over-Evaluation

We introduce a global mutable variable `finalisers` that stores a list of pending assertions, to be checked at the end of the main computation.

```
finalisers :: IORef [IO ()]
finalisers = unsafePerformIO $ newIORef []
```

The function `assert` simply adds an assertion to the `finalisers` list. The function also takes a string as argument to simplify identification when an assertion fails.

```
assert :: Assert a => String -> (a -> Bool) -> a -> a
assert s p x = unsafePerformIO $ do
  r <- newIORef Blocked
  fins <- readIORef finalisers
  writeIORef finalisers (evalAssertion s p (listen r) : fins)
  return (demand r x)
```

Only evaluation of `evalAssertion n p x` actually evaluates the assertion of name `n` and predicate `p` with test argument `x`. The function `evalAssertion` has to catch exceptions to ensure that an exception in one assertion does not prevent the remaining pending assertions from being tested. The function `evalAssertion` also has to handle the case that it is blocked to avoid over-evaluation:

```
evalAssertion :: String -> (a -> Bool) -> a -> IO ()
evalAssertion n p x = do
  Control.Exception.catch
    (when (not (p x))
      (hPutStrLn stderr ("\nAssertion " ++ show n ++ " failed.")))
```

```
(\e -> case e of
        ErrorCall "blocked" -> return ()
        _ -> hPutStrLn stderr ("\nAssertion " ++ show n ++
                              " raised exception: " ++
                              show e))
```

To use assertions we have to wrap the action corresponding to the underlying program by applying runA to it. To ensure that the assertions are always run at the end of the computation, the definition of runA has to catch any exception occurring in the main computation[2].

```
runA :: IO a -> IO ()
runA io = do
  Control.Exception.catch io
    (const (putStrLn "Exception occurred in main computation" >>
            return undefined))
  fins <- readIORef finalisers
  sequence_ fins
```

Finally the functions demand and listen implement the demand driven copying of a tested value by the main computation for the assertion.

```
data ValState a = Blocked | Unblocked a

class Assert a where
  demand :: IORef (ValState a) -> a -> a

instance Assert a => Assert [a] where
  demand r [] = unsafePerformIO $ do
    writeIORef r (Unblocked [])
    return []
  demand r (x:xs) = unsafePerformIO $ do
    r1 <- newIORef Blocked
    r2 <- newIORef Blocked
    writeIORef r (Unblocked (listen r1 : listen r2))
    return (demand r1 x : demand r2 xs)

listen :: IORef (ValState a) -> a
listen r = unsafePerformIO $ do
  val <- readIORef r
  case val of
    Blocked -> error "blocked"
    Unblocked x -> return x
```

---

[2] The variable finalisers is initialised with the empty list. However, interactive interpreters may not reevaluate a CAF such as finalisers every time a new expression is interactively evaluated. Hence to ensure correct initialisation we have to insert writeIORef finalisers [] as first line in the do block of runA.

B   Concurrent Implementation: Assertions with Priority

To control the running status of a pair of threads we introduce a `Switch` of two
binary semaphores and associated functions for passing control. The function
`waitQSem` blocks a thread until a 'unit' of a semaphore becomes available, and
`signalQSem` makes a 'unit' available.

```
data Switch = S QSem QSem

initSwitch :: IO Switch
initSwitch = do mainS <- newQSem (-1)
                assertS <- newQSem (-1)
                return (S mainS assertS)

continueAssert :: Switch -> IO ()
continueAssert (S mainS assertS) = do signalQSem assertS
                                      waitQSem mainS

continueMain :: Switch -> IO ()
continueMain (S mainS assertS) = do signalQSem mainS
                                    waitQSem assertS

finishAssert :: Switch -> IO ()
finishAssert (S mainS _) = signalQSem mainS
```

A part of a tested value can be in any of three states: (1) not yet demanded
by either the main or the assertion thread, (2) demanded by the assertion thread
which is hence blocked, and (3) evaluated, because it was demanded by the main
thread:

```
data ValState a = Untouched | DemandedByAssert | Evaluated a
```

The basic idea of copying the test value on demand is still the same as
before. As a helper for the function `demand` we introduce the function `copy`. It
distinguishes the states `DemandedByAssert` and `Evaluated` and passes control
to the assertion thread in the first case. Similarly the function `listen` passes
control according to the state.

```
class Assert a where
  demand :: a -> Switch -> IORef (ValState a) -> a

instance Assert a => Assert [a] where
  demand [] s =  unsafePerformIO $ do
    copy s r []
    return []
  demand (x:xs) s = unsafePerformIO $ do
    r1 <- newIORef Untouched
    r2 <- newIORef Untouched
```

```
      copy s r (listen s r1 : listen s r2)
      return (demand x s r1 : demand xs s r2)


copy :: Switch -> IORef (ValState a) -> a -> IO ()
copy s r x =  do
  state <- readIORef r
  case state of
    Untouched -> writeIORef r (Evaluated x)
    DemandedByAssert -> do
      writeIORef r (Evaluated x)
      continueAssert s

listen :: Switch -> IORef (ValState a) -> a
listen s r = unsafePerformIO $ do
  state <- readIORef r
  case state of
    Untouched -> do
      writeIORef r DemandedByAssert
      continueMain s
      state <- readIORef r
      case state of
        Evaluated x -> return x
    Evaluated x -> return x
```

Finally we adapt the definitions of the function `assert` and `evalAssertion` to the concurrent setting. The function `forkIO` starts a new thread.

```
assert :: Assert a => String -> (a -> Bool) -> a -> a
assert n p x = unsafePerformIO $ do
  r <- newIORef Untouched
  s <- initSwitch
  forkIO (evalAssertion n p (listen s r) >> finishAssert s)
  continueAssert s
  return (demand x s r)

evalAssertion :: String -> (a -> Bool) -> a -> IO ()
evalAssertion n p x = do
  Control.Exception.catch
    (when (not (p x))
      (hPutStrLn stderr ("\nAssertion " ++ show n ++ " failed.")))
    (\e -> hPutStrLn stderr
            ("\nAssertion " ++ show n ++
              " failed with exception: " ++ show e)
```

This implementation does not need a wrapper function `runA`.

C   The Class Assert and Its Instances

In both sequential and concurrent implementations there is a class Assert. We
need an instance of Assert for every type of value that we wish to make assertions about. To simplify the writing of new instances we define a family of
$demand_n$ functions. For the concurrent implementation they are defined as follows:

```
demand0 :: Switch -> IORef (ValState a) -> a -> a
demand0 x s r = unsafePerformIO $ do
  copy s r x
  return x

demand1 :: (Assert b) => (b -> a) -> b
                         -> Switch -> IORef (ValState a) -> a
demand1 c x1 s r = unsafePerformIO $ do
  r1 <- newIORef Untouched
  copy s r (c (listen s r1))
  return (c (demand x1 s r1))

demand2 :: (Assert b, Assert c) => (c -> b -> a) -> c -> b
                         -> Switch -> IORef (ValState a) -> a

demand2 c x1 x2 s r = unsafePerformIO $ do
  r1 <- newIORef Untouched
  r2 <- newIORef Untouched
  copy s r (c (listen s r1) (listen s r2))
  return (c (demand x1 s r1) (demand x2 s r2))
```

Instances thus become short and easy to write:

```
instance Assert a => Assert [a] where
  demand [] = demand0 []
  demand (x:xs) = demand2 (:) x xs

instance (Assert a,Assert b) => Assert (a,b) where
  demand (x,y) = demand2 (,) x y

instance Assert Char where
  demand c = c 'seq' demand0 c
```

The use of seq is needed in the last case where no pattern matching takes place
to ensure that the value is always evaluated by the main thread, not the assertion
thread.

Although this is an improvement, a tool such as DrIFT[3] is still useful to
derive what may be a large number of instances.

---

[3] http://repetae.net/john/computer/haskell/DrIFT/

A different problem is that the class context of the function `assert` restricts its use in the definition of polymorphic functions. For our running example we obtain the type

```
checkedWith :: (Ord a, Assert a) => Set a -> a -> Set a
```

Users of HOOD seem to be able to live with a similar restriction.

For Hugs there is a special version of HOOD that provides a built-in polymorphic function `observe`. Likewise a built-in polymorphic function `assert` is feasible. Even better, since the implementations of `observe` and `assert` are based on the same technique, it is desirable to identify the functionality of a single built-in polymorphic function in terms of which both `observe`, `assert` and possibly further testing and debugging functions could be defined. A built-in polymorphic function removes both the annoying need for a large number of similar instances and the restricting class context.

Interfacing Haskell with Object-Oriented Languages

André T.H. Pang[1,2] and Manuel M.T. Chakravarty[1,3]

[1] University of New South Wales
School of Computer Science & Engineering
Sydney, Australia
{andrep,chak}@cse.unsw.edu.au
[2] CSIRO, Information & Communication Technologies
[3] National ICT Australia, ERTOS

Abstract. The interfacing of object-oriented languages with functional languages, in general, and with Haskell, in particular, has received a considerable amount of attention. Previous work, including Lambada, a Haskell to Java bridge, showed how an object-oriented class hierarchy can be modeled using Haskell type classes, such that Java libraries can be used conveniently from Haskell.

The present paper extends this previous work in two major directions. Firstly, we describe a new implementation of object-oriented style method calls and overloading in Haskell, using multi-parameter type classes and functional dependencies. This enables calling of a foreign object's methods in a syntactically convenient, type-safe manner. Secondly, we sketch an approach to automating the generation of library bindings using compile-time meta-programming for object-oriented frameworks featuring reflection. We have evaluated the practicality of our approach by implementing a Haskell binding to the Objective-C language on the Mac OS X platform.

1   Introduction

The usability of programming languages is dependent on the ability to inter-operate with existing software infrastructures: modern application development requires access to libraries which enable operating system functionality, graphical user interfaces, and access to component frameworks. Conversely, we want to extend those existing libraries using code written in advanced high-level languages. All this leads to two main challenges: (1) foreign language structures need to be modeled and (2) interface code that enables access to existing libraries and components needs to be written. The former is difficult due to the mismatch of data abstractions and type systems between languages, whereas the latter is a practical challenge due to the plain size of modern software infrastructures.

This paper contributes to the interoperation of statically typed functional programming languages – in particular, Haskell – with infrastructure software developed for object-oriented languages. Our motivation for such interoperability

P. Trinder, G. Michaelson, and R. Peña (Eds.): IFL 2003, LNCS 3145, pp. 20–35, 2004.

is to access and re-use existing object-oriented frameworks, such as the Cocoa framework of Mac OS X. Using Cocoa, we can implement a program in the Objective-C language to dump the contents of a document referred to by a URL to standard output as follows:

```
int main (int argc, char **argv) {
  NSURL *url = [NSURL urlWithString:
    [NSString stringWithCString:argv[1]]];
  NSString *urlData = [NSString stringWithContentsOfURL:url];
  fputs ([urlData cString]);}
```

The conciseness of the code hinges on the comprehensive infrastructure provided by Cocoa. Haskell cannot match the simplicity of the above program if we have to re-implement the infrastructure – i.e., the function `stringWithContentsOfURL:` of the class `NSString`. Hence, we would like to use such classes from Haskell as elegantly and conveniently as using them from the framework's native object-oriented language. For the above URL fetcher code, we would like to write:

```
main = do
  (arg:_) ← System.getArgs
  url ← _NSURL_ # urlWithString arg
  urlData ← _NSString_ # stringWithContentsOfURL url
  putStr urlData
```

Interfacing Haskell with object-oriented languages presents a number of problems, one of which is the mismatch between the respective type systems. In particular, Haskell lacks a defining feature of such languages: it does not have class inheritance (subtyping). Some object-oriented systems (e.g. Java, Smalltalk, Objective-C) also use *class objects*, which act as objects that are concretised representations of the class. This mapping from OO classes to Haskell types must also ensure that type-safe method invocation on those objects can be performed – preferably with a simple syntax – and also ensure that it is possible to model the external API automatically via an *interface generator*.

1.1   Our Approach

In this paper, we advocate the use of multi-parameter type classes [1] to enable syntactically convenient upcasting and downcasting of objects between types, and present a generic approach to representing class objects in Haskell. We show that multi-parameter type classes in combination with functional dependencies [2] can provide full object-oriented style overloading in Haskell, enabling interaction with object-oriented APIs as fluidly as one would expect from the API's native language. Moreover, we use recent advances in compile-time meta-programming – and specifically Template Haskell [3] – to provide direct access to existing component software whose interfaces can be enquired via reflection, and hence avoid the need for extra tool support, including the configuration and maintenance problems associated with it.

In summary, the main contributions of the present paper are the following:

1. type-safe and syntactically convenient upcasting and downcasting (Sect 2.2),
2. an encoding of class objects (Sect 2.4),
3. a novel encoding of object-oriented method overloading into multi-parameter type classes (Sect 3),
4. the automated generation of library bindings by way of compile-time meta-programming for frameworks featuring reflection (Sect 4), and
5. an outline of a Haskell binding to Objective-C, in general, and the Cocoa framework of Mac OS X, in particular (Sect 5).

Throughout the paper, we will summarise methods used in the work on Lambada [4] as well as Shields & Peyton Jones's work on object-oriented style overloading [5], as this forms the basis for our work. We will clearly state where our approach moves beyond this previous work.

1.2 Related Work

Previous work, in particular that which has culminated in Lambada [4,6–8], has modeled aspects of object-oriented class hierarchies and overloading in Haskell. Lambada concentrates on Java as the foreign language and uses tuples and type classes to pass an arbitrary number of method arguments from Haskell and to invoke Java methods with varying return types. Moreover, it encodes class inheritance via phantom types and type classes. Lambada is based on the interface generator H/Direct [9] and is the basis for Haskell-Java bridges such as GCJNI [10] and the Haskell/Java VM Bridge [11]. However, the Haskell API presented in Lambada does not provide the same elegance nor convenience as the framework language. Our aim is to close that gap further.

Shields and Peyton Jones [5] extend the approach of Lambada where type classes encode object-oriented class hierarchies. They provide object-oriented style method overloading by introducing several non-trivial extensions of the type system. In contrast, we confine ourselves to multi-parameter type classes with functional dependencies – a Haskell extension already implemented by Hugs and the Glasgow Haskell Compiler.

Haskell *interface generators* such as GreenCard [12], C→Haskell [13], and `hsc2hs` [14] partially automate the development of Haskell bindings to external libraries. These tools are pre-processors which are separate from the compilation process, whereas we concentrate on using compile-time meta-programming facilities such as Template Haskell to provide such functionality. Alastair Reid [15] has also recently taken a similar approach, re-implementing GreenCard as *Template GreenCard* using compile-time meta-programming. Reid's and our work has been done concurrently and independently.

2   Modeling an Object-Oriented Class Hierarchy

With regard to the mismatch between the data structures of the two interoperating languages, the main challenge is the lack of subtyping – class inheritance –

in Haskell. Hence, we need a scheme to encode subtyping with Haskell's existing features, such that we can handle (1) multiple inheritance and interfaces, (2) up and down casts, and (3) class objects. Moreover, the encoding should enable to accurately type check code which uses objects or invokes methods on objects. Previous research has shown how to model multiple inheritance in Haskell, which we will summarise in the next subsection as it forms the basis for the discussion of casts, class objects, and object representations in the remainder of this section.

2.1   Class Hierarchy Encoding Techniques

Many previous approaches use *phantom types* to model inheritance [4,6–8], which we mention here for completeness. The idea here is to have both a data type and a type synonym for each class, where the data type has an unused – i.e., a *phantom* – type parameter. Then, chains of nested types represent inheritance chains, as is done in the following example where a `Coffee` class inherits from a `Drink` class:

```
data DrinkT a = DrinkT; type Drink a = DrinkT a
data CoffeeT a = CoffeeT; type Coffee a = Drink (CoffeeT a)
```

Here, the type `Drink` () stands for an instance of the `Drink` class and `Drink a` stands for any instances of `Drink` or any instances of its subclasses. The main shortcomings of this approach are obscure type errors when inheritance is used extensively and the inability to encode multiple inheritance. Thus, we reject phantom types for our purposes.

Instead, we advocate the use of type classes to encode multiple inheritance, similar to how Lambada encodes Java interfaces in Haskell and to the approaches outlined by Shields and Peyton Jones [5]. In this scheme, we have one data type and one type class per encoded OO class. The type class associated with an OO class X, which we name $\mathrm{Sub}X$ below, has an instance for each subclass of that OO class. This is illustrated in the following example, where a class D inherits from two classes B and C, and B and C both inherit from a class A:

```
data A; class SubA a; instance SubA A
data B; class SubB a; instance SubA B; instance SubB B
data C; class SubC a; instance SubA C; instance SubC C
data D; class SubD a; instance SubA D; instance SubB D
  instance SubC D; instance SubD D
```

Multiple inheritance presents no challenge with this encoding. In fact, the encoding is appropriate when instances of B and C each inherit from *separate* instances of A (e.g., non-`virtual` multiple inheritance in C++) as well as if they inherit from the same instance of A (e.g., as is done in Java, or using the `virtual` keyword in C++). In both cases, the base class A is still of the same *type*, even if there are multiple instances of A, one for B and one for C.

2.2   Upcasting and Downcasting Objects

Two central operations in a class hierarchy are upcasts and downcasts, where the object of a class is used as the object of a superclass or specialised to a subclasses, respectively. Such casting (or coercing) operations define a binary relation between two types, which is why we will use a two-parameter type class to model that relationship and the corresponding operations in Haskell. This is preferable to an encoding based on single-parameter classes where the second class is part of the function name. For example, Haskell 98 defines the `fromInteger` and `toInteger` functions, which coerce between values of `Integer` and other numerals. This approach is reasonable for the base language Haskell 98, as it only supports single-parameter type classes. However, it is problematic when modeling object hierarchies as it is less generic and leads to a much larger number of classes. Consequently, we introduce the two-parameter class `Cast` and instantiate it as follows for the earlier `Drink` example:

```
class Cast sub super where
    upcast :: sub → super; downcast :: super → sub
instance Cast Coffee Drink where
    upcast Coffee = Drink; downcast Drink = Coffee

upcastingUsage = upcast Coffee :: Drink
downcastingUsage = downcast Drink :: Coffee
```

Languages, such as Objective-C, check the validity of casts at runtime. Hence, the above `upcast` and `downcast` functions need to implement a similar check that verifies the validity of a cast in a given object hierarchy. We realise this by calling a function provided by the object-oriented language, via the FFI. An appropriate action – such as throwing a Haskell exception – can be taken if the cast fails.

2.3   Representing References to Objects in Haskell

Most object-oriented languages use memory references or pointers as an abstract object representation. On the Haskell side, it is easy to use type synonyms such as `type Drink = Ptr ()` and `type Coffee = Ptr ()`, and hence, use void (untyped) pointers to represent objects. However, this approach prevents the type system from distinguishing between different objects. To improve this situation, we use recursive `newtype` declarations, such as `newtype Coffee = Coffee (Ptr Coffee)`. As a result, pointers to objects are typed; we can then use different type class instances for different objects (which is not possible with type synonyms).

2.4   Class Objects

In some languages – e.g., Java, Smalltalk, Objective-C – defining a class has a dual purpose: it creates a new type with the name of that class and it also creates an instantiated object known as a *class object*. Class objects are concrete objects that represent the class: they store details such as method implementations, the name of the class, and which superclasses they inherit from.

In Haskell, we propose to make class objects accessible via a toplevel function `getClassObj` that obtains an abstract handle to the class object from the foreign language. We statically distinguish class objects from the standard *instance objects* by extending the class hierarchy on the Haskell side to include two separate *inheritance trees*: one tree for instance objects and another one for class objects. Two new data types – `InstanceObj` and `ClassObj` – act as the *roots* of the two trees, respectively. Listing 1.1 shows the setup for the `Drink` example, which we already used earlier. By convention, we use function names following the scheme `_classname_` to denote class objects.

Carrying the idea of class objects even further, some languages also have *metaclass objects*, which serve as class objects of class objects. We encode them in Haskell by a third inheritance tree, the `MetaclassObj` inheritance tree, and by extending the naming scheme of class objects to `__classname__` for metaclass objects.

3 Method Invocation on Objects

Given a design for modeling an object-oriented class hierarchy, we now address the question of how to invoke methods on those objects. This is non-trivial, as we wish to arrive at an invocation interface that is as concise and simple as method invocation from the object framework's native language. At the same time, we need to retain object-oriented style overloading, polymorphism, and also Haskell features, such as strong typing and type inference.

3.1 Message Expressions: The Low-Level Interface

A method invocation `anObject.aMethod (argument1, argument2, ...)` contains several entities. We call the name of the method along with its arguments – i.e., `aMethod(argument1, argument2, ...)` – a *message*. Moreover, we call the object or component receiving the message, i.e. `anObject`, the *receiver* of the message. Finally, we call a particular instance of a message together with its receiver, i.e. a concrete representation of a method invocation, a *message expression*. Thus, to send a *message*, it needs to be paired with a *receiver* to give a *message expression*.

On the lowest level, Haskell code interacts with other languages by using the standard *Foreign Function Interface (FFI)* [16]. The FFI, although conceptually more general, is currently only defined for interaction with C code. Bindings to object-oriented or component systems could in principle be achieved by extending the FFI to cover a wider range of calling conventions. However, this is an involved endeavour; so, given the current standard, it is more attractive to make use of the existing interface to C and to use it as a *proxy language*, or *bridge*, to enable Haskell code to communicate with the object-oriented system. We take this route and leave the exact representation of message expressions to the bridge, which gives us more flexibility in how such expressions can be represented, and also allows us to take advantage of existing language bindings from our target language to C. On the Haskell side, we provide a low-level Haskell API, outlined in Figure 1.2, to access C functions that manipulate message expressions as an abstract data type, shown in this example as simple C pointers.

Listing 1.1. Modeling a class hierarchy which includes class objects

```
class Obj o
-- the root of all objects (both class and non-class objects)
newtype AnyObj = AnyObj (Ptr AnyObj)
instance Obj AnyObj

class Obj i ⇒ Instance i
-- the root of all instance (non-class) objects
newtype InstanceObj = InstanceObj (Ptr InstanceObj)
instance Obj InstanceObj; instance Instance InstanceObj

class Instance s ⇒ SubDrink s
newtype Drink = Drink (Ptr Drink)
instance Obj Drink; instance Instance; instance SubCoffee Drink

class Instance s ⇒ SubCoffee s
newtype Coffee = Coffee (Ptr Coffee)
instance Obj Coffee; instance Instance Coffee; instance SubDrink
  Coffee; instance SubCoffee Coffee

-- the inheritance tree for class objects (the "class of classes")
class Obj c ⇒ Class c where
  -- Given the name of a class, returns its class object
  getClassObjFromName :: String → c
  -- Given a class object, returns its name
  classObjName :: c → String

-- the root of all class objects
newtype ClassObj = ClassObj (Ptr ClassObj)
instance Obj ClassObj; instance Class ClassObj

class Class s ⇒ DrinkClass s
newtype DrinkClassObj = DrinkClassObj (Ptr DrinkClassObj)
instance Obj DrinkClassObj
instance Class DrinkClassObj where { ... }
instance DrinkClass DrinkClassObj

class Class s ⇒ CoffeeClass s
newtype CoffeeClassObj = CoffeeClassObj (Ptr CoffeeClassObj)
instance Obj CoffeeClassObj; instance Class CoffeeClassObj; instance
  DrinkClass CoffeeClassObj; instance CoffeeClass CoffeeClassObj

getClassObj :: Class c ⇒ c
getClassObj =
  let x = upcast (getClassObjectFromName (classObjectName x)) in x

-- usage:
_Coffee_ = getClassObj :: CoffeeClassObj
_Drink_ = getClassObj :: DrinkClassObj
```

Listing 1.2. Low-Level Messaging Interface

```
newtype AnyObj = AnyObj (Ptr AnyObj); type Receiver = AnyObj
newtype MsgExpr = MsgExpr (Ptr MsgExpr)

foreign import ccall makeMsgExpr :: IO MsgExpr
foreign import ccall setReceiver :: MsgExpr → Receiver → IO ()
foreign import ccall setMethodName :: MsgExpr → CString → IO ()
  -- assuming that the method name to invoke is a C string

foreign import ccall setCIntArg :: MsgExpr → Int → CInt → IO ()
  -- the 'Int' arg specifies which index in the argument list to set
foreign import ccall setCCharArg :: MsgExpr → Int → CChar → IO ()
-- (repeat for the rest of the C basic foreign types) ...

-- send a message expression to its designated receiver
foreign import ccall sendMsgExprWithNoReply :: MsgExpr → IO ()
foreign import ccall sendMsgExprWithIntReply :: MsgExpr → IO Int
-- (repeat for the rest of the C basic foreign types) ...
```

3.2 A Higher-Level Message Sending Interface

On top of this low-level messaging API, we build a more convenient high-level
API in two steps. We will take the first step in this subsection where we construct
a generic `sendMsg` function, which can send a message with an arbitrary number
of arguments to an arbitrary receiver. The construction of the generic `sendMsg`
function is rather similar to the approach take in Lambada [4], but it is necessary
to summarise them here since we will build on them later, in our contribution
of the direct messaging interface. Let us turn to the generic messaging function
first, which we would like to use as illustrated in the following three example
invocations:

```
sendMsg receiver "methodName" (arg1, arg2, arg3) -- :: IO ()
sendMsg receiver' "anotherMethod" arg1 -- IO ()
-- sendMsg may also return a value:
num ← sendMsg receiver'' "yetAnotherMethod" (arg1, arg2) -- IO Int
```

Setting the Message Arguments. We use type classes to unify the various
set *Type* Arg functions from Section 3.1 into a single, overloaded `setArg` function:

```
class Storable a ⇒ Arg a where
   setArg :: MsgExpr → Int → a → IO ()
instance Arg CInt where setArg = setCIntArg
instance Arg CString where setArg = setCStringArg
-- etc ...
```

Sending Variable Arguments in a Message. As Haskell does not directly
support for functions with a variable number of parameters, we use tuples to
avoid the need for a whole family of `sendMsg` functions.

```
class Args args where
  setArgs :: MsgExpr → args → IO (); setArgs = setArg 1
instance Args Char where setArgs = setArg 1
instance Args Int where setArgs = setArg 1
instance Args CString where setArgs = setArg 1

instance (Arg a, Arg b) ⇒ Args (a, b) where
  setArgs expr (a, b) = do { setArg 1 expr a; setArg 2 expr b; }
instance (Arg a, Arg b, Arg c) ⇒ Args (a, b, c) where
  setArgs expr (a, b, c) = do { setArg 1 expr a; setArg 2 expr b;
    setArg 3 expr c; } -- (repeat for n-sized tuples)
```

It is also possible to use a list containing *existential data types* (an extension of Haskell 98 supported by many Haskell compilers) instead of a tuple, but the syntax to use such an existential list in practice is far more unwieldy.

Overloading the Message Reply Type. Just as we use type classes to unify the various set*Type*Arg functions into a single **setArg** function, we proceed to similarly obtain a function **sendMsgExpr** that can receive replies of varying type. We simply invoke the appropriate sendMsgExprWith*Type*Reply function:

```
class MsgReply r where sendMsgExpr :: MsgExpr → IO r
instance MsgReply () where sendMsgExpr = sendMsgExprWithNoReply
instance MsgReply Int where sendMsgExpr = sendMsgExprWithIntReply
instance MsgReply Float where sendMsgExpr = sendMsgExprWithFloatReply
-- etc ...
```

Implementing sendMsg. We implement **sendMsg** by combining the components discussed in this subsection. Thanks to liberal use of ad-hoc polymorphism via type classes, its implementation is (perhaps surprisingly) short and straightforward – especially considering how many lines of code this polymorphism saves us from writing when compared to directly using the low-level API to send messages:

```
sendMsg :: (Args args, MsgReply r)
        ⇒ Receiver → MethodName → args → IO r
sendMsg receiver methodName args = do
  e ← makeMsgExpr; setReceiver e receiver; setMethodName e methodName
  setArgs e args; r ← sendMsgExpr e; return r
```

3.3   Direct Messaging: Statically Type-Checked Message Sending

Unfortunately, while the definition of **sendMsg** enables any type of message with an arbitrary reply type to be sent to any receiving object, it also has the unpleasant side-effect that whenever the **sendMsg** function is called, the type system must be told explicitly what the reply type will be (i.e. the resulting type variable must be *fixed*), otherwise the type of **sendMsg** will be indeterminate. The receiving object and any objects in the argument list must also be upcast to the

`AnyObj` type, and if the message reply is an object, an explicit downcast must be performed on the reply type from `AnyObj` to its correct type. Thus, using `sendMsg`, the Haskell version of the simple Java statements `aHashtable.put(aKey, aValue); v = aHashtable.get(aKey)` is rather unattractive:

```
sendMsg (upcast aHashtable :: AnyObj) "put" (upcast aKey :: AnyObj,
   upcast aValue :: AnyObj) :: IO ()
valueAnyObj ← sendMsg (upcast aHashtable :: AnyObj) "get" (upcast
   aKey :: AnyObj) :: IO AnyObj
let v = downcast valueAnyObj :: IO SomeValue
```

It is clear that the Haskell version does not meet the two goals of allowing elegant and convenient communication with object-oriented frameworks. Ideally, the Haskell code to perform message sending should be as succinct as possible: `put aHashtable (aKey, aValue); v <- get aHashtable aKey`. This is how one would expect to use those functions if they were implemented in a native Haskell `Hashtable` module. The goal is therefore to have functions which automatically perform any typecasting and type fixing necessary to send a message, so that the programmer does not have to explicitly perform those tasks. To implement these functions, the dynamic `sendMsg` function can have its dynamism constrained by wrapper functions such as `put` and `get`, when there is knowledge of all the message expression's types at compile-time. Let us call these static wrapper functions *direct messaging functions*.

Automatically Upcasting Objects in the Argument List. We avoid explicit upcasts for objects sent via an argument list by making the relevant object data type (e.g. `HashtableObj`) an instance of the `Arg` type class. By making the `Obj` type class inherit from the `Arg` type class and implementing a *default method* in `Obj` named `setObjArg`, it is possible to do this generically for all objects:

```
class Arg arg ⇒ Obj arg where
  setObjArg :: Int → MsgExpr → arg → IO ()
  setObjArg idx exp arg = setAnyObjArg idx exp (upcast arg :: AnyObj)
instance Obj AnObj; instance Arg AnObj where setArg = setObjArg
```

Implementing Object-Oriented Style Overloading. In an object-oriented language, each class has a separate name space for method names. Moreover, it is possible to have two classes `Foo` and `Bar`, which both contain a method named m – and not only can m be overloaded within the class so that it can be called with different types of arguments, but the two classes may contain completely different return types for m:

```
class Foo { int m (float f, char c) { ... }; int m (int i) { ... } }
class Bar { void m (Object o) { ... }; void m () { ... } }
```

Since Haskell does not have namespace separation between objects, a method invocation of m on an instance of `Foo` or `Bar` would be written as `m Foo (3.14, 'a')` or `m Bar anObj` instead. We can implement such a function m by wrapping `sendMsg` in the following manner:

```
m :: (Obj receiver, Args args, MsgReply reply) =>
    receiver -> args -> reply
m receiver args reply = sendMsg receiver "m" args
data Foo = Foo; data Bar = Bar -- some ADT class instances
usage = do -- note that we must still fix the return type of m
  i <- m Foo (3.14, 'c') :: IO Int; i' <- m Foo (69 :: Int) :: IO Int
  m Bar anObj :: IO (); m Bar () :: IO ()
```

We can implement the hashtable functions put and get similarly to m. However, then, put and get will inherit the problem of requiring explicit type annotations from sendMsg. What is required is a way to *constrain* the type variables
which put and get can operate on. We do so by using a *multi-parameter type
class*: one parameter is used for each type variable that needs to be constrained.
The functions put, get, and any other method invocation have three parameters which need to be constrained: (1) the receiving object, (2) the types of the
argument list, and (3) the reply type. Additionally, the type system must be
told that the reply type is uniquely determined by the receiving object and the
argument list; otherwise, the result type will not be properly *fixed* by usage of
the put and get functions. We specify this type dependency using *functional
dependencies*. Now we have all the ingredients for implementing put and get:

```
class (Obj receiver, Args args, MsgReply reply) =>
  Put receiver args reply | receiver args -> reply
put :: (Put receiver args reply) => receiver -> args -> reply
put = sendMsg (upcast receiver :: AnyObj) "put" args

class (Obj receiver, Args args, MsgReply reply) =>
  Get receiver args reply | receiver args -> reply
get :: (Get receiver args reply) => receiver -> args -> reply
get = sendMsg (upcast receiver :: AnyObj) "get" args

-- specifying which types can be used with put and get
instance Put HashtableObj (AnyObj, AnyObj) ()
instance Get HashtableObj AnyObj AnyObj
instance Put FiniteMapObj (AnyObj, AnyObj) ()
instance Get FiniteMapObj AnyObj AnyObj
```

The DirectMsg Type Class. The above Put and Get type classes share many
similarities: the only difference between them is that Put is used to constrain the
type variables of the put function, and Get constrains the type variables of the
get function. We can eliminate these per method type classes by introducing
a DirectMsg type class which, as a new argument, gets the *method name* as
a *phantom parameter*, and declare a unique *method data type* for each method
name. Each instance of DirectMsg uses the method data type in its instance
declaration, and each direct messaging function *fixes* the phantom parameter
using the method data type, as in this example:

```
class (Obj rcvr, Args args, MsgReply reply) =>
  DirectMsg rcvr methodName args reply | rcvr methodName args -> reply
```

```
data Method_put; data Method_get
put :: (DirectMsg rcvr Method_put args reply) ⇒ rcvr → args → reply
put receiver args = sendMsg (upcast receiver :: AnyObj) "put" args
get :: (DirectMsg rcvr Method_get args reply) ⇒ rcvr → args → reply
get receiver args = sendMsg (upcast receiver :: AnyObj) "get" args

-- specifying which types can be used with put and get
instance DirectMsg HashtableObj MethodName_put (AnyObj, AnyObj) ()
instance DirectMsg HashtableObj MethodName_get (AnyObj) AnyObj
instance DirectMsg FiniteMapObj MethodName_put (AnyObj, AnyObj) ()
instance DirectMsg FiniteMapObj MethodName_get (AnyObj) AnyObj
```

This design using a single `DirectMsg` type class for all methods is sufficiently lightweight to be used with thousands of direct messaging functions. Moreover, it is easy to generate all the required declarations automatically. For languages which feature multiple inheritance and require disambiguation at the call site of the method invocation to determine which method to invoke, multiple Haskell method invocation functions can be provided, possibly with a simple name mangling scheme, e.g. the two C++ methods `foo.parent1::bar()` and `foo.parent2::bar()` can be translated to Haskell as `foo_parent1` and `foo_parent2`.

3.4   Transparent Marshaling

The `Arg` and `MsgReply` type classes can also perform *transparent marshaling*. For example, the following code demonstrates how the Haskell `String` type can be transparently marshaled to and from a foreign `StringObj` type before a message is sent or a message reply is retrieved:

```
instance Arg String where setArg expr index arg = do
  cString ← newCString arg; stringObj ← new _StringObj_ cString
  setArg expr index stringObj
instance MsgReply String where sendMsgExpr rcvr methodName args = do
  o ← sendMsgExprWithAnyObjReply rcvr methodName args
  let stringObj = downcast o :: StringObj
  cString ← getCString stringObj; peekCString cString
```

3.5   Monadic Binding and Object-Oriented Syntax

For clarity, the `sendMsg` function has been used so far with the receiving object as the first parameter in the argument list. However, we get a more natural notation if we place the receiving object *last* in the argument list, because then it is possible to create a function (`#`) as follows:

```
(#) :: obj → (obj → reply) → reply; obj # method = method obj
```

It allows us to write `object # method` rather than `method object`. This more closely resembles object-oriented notation. We can also use the monadic bind operator ($\gg=$) to build *message chains*, where the result of a method invocation is used as the receiver of the next method invocation. For example, equivalent to `foo.bar(a).baz(b)` in Java or `[[foo bar:a] baz:b]` in Objective-C, we can write `foo # bar a >>= baz b` in Haskell.

4   Meta-programming an Interface Generator

The majority of Haskell language binding tools are implemented as pre-processors that generate a Haskell version of the desired component system's API functions: such tools are called *interface generators*. The Glorious Glasgow Haskell Compiler recently introduced facilities for *compile-time meta-programming*, called *Template Haskell*, that provide an alternative to interface generators implemented as pre-processors. Compile-time meta-programming restricts meta-programming – i.e., program generation – to compile time, which means that interface generation can be folded into the compilation process of the interface and possibly its client; thus, the interface generator becomes a meta-program. In Template Haskell, a meta-program is standard Haskell code that can inspect, modify, and generate other Haskell code translated in the some compilation run.

In other words, we can program the Haskell compiler itself to take the role of an interface generator (such as H/Direct, GreenCard, or C→Haskell). Instead of generating text files, such an interface generator produces an internal representation of the generated Haskell code, which is, then, immediately translated to object code. If such a meta-programming-based interface generator can automatically find the interfaces presented by the target API, then the task of mapping a component system's API in Haskell can be completely automated at compile-time, and all that is required from the programmer are a few extra lines of code to splice in the instructions to the meta-program implementing the interface generator. Finding the target API can happen in either of two ways:

1. If the API is available in the form of a machine readable interface files, the meta-program can analyse these interface files and synthesise a matching Haskell API together with the required marshaling code.
2. If the API can be queried using the reflective capabilities of the target framework, the meta-program can use the FFI to retrieve the API at compile time.

The later method, i.e. the use of reflection, is attractive as it removes any scope for a mismatch between the API version used for interface generation and that used on execution of the interface. However, it at the same time also complicates cross-compilation.

Interface Files. To illustrate the use of interface files for binding generation with meta-programming, let us consider the case of generating bindings to C libraries using Template Haskell [3]. In this case, the Haskell meta-program needs to read the C header files of the library, which Template Haskell supports via I/O actions in the *quotation monad*. This monad, called `Q`, is a state transformer realised as an extension of the standard Haskell `IO` monad. Hence, standard `IO` routines can be lifted into the quotation monad. In this setting, the following skeleton outlines the generation of FFI import declarations from a C header file:

```
importC :: FilePath → Q Dec
importC headerFile = do
  -- generate an abstract syntax tree from the C header file
  headerAST ← parseC headerFile
  -- make "foreign import" declarations from C function prototypes
  foreignImportDecls ← cPrototypesToHaskellDecls headerAST
  return foreignImportDecls
```

In practice, we need additional code to generate marshaling code, in addition to the FFI declarations. In any case, a function, such as `importC`, might then be used by way of a Template Haskell *toplevel splice*, which glues the generated code into the currently compiled program, such as `$(importC "<math.h>")` to provide access to a C library.

Reflection. To illustrate the use of reflection for the same task, we shall consider the case of interfacing to Objective-C, which is what we do for the Mocha binding described in Section 5. In this case, the meta-program needs access to the targeted object-oriented framework itself, while generating the required Haskell API and marshaling code. This access requires the interoperation of Haskell with the target language (in our case, with Objective-C), and hence, requires the use of the FFI. In Haskell, this will usually require IO operations, which are realised via the quotation monad, just as in the case of accessing interface files. As an example, consider the following:

```
-- the root of all class objects (as in Listing 1.1)
newtype ClassObj = ClassObj (Ptr ClassObj)
-- C proxy language function to retrieve ObjC classes via reflection
foreign import lookupObjCClasses :: IO [ObjCClass]
-- declares a Haskell API from an ObjC class (e.g. with marshaling
-- code and direct messaging functions)
declareHaskellAPIForObjCClass :: ObjCClass → Q Exp
importObjCClasses :: Q Exp
importObjCClasses = do
  classes ← lookupObjCClasses
  haskellAPIDeclarations ← map declareHaskellAPIForObjCClass classes
  sequence haskellAPIDeclarations
```

One can then splice in the Haskell API declarations for the Objective-C classes by writing `$(importObjCClasses)`.

5   Mocha: A Haskell to Objective-C Binding

We implemented the methods described in this paper to realise a language binding between Haskell and Objective-C, which we named Mocha. Objective-C is used extensively in the Mac OS X, NeXTStep and GNUstep environments, and features two object frameworks – *Foundation* and *AppKit* – which together facilitate rapid software development. *Cocoa* is the name that Apple® has given to the combination of the *Foundation* and *AppKit* frameworks in association with several more Objective-C classes specific to the Mac OS X platform.

Modeling Cocoa Classes. To model the class hierarchy, Mocha generates four class hierarchy trees for the Haskell programmer: one to represent instance objects, one for class objects, one for meta-class objects, and one for Objective-C's *formal protocol* objects[1] – this follows the method described in Section 2. Explicit upcasting and downcasting of objects is provided, so that objects retrieved from Cocoa container objects (such as **NSArray** or **NSDictionary**) can be cast appropriately – following Section 2.2.

Interface definitions are provided for the entire Cocoa framework, and on-the-fly interface generation is provided via Template Haskell, so that user-written Objective-C frameworks can easily be used when writing a Haskell program. (The Template Haskell-based interface generator was also used to generate the interface definitions for Cocoa.)

Communication with Objective-C. Mocha enables Haskell to send messages to Objective-C objects and also facilitates Objective-C objects written in Haskell. Message sending from Haskell to Objective-C is based on the techniques described in Section 3, with the exception that an additional type class has been used in Mocha to integrate Objective-C's *type encodings* scheme with the messaging functions.

The abstract **MsgExpr** data type is implemented in Mocha using Cocoa's **NSInvocation** class, which exactly fulfills the properties required of a **MsgExpr**. Mocha implements transparent marshaling between many analogous data types, such as a Haskell **Strings** and the Cocoa framework's **NSString** class, and provides *direct messaging functions* for the entire Cocoa framework.

Mocha uses *surrogate objects* to forward messages from the Objective-C environment to the Haskell environment, and these surrogate objects are capable of masquerading as any type of object in Objective-C. As a result, it is possible for the Haskell environment to respond to actions produced by a user in a GUI interface, or even for Haskell code to function as a fully-fledged **NSDocument** or **NSWindow** controller.

Building Cocoa Applications. The Haskell URL fetcher introduced in Section 1 of this paper is a complete, working program and is one of the examples included with Mocha. Mocha can be used to build complete GUI applications on Mac OS X that are written purely in Haskell, using the Cocoa framework. Mocha is currently only implemented on the Mac OS X platform, but it should be possible to port it to other Objective-C systems such as GNUstep without much difficulty.

The homepage for Mocha is at http://www.algorithm.com.au/mocha/. In accordance with the Haskell and Apple open-source developer and research communities, it has been provided under the liberal BSD license.

---

[1] A *formal protocol* is similar to a Java *interface* or a C++ *pure virtual class*. Formal protocols enable objects to inherit multiple interface definitions, but not inherit multiple implementation definitions.

Acknowledgments

We are grateful to Wolfgang Thaller for the many technical discussions about the topics discussed in this paper and the inspiration provided by his HOC binding. Moreover, we thank Roman Leshchinskiy for his helpful feedback on an earlier version of the paper.

References

1. Simon Peyton Jones, M.J., Meijer, E.: Type classes: exploring the design space. In: Haskell Workshop. (1997)
2. Jones, M.P.: Type classes with functional dependencies. In: Proceedings of the 9th European Symposium on Programming (ESOP 2000). Number 1782 in Lecture Notes in Computer Science, Springer-Verlag (2000)
3. Sheard, T., Peyton Jones, S.: Template meta-programming for haskell. In: Proceedings of the Haskell Workshop. (2002)
4. Meijer, E., Finne, S.: Lambada: Haskell as a better Java. In: Electronic Notes in Theoretical Computer Science 41 No. 1. (2001)
5. Shields, M., Peyton Jones, S.: Object-oriented style overloading for Haskell. In: First Workshop on Multi-language Inferastructure and Interoperability (BABEL'01), Firenze, Italy. (2001)
6. Leijen, D., Meijer, E., Hook, J.: Haskell as an automation controller. In: Advanced Functional Programming. (1998) 268–289
7. Finne, S., Leijen, D., Meijer, E., Jones, S.P.: Calling hell from heaven and heaven from hell. In: Proceedings of the ACM SIGPLAN International Conference on Functional Programming, ACM Press (1999)
8. Peyton Jones, S., Meijer, E., Leijen, D.: Scripting COM components in Haskell. In: Proceedings of the Fifth International Conference on Software Reuse, IEEE Computer Society (1998)
9. Finne, S., Leijen, D., Meijer, E., Peyton Jones, S.L.: H/Direct: A binary foreign language interface for Haskell. In: Proceedings of the ACM SIGPLAN International Conference on Functional Programming (ICFP'98), ACM Press (1998) 153–162
10. Courtney, A.: GCJNI (2002) http://haskell.cs.yale.edu/gcjni/.
11. Yakeley, A.: Haskell/Java VM Bridge (2003)
   http://sourceforge.net/projects/jvm-bridge/.
12. Nordin, T., Peyton Jones, S.L., Reid, A.: Green Card: a foreign-language interface for Haskell. In: Proceedings of the Haskell Workshop. (1997)
13. Chakravarty, M.M.T.: C→Haskell, or yet another interfacing tool. In Koopman, P., ed.: Proceedings of Implementation of Functional Languages, 11th. International Workshop (IFL'99). (1999)
14. The GHC Team: The Glasgow Haskell Compiler user's guide: Writing Haskell interfaces to C code: hsc2hs (2001)
   http://www.haskell.org/ghc/docs/latest/html/users_guide/hsc2hs.html.
15. Reid, A.: Template Greencard (draft) (2003) Presented at Implementation of Functional Languages, 15th International Workshop (IFL'03).
16. The Haskell FFI Team: A primitive foreign function interface.
   http://www.cse.unsw.edu.au/~chak/haskell/ffi/ (1998)

A Functional Shell
That Dynamically Combines Compiled Code

Arjen van Weelden* and Rinus Plasmeijer

Computer Science Institute, University of Nijmegen
Toernooiveld 1, 6525 ED Nijmegen, The Netherlands
{arjenw,rinus}@cs.kun.nl

Abstract. We present a new shell that provides the full basic functionality of a strongly typed lazy functional language, including overloading.
The shell can be used for manipulating files, applications, data and processes at the command line. The shell does type checking and only executes well-typed expressions. Files are typed, and applications are simply
files with a function type. The shell executes a command line by combining existing code of functions on disk. We use the hybrid static/dynamic
type system of Clean to do type checking/inference. Its dynamic linker
is used to store and retrieve any expression (both data and code) with
its type on disk. Our shell combines the advantages of interpreters (direct response) and compilers (statically typed, fast code). Applications
(compiled functions) can be used, in a type safe way, in the shell, and
functions defined in the shell can be used by any compiled application.

1   Introduction

Programming languages, especially pure and lazy functional languages like Clean
[1] and Haskell [2], provide good support for abstraction (e.g. subroutines, overloading, polymorphic functions), composition (e.g. application, higher-order
functions, module systems), and verification (e.g. strong type checking and inference).

In contrast, command line languages used by operating system shells usually
have little support for abstraction, composition, and especially verification. They
do not provide higher-order subroutines, complex data structures, type inference,
or even type checking at all before evaluation. Given their limited set of types
and their specific area of application, this has not been recognized as a serious
problem in the past.

We think that command line languages can benefit from some of the programming language facilities, as this will increase their flexibility, reusability
and security. We have previously done research on reducing run-time errors (e.g.
memory access violations, type errors) in operating systems by implementing a
micro kernel in Clean that provides type safe communication of any value of any
type between functional processes, called Famke [3]. This has shown that (moderate) use of dynamic typing [4], in combination with Clean's dynamic run-time

---

* Part of this work was supported by InterNLnet.

P. Trinder, G. Michaelson, and R. Peña (Eds.): IFL 2003, LNCS 3145, pp. 36–52, 2004.
© Springer-Verlag Berlin Heidelberg 2004

system and dynamic linker [5, 6], enables processes to communicate any data (and even code) of any type in a type safe way.

During the development of a shell/command line interface for our prototype functional operating system it became clear that a normal shell cannot really make use (at run-time) of the type information derived by the compiler (at compile-time). To reduce the possibility of run-time errors during execution of scripts or command lines, we need a shell that supports abstraction and verification (i.e. type checking) in the same way as the Clean compiler does. In order to do this, we need a better integration of compile-time (i.e. static typing) and run-time (i.e. interactivity) concepts.

In this paper we present a shell for a functional language-based operating system that combines the best of both worlds: the interactivity of an interpreter and the efficiency and type safety of a compiler. This shell is used as the user interface for Famke, the above mentioned kernel of a prototype functional operating system in development. The shell can make use of compiled functions/programs, without losing type information. Functions defined in the shell can also be used by compiled applications.

The shell is built on top of Clean's hybrid static/dynamic type system and its dynamic I/O run-time support. It allows programmers to save any Clean expression, i.e. a graph that can contain data, references to functions, and closures, to disk. Clean expressions can be written to disk as a *dynamic*, which contains a representation of their (polymorphic) static type, while preserving sharing. Clean programs can load dynamics from disk and use run-time type pattern matching to reintegrate it into the statically typed program. In this way, new functionality (e.g. plug-ins) can be added to a running program in a type safe way.

The shell is called Esther (*Extensible Shell with Type cHecking ExpeRiment*), and is capable of:

- reading an expression from the console, using Clean's syntax for a basic, but complete, functional language. It offers application, lambda abstraction, recursive let, pattern matching, function definitions, and even overloading;
- using compiled Clean programs as typed functions at the command line;
- defining new functions, which can be used by other compiled Clean programs (without using the shell or an interpreter);
- extracting type information (and indirectly, code) from dynamics on disk;
- type checking the expression, and solving overloading, before evaluation;
- constructing a new dynamic containing the correct type and code of the expression.

First, we introduce the static/dynamic hybrid type system of Clean in Sect. 2. Section 3 gives a global description of how Esther uses dynamics to type check an expression. It also give examples of the use of dynamics. In Sect. 4 we show how to construct a dynamic for each kind of subexpression such that it has the correct semantics and type, and how to compose them in a type checked way. Related work is discussed in Sect. 5 and we conclude and mention future research in Sect. 6.

2   Dynamics in Clean

In addition to its static type system, Clean has recently been extended with
a (polymorphic) dynamic type system [4–6]. A dynamic in Clean is a value of
static type *Dynamic*, which contains an expression as well as a representation of
the (static) type of that expression. Dynamics can be formed (i.e. lifted from the
static to the dynamic type system) using the keyword `dynamic` in combination
with the value and an optional type. The compiler will infer the type if it is
omitted[1].

```
dynamic 42 :: Int²
dynamic map fst :: A³.a b: [(a, b)] -> [a]
```

Function alternatives and case patterns can pattern match on values of type
Dynamic (i.e. bring them from the dynamic back into the static type system).
Such a pattern match consist of a value pattern and a type pattern. In the
example below, `matchInt` returns `Just` the value contained inside the dynamic
if it has type *Int*; and `Nothing` if it has any other type. The compiler translates
a pattern match on a type into run-time type unification. If the unification fails,
the next alternative is tried, as in a common (value) pattern match.

```
::⁴ Maybe a = Nothing | Just a

matchInt :: Dynamic -> Maybe Int
matchInt (x :: Int) = Just x
matchInt   other    = Nothing
```

A type pattern can contain type variables which, provided that run-time
unification is successful, are bound to the offered type. In the example below,
`dynamicApply` tests if the argument type of the function `f` inside its first argument can be unified with the type of the value `x` inside the second argument. If
this is the case then `dynamicApply` can safely apply `f` to `x`. The type variables
a and *b* will be instantiated by the run-time unification. At compile time it is
generally unknown what type *a* and *b* will be, but if the type pattern match
succeeds, the compiler can safely apply `f` to `x`. This yields a value with the type
that is bound to *b* by unification, which is wrapped in a dynamic.

```
dynamicApply :: Dynamic Dynamic -> Dynamic⁵
dynamicApply (f :: a -> b) (x :: a) = dynamic f x :: b⁶
dynamicApply     df            dx   = dynamic "Error: cannot apply"
```

Type variables in dynamic patterns can also relate to a type variable in the
static type of a function. Such functions are called type dependent functions [7].
A caret (ˆ) behind a variable in a pattern associates it with the type variable with

---

[1] Types containing universally quantified variables are currently not inferred by the
  compiler. We will not always write these types for ease of presentation.
[2] Numerical denotations are not overloaded in Clean.
[3] Clean's syntax for Haskell's `forall`.
[4] Defines a new data type in Clean, Haskell uses the `data` keyword.
[5] Clean separates argument types by whitespace, instead of `->`.
[6] The type *b* is also inferred by the compiler.

the same name in the static type of the function. The static type variable then becomes overloaded in the predefined TC (or type code) class. The TC class is used to 'carry' the type representation. In the example below, the static type variable t will be determined by the (static) context in which it is used, and will impose a restriction on the actual type that is accepted at run-time by matchDynamic. It yields Just the value inside the dynamic (if the dynamic contains a value of the required context dependent type) or Nothing (if it does not).

```
matchDynamic :: Dynamic -> Maybe t | TC t⁷
matchDynamic (x :: t^) = Just x
matchDynamic  other    = Nothing
```

The dynamic run-time system of Clean supports writing dynamics to disk and reading them back again, possibly in another program or during another execution of the same program. The dynamic will be read in lazily after a successful run-time unification (triggered by a pattern match on the dynamic). The amount of data and code that the dynamic linker will link, is therefore determined by the amount of evaluation of the value inside the dynamic. Dynamics written by a program can be safely read by any other program, providing a simple form of persistence and some rudimentary means of communication.

```
writeDynamic :: String Dynamic *⁸World -> (Bool, *World)
readDynamic :: String *World -> (Bool, Dynamic, *World)
```

Running prog1 and prog2 in the example below will write a function and a value to dynamics on disk. Running prog3 will create a new dynamic on disk that contains the result of 'applying' (using the dynamicApply function) the dynamic with the name "function" to the dynamic with the name "value". The closure 40 + 2 will not be evaluated until the * operator needs it. In this case, because the 'dynamic application' of df to dx is lazy, the closure will not be evaluated until the value of the dynamic on disk named "result" is needed. Running prog4 tries to match the dynamic dr, from the file named "result", with the type *Int*. After this succeeds, it displays the value by evaluating the expression, which is semantically equal to let x = 40 + 2 in x * x, yielding 1764.

```
prog1 world = writeDynamic "function" (dynamic * :: Int Int -> Int) world

prog2 world = writeDynamic "value" (dynamic 40 + 2) world

prog3 world = let (ok1, df, world1) = readDynamic "function" world
                  (ok2, dx, world2) = readDynamic "value" world1
              in  writeDynamic "result" (dynamicApply df dx) world2

prog4 world = let (ok, dr, world1) = readDynamic "result" world
              in  (case dr of (x :: Int) -> x, world1)
```

---

[7] Clean uses | to denote overloading. In Haskell this would be written as (TC t) => Dynamic -> Maybe t.

[8] This is a uniqueness attribute, indicating that the world environment is passed around in a single threaded way. Unique values allow safe destructive updates and are used for I/O in Clean. The value of type World corresponds with the hidden state of the IO monad in Haskell.

3   An Overview of Esther

The last example of the previous section shows how one can store and retrieve values, expressions, and functions of any type to and from the file system. It also shows that the `dynamicApply` function can be used to type check an application at run-time using the static types stored in dynamics. Combining both in an interactive 'read expression – apply dynamics – evaluate and show result' loop gives a very simple shell that already supports the type checked run-time application of programs to documents.

Obviously, we could have implemented type checking ourselves using one of the common algorithms involving building and solving a list of type equations. Instead, we decided to use Clean's dynamic run-time unification, for this has several advantages: 1) Clean's dynamics allow us to do type safe and lazy I/O of expressions; 2) we do not need to convert between the (hidden) type representation used by dynamics and the type representation used by our type checking algorithm; 3) it shows whether Clean's current dynamics interface is powerful enough to implement basic type inference and type checking; 4) we get future improvements of Clean's dynamics interface for free (e.g. uniqueness attributes or overloading).

Unlike common command interpreters or shells, our shell Esther does not work on untyped files that consist of executables and streams of characters. Instead, all functions/programs are stored as dynamics, forming a rudimentary typed file system.

Moreover, instead of evaluating the expression by interpretation of the source code, Esther generates a new dynamic that contains a closure that refers to the compiled code of other programs. The shell, therefore, is a hybrid interpreter that generates compiled code. The resulting dynamic can be used by any other compiled Clean program without using an interpreter or the shell. Dynamics can contain closures, which refer to code and data belonging to other compiled Clean programs. When needed for evaluation, the code is automatically linked to the running program by Clean's dynamic linker. This approach results in less overhead during evaluation of the expression than using a conventional source code interpreter.

Esther performs the following steps in a loop:

- it reads a string from the console and parses it like a Clean expression. It supports denotations of Clean's basic and predefined types, application, infix operators, lambda abstraction, overloading, let(rec), and case expressions;
- identifiers that are not bound by a lambda abstraction, a let(rec), or a case pattern are assumed to be names of dynamics on disk, and they are read from disk;
- type checks the expression using dynamic run-time unification and type pattern matching, which also infers types;
- if the command expression does not contain type errors, Esther displays the result of the expression and the inferred type. Esther will automatically be extended with any code necessary to display the result (which requires evaluation) by the dynamic linker.

Fig. 1. A combined screenshot of two incarnations of Esther.

3.1 Example: A Session with Esther

To illustrate the expressive power of Esther, we show an Esther session in Fig. 1 (the left window with the white title bar) and explain what happens:

1. 'Simple' arithmetic. The shell looks in the current search-path to find the infix function +. The + is overloaded, and the shell searches again for an instance for + for type *Int*. Finally, it responds with the value and inferred type of the result.
2. Typing the name of a dynamic at the prompt shows its contents, which can contain unnamed lambda functions (\), and its type.
3. The dynamic map is applied to the dynamic fst yielding the expected type.
4. The infix operator + cannot be applied to an integer and a string.
5. The overloaded function inc is revealed to be overloaded in + and one. The \ id id is caused by the way Esther handles overloading (see Sect. 4.6.).
6. The lambda expression \f x -> f (f x) is written to disk, using the >> operator, and named twice. It is defined as a left associative infix operator with priority 9. Esther shows the internal code and type of the lambda expression, exposing the fact that it uses combinators (see Sect. 4.2).
7. The dynamic inc is applied to 1.14 via the previously defined operator twice.
8. Defines a function named head that selects the first argument of a list using a case expression.
9. Applies head to an empty list yielding a pattern mismatch exception.
10. Defines a function named fac that yields the factorial of its argument.

11. `fac 10` is evaluated to 3628800.
12. `famkeNewProcess` is used to start Esther (which is also stored as a dynamic) as new process, on the same computer (right window with black title bar):

1 Evaluates `cd "/programs/StdEnv"` to 'change directory' to the directory that provides Clean's standard library to Esther, by storing the functions as dynamics in the file system. Because `cd` has type $String$ $*World \rightarrow *World$ and therefore no result, Esther shows UNIT (i.e. $void$).

2 Evaluates the application of `ls` to the empty string, showing all files in the current directory: the functions in the standard library.

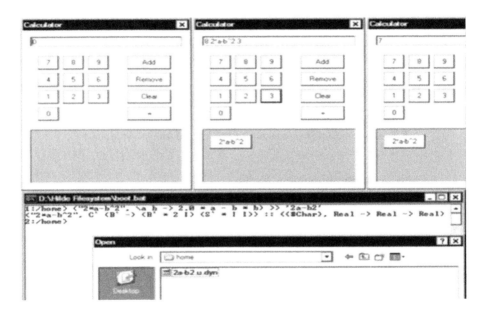

Fig. 2. A combined screenshot of the calculator in action and Esther.

3.2   Example: A Calculator That Uses a Shell Function

Figure 2 shows a sequence of screenshots of a calculator program written in Clean. Initially, the calculator has no function buttons. Instead, it has buttons to add and remove function buttons. These will be loaded dynamically after adding dynamics that contain tuples of $String$ and $Real\ Real \rightarrow Real$.

The lower half of Fig. 2 shows a command line in the Esther shell that writes such a tuple as a dynamic named "2a-b2.u.dyn" to disk. The extension ".dyn" is added by Clean dynamic linker, the ".u" before the extension is used to store the file fixity attributes ("u" means prefix). Esther pretty prints these attributes, but the Microsoft Windows file selector shows the file name in a raw form.

Its button name is 2*a-b^2 and the function is \a b -> 2.0 * a - b * b. Pressing the Add button on the calculator opens a file selection dialog, shown at the bottom of Fig. 2. After selecting the dynamic named "2a-2b.u.dyn", it becomes available in the calculator as the button 2*a-b^2, and it is applied to 8 and 3 yielding 7.

The calculator itself is a separately compiled Clean executable that runs without using Esther. Alternatively, one can write the calculator, which has type [(*String*, *Real Real* → *Real*)] *World* → *World*, to disk as a dynamic. The calculator can then be started from Esther, either in the current shell or as a separate process.

4 Type Checking with Dynamics

In this section, we show how one can use the type unification of Clean's dynamic run-time system to type check a common syntax tree, and how to construct the corresponding Clean expression. The parsing is trivial and we will assume that the string has already been successfully parsed. In order to support a basic, but complete, functional language in our shell we need to support function definitions, lambda, let(rec), and case expressions.

We will introduce the syntax tree piecewise and show for each kind of expression how to construct a dynamic that contains the corresponding Clean expression and the type for that expression. Names occurring free in the command line are read from disk as dynamics before type checking. The expression can contain references to other dynamics, and therefore to the compiled code of functions, which will be automatically linked by Clean's run-time system.

4.1 Application

Suppose we have a syntax tree for constant values and function applications that looks like:

```
:: Expr = (@) infixl 9⁹ Expr Expr  //¹⁰ Application
        | Value Dynamic            // Constant or dynamic value from disk
```

We introduce a function compose, which constructs the dynamic containing a value with the correct type that, when evaluated, will yield the result of the given expression.

```
compose :: Expr -> Dynamic
compose (Value d) = d
compose (f @ x)   = case (compose f, compose x) of
    (f :: a -> b, x :: a) -> dynamic f x :: b
    (df, dx)              -> raise¹¹ ("Cannot apply " +++ typeOf df
                                     +++ " to " +++ typeOf dx)
```

---

[9] This defines an infix constructor with priority 9 that is left associative.

[10] This a Clean comment to end-of-line, like Haskell's --.

[11] For easier error reporting, we implemented imprecise user-defined exceptions à la Haskell [8]. We used dynamics to make the set of exceptions extensible.

```
typeOf :: Dynamic -> String
typeOf dyn = toString (typecodeOfDynamic dyn) // pretty print type
```

Composing a constant value, contained in a dynamic, is trivial. Composing an application of one expression to another is a lot like the dynamicApply function of Sect. 2. Most importantly, we added error reporting using the typeOf function for pretty printing the type of a value inside a dynamic.

4.2 Lambda Expressions

Next, we extend the syntax tree with lambda expressions and variables.

```
:: Expr = ...                        // Previous def.
        | (-->) infixr 0 Expr Expr   // Lambda abstraction: \ .. -> ..
        | Var String                 // Variable
        | S | K | I                  // Combinators
```

At first sight, it looks as if we could simply replace a Lambda constructor in the syntax tree with a dynamic containing a lambda expression in Clean:

```
compose (Var x --> e) = dynamic (\y -> composeLambda x y e :: ?)
```

The problem with this approach is that we have to specify the type of the lambda expression before the evaluation of composeLambda. Furthermore, composeLambda will not be evaluated until the lambda expression is applied to an argument. This problem is unavoidable because we cannot get 'around' the lambda. Fortunately, bracket abstraction [9] solves both problems.

Applications and constant values are composed to dynamics in the usual way. We translate each lambda expression (-->) to a sequence of combinators (S, K, and I) and applications, with the help of the function ski.

```
compose ...        // Previous def.
compose (x --> e) = compose (ski x e)
compose I         = dynamic \x -> x
compose K         = dynamic \x y -> x
compose S         = dynamic \f g x -> f x (g x)

ski :: Expr Expr -> Expr  // common bracket abstraction
ski x       (y --> e) = ski x (ski y e)
ski (Var x) (Var y)   |¹² x == y = I
ski x       (f @ y)   = S @ ski x f @ ski x y
ski x       e         = K @ e
```

Composing lambda expressions uses ski to eliminate the Lambda and Variable syntax constructors, leaving only applications, dynamic values, and combinators. Composing a combinator simply wraps its corresponding definition and type as a lambda expression into a dynamic.

Special combinators and combinator optimization rules are often used to improve the speed of the generated combinator code by reducing the number of

---

¹² If this guard fails, we end up in the last function alternative.

combinators [10]. One has to be careful not to optimize the generated combinator expressions in such a way that the resulting type becomes too general. In an untyped world this is allowed because they preserve the intended semantics when generating untyped (abstract) code. However, our generated code is contained within a dynamic and is therefore typed. This makes it essential that we preserve the principal type of the expression during bracket abstraction. Adding common η-conversion, for example, results in a too general type for `Var "f" -->` `Var "x" --> f x`: $\forall a.a \rightarrow a$, instead of $\forall ab.(a \rightarrow b) \rightarrow a \rightarrow b$. Such optimizations might prevent us from getting the principal type for an expression. Simple bracket abstraction using `S`, `K`, and `I`, as performed by `ski`, does preserves the principal type [11].

Code combined by Esther in this way is not as fast as code generated by the Clean compiler. Combinators introduced by bracket abstraction are the main reason for this slowdown. Additionally, all applications are lazy and not specialized for basic types. However, these disadvantages only hold for the small (lambda) functions written at the command line, which are mostly used for plumbing. If faster execution is required, one can always copy-paste the command line into a Clean module that writes a dynamic to disk and running the compiler.

In order to reduce the number of combinators in the generated expression, our current implementation uses Diller's algorithm C [12] without η-conversion in order to preserve the principal type, while reducing the number of generated combinators from exponential to quadratic. Our current implementation seems to be fast enough, so we did not explore further optimizations by other bracket abstraction algorithms.

4.3 Irrefutable Patterns

Here we introduce irrefutable patterns, e.g. (nested) tuples, in lambda expressions. This is a preparation for the upcoming let(rec) expressions.

```
:: Expr = ...              // Previous def.
          | Tuple Int      // Tuple constructor

compose ...        // Previous def.
compose (Tuple n) = tupleConstr n

tupleConstr :: Int -> Dynamic
tupleConstr 2 = dynamic \x y -> (x, y)
tupleConstr 3 = dynamic \x y z -> (x, y, z)
tupleConstr ... // and so on...13

ski :: Expr Expr -> Expr
ski (f @ x)  e = ski f (x --> e)
ski (Tuple n) e = Value (matchTuple n) @ e
ski ...        // previous def.
```

---

[13] ...until 32. Clean does not support functions or data types with arity above 32.

```
matchTuple :: Int -> Dynamic
matchTuple 2 = dynamic \f t -> f (fst t) (snd t)
matchTuple 3 = dynamic \f t -> f (fst3 t) (snd3 t) (thd3 t)
matchTuple ... // and so on...
```

We extend the syntax tree with `Tuple` n constructors (where n is the number of elements in the tuple). This makes expressions like `Tuple 3 @ Var "x" @ Var "y" @ Var "z" --> Tuple 2 @ Var "x" @ Var "z"` valid expressions. This example corresponds with the Clean lambda expression `\(x, y, z) -> (x, z)`.

When the `ski` function reaches an application in the left-hand side of the lambda abstraction, it processes both sub-patterns recursively. When the `ski` function reaches a `Tuple` constructor it replaces it with a call to the `matchTuple` function. Note that the right-hand side of the lambda expression has already been transformed into lambda abstractions, which expect each component of the tuple as a separate argument. We then use the `matchTuple` function to extract each component of the tuple separately. It uses lazy tuple selections (using `fst` and `snd`, because Clean tuple patterns are always eager) to prevent non-termination of recursive let(rec)s in the next section.

4.4 Let(rec) Expressions

Now we are ready to add irrefutable let(rec) expressions. Refutable let(rec) expressions must be written as cases, which will be introduced in next section.

```
:: Expr = ...                    // Previous def.
        | Letrec [Def] Expr      // let(rec) .. in ..
        | Y                      // Combinator

:: Def = (::=) infix 0 Expr Expr   // .. = ..

compose ...             // Previous def.
compose (Letrec ds e) = compose (letRecToLambda ds e)
compose Y             = dynamic y where y f = f (y f)

letRecToLambda :: [Def] Expr -> Expr
letRecToLambda ds e = let (p ::= d) = combine ds
                      in  ski p e @ (Y @ ski p d)

combine :: [Def] -> Def
combine [p ::= e]    = p ::= e
combine [p1 ::= e1:ds] = let (p2 ::= e2) = combine ds
                         in  Tuple 2 @ p1 @ p2 ::= Tuple 2 @ e1 @ e2
```

When `compose` encounters a let(rec) expression it uses `letRecToLambda` to convert it into a lambda expression. The `letRecToLambda` function `combines` all (possibly mutually recursive) definitions by pairing definitions into a single (possibly recursive) irrefutable tuple pattern. This leaves us with just a single definition that `letRecToLambda` converts to a lambda expression in the usual way [13].

4.5   Case Expressions

Composing a case expression is done by transforming each alternative into a lambda expression that takes the expression to match as an argument. If the expression matches the pattern, the right-hand side of the alternative is taken. When it does not match, the lambda expression corresponding to the next alternative is applied to the expression, forming a cascade of if-then-else constructs. This results in a single lambda expression that implements the case construct, and we apply it to the expression that we wanted to match against.

```
:: Expr = ...                        // Previous def.
        | Case Expr [Alt]            // case .. of ..

:: Alt = (==>) infix 0 Expr Expr    // .. -> ..

compose ...            // Previous def.
compose (Case e as) = compose (altsToLambda as @ e)
```

We translate the alternatives into lambda expressions below using the following rules. If the pattern consists of an application we do bracket abstraction for each argument, just as we did for lambda expressions, in order to deal with each subpattern recursively. Matching against an irrefutable pattern, such as variables of tuples, always succeeds and we reuse the code of ski that does the matching for lambda expressions. Matching basic values is done using ifEqual that uses Clean's built-in equalities for each basic type. We always add a default alternative, using the mismatch function, that informs the user that none of the patterns matched the expression.

```
altsToLambda :: [Alt] -> Expr
altsToLambda []                      = Value mismatch
altsToLambda [f @ x ==> e:as]        = altsToLambda [f ==> ski x e:as]
altsToLambda [Var x ==> e:_]         = Var x --> e
altsToLambda [Tuple n ==> e:_]       = Tuple n --> e
altsToLambda [Value dyn ==> th:as] = let el = altsToLambda as
     in case dyn of
          (i :: Int)  -> Value (ifEqual i) @ th @ el
          (c :: Char) -> Value (ifEqual c) @ th @ el
          ... // for all basic types

ifEqual :: a -> Dynamic | TC a & Eq a
ifEqual x = dynamic \th el y -> if (x == y) th (el y)
                   :: A.b: b (a^ -> b) a^ -> b

mismatch = dynamic raise "Pattern mismatch" :: A.a: a
```

Matching against a constructor contained in a dynamic takes more work. For example, if we put Clean's list constructor [:] in a dynamic we find that it has type $\forall a.a \rightarrow [a] \rightarrow [a]$, which is a function type. In Clean, one cannot match closures or functions against constructors. Therefore, using the function makeNode below, we construct a node that contains the right constructor by adding dummy arguments until it has no function type anymore. The function ifMatch uses some low-level code to match two nodes to see if the constructor of the pattern matches the outermost constructor of the expression. If it matches, we need to extract the arguments from the node. This is done by the `applyTo` function, which decides how many arguments need to be extracted (and what their types are) by inspection of the type of the curried constructor. Again, we use some low-level auxiliary code to extract each argument while preserving laziness.

```
altsToLambda [Value dyn ==> th:as] = let el = altsToLambda as
    in case dyn of
        ... // previous definition for basic types
        constr -> Value (ifMatch (makeNode constr))
                                  @ (Value (applyTo dyn) @ th) @ el

ifMatch :: Dynamic -> Dynamic
ifMatch (x :: a) = dynamic \th el y -> if (matchNode x y) (th y) (el y)
                        :: A.b: (a -> b) (a -> b) a -> b

makeNode :: Dynamic -> Dynamic
makeNode (f :: a -> b) = makeNode (dynamic f undef :: b)
makeNode (x :: a)      = dynamic x :: a

applyTo :: Dynamic -> Dynamic
applyTo ...              // and so on, most specific type first...
applyTo (_ :: a b -> c) = dynamic \f x -> f (arg1of2 x) (arg2of2 x)
                        :: A.d: (a b -> d) c -> d
applyTo (_ :: a -> b)   = dynamic \f x -> f (arg1of1 x)
                        :: A.c: (a -> c) b -> c
applyTo (_ :: a)        = dynamic \f x -> f :: A.b: b a -> b

matchNode :: a a -> Bool // low-level code; compares two nodes.

argiofn :: a -> b // low-level code; selects ith argument of n-ary node
```

Pattern matching against user defined constructors requires that the constructors are available from (i.e. stored in) the file system. Esther currently does not support type definitions at the command line, and the Clean compiler must be used to introduce new types and constructors into the file system. The example below shows how one can write the constructors C, D, and E of the type T to the file system. Once the constructors are available in the file system, one can write command lines like \x -> case x of C y -> y; D z -> z; E -> 0 (for which type $(T\ Int) \to Int$ is inferred).

```
:: T a = C a | D Int | E

Start world =
    let (_, w1) = writeDynamic "C" (dynamic C :: A.a: a -> T a) world
        (_, w2) = writeDynamic "D" (dynamic D :: A.a: Int -> T a) w1
        (_, w3) = writeDynamic "E" (dynamic E :: A.a: T a) w2
    in  w3
```

4.6 Overloading

Support for overloaded expressions within dynamics in Clean is not yet implemented (e.g. one cannot write `dynamic (==)` `:: A.a: a a -> Bool | Eq a`). Even when a future dynamics implementation supports overloading, it cannot be used in a way that suits Esther. We want to solve overloading using instances/dictionaries from the file system, which may change over time, and which is something we cannot expect from Clean's dynamic run-time system out of the box.

Below is the Clean version of the overloaded functions `==` and `one`. We will use these two functions as a running example.

```
class Eq  a where (==) infix 4 :: a a -> Bool
class one a where one :: a

instance Eq  Int where (==) x y = // low-level code to compare integers
instance one Int where one    = 1
```

To mimic Clean's overloading, we introduce the type O to differentiate between 'overloaded' dynamics and 'normal' dynamics. The type O, shown below, has four type variables which represent: the variable the expression is overloaded in (v), the dictionary type (d), the 'original' type of the expression (t), and the type of the name of the overloaded function (n). Values of the type O consists of a constructor `O` followed by the overloaded expression (of type $d \rightarrow t$), and the name of the overloaded function (of type n). We motivate the design of this type later on in this section.

```
:: O v d t n = O (d -> t) n     // Overloaded expression

==  = dynamic O id "Eq"  :: A.a: O a (a a -> Bool) (a a -> Bool) String
one = dynamic O id "one" :: A.a: O a a a String

instance_Eq_Int  = dynamic \x y -> x == y :: Int Int -> Bool
instance_one_Int = dynamic 1              :: Int
```

The dynamic `==`, in the example above, is Esther's representation of Clean's overloaded function `==`. The overloaded expression itself is the identity function because the result of the expression *is* the dictionary of `==`. The name of the class is `Eq`. The dynamic `==` is overloaded in a single variable a, the type of the dictionary is $a \rightarrow a \rightarrow Bool$ as expected, the 'original' type is the same, and the type of the name is $String$. Likewise, the dynamic `one` is Esther's representation of Clean's overloaded function `one`.

By separating the different parts of the overloaded type, we obtain direct access to the variable in which the expression is overloaded. This makes it easy to detect if the overloading has been resolved (i.e. the variable no longer unifies with $\forall a.a$). By separating the dictionary type and the 'original' type of the expression, it becomes easier to check if the application of one overloaded dynamic to another is allowed (i.e. can a value of type O _ _ $(a \rightarrow b)$ _ be applied to a value of type O _ _ a _).

To apply one overloaded dynamic to another, we combine the overloading information using the P (pair) type as shown below in the function `apply0`.

```
:: P a b = P a b                // Just a pair

apply0 :: Dynamic Dynamic -> Dynamic
apply0 ((O f nf) :: O vf df (a -> b) sf) ((O x nx) :: O vx dx a sx)
   = dynamic O (\d_f d_x -> f d_f (x d_x)) (P nf nx)
                                :: O (P vf vx) (P df dx) b (P sf sx)
```

We use the (private) data type P instead of tuples because this allows us to differentiate between a pair of two variables and a single variable that has been unified with a tuple. Applying `apply0` to `==` and `one` yields an expression semantically equal to `isOne` below. `isOne` is overloaded in a pair of two variables, which are the same. The overloaded expression needs a pair of dictionaries to build the expression `(==)` `one`. The 'original' type is $a \to Bool$, and it is overloaded in `Eq` and `one`. Esther will pretty print this as: `isOne :: a -> Bool |` `Eq a & one a`.

```
isOne = dynamic O (\(P d_Eq d_one) -> id d_Eq (id d_one)) (P "Eq" "one")
     :: A.a: O (P a a) (P (a a -> Bool) a) (a -> Bool) (P String String)
```

Applying `isOne` to the integer 42 will bind the variable a to Int. Esther is now able to choose the right instance for both `Eq` and `one`. It searches the file system for the files named "instance Eq Int" and "instance one Int", and applies the code of `isOne` to the dictionaries after applying the overloaded expression to 42. The result will look like `isOne10` in the example below, where all overloading has been removed.

```
isOne42 = dynamic (\(P d_Eq d_one) -> id d_Eq (id d_one) 42)
                            (P d_Eq_Int d_one_Int) :: Bool
```

Although overloading is resolved in the example above, the plumbing/dictionary passing code is still present. This will increase evaluation time, and it is not clear yet how this can be prevented.

5   Related Work

We have not yet seen an interpreter or shell that equals Esther's ability to use pre-compiled code, and to store expressions as compiled code, which can be used in other already compiled programs, in a type safe way.

Es [14] is a shell that supports higher-order functions and allows the user to construct new functions at the command line. A UNIX shell in Haskell [15] by Jim Mattson is an interactive program that also launches executables, and provides pipelining and redirections. Tcl [16] is a popular tool to combine programs, and to provide communications between them. None of these programs provides a way to read and write typed objects, other than strings, from and to disk. Therefore, they cannot provide our level of type safety.

A functional interpreter with a file system manipulation library can also provide functional expressiveness and either static or dynamic type checking of part of the command line. For example, the Scheme Shell (ScSh) [17] integrates common shell operations with the Scheme language to enable the user to use the full expressiveness of Scheme at the command line. Interpreters for statically typed functional languages, such as Hugs [18], even provide static type checking in advance. Although they do type check source code, they cannot type check the application of binary executables to documents/data structures because they work on untyped executables.

The BeanShell [19] is an embeddable Java source interpreter with object scripting language features, written in Java. It is able of type inference for variables and to combine shell scripts with existing Java programs. While Esther generates compiled code via dynamics, the BeanShell interpreter is invoked each time a script is called from a normal Java program.

Run-time code generation in order to specialize code at run-time to certain parameters is not related to Esther, which only combines existing code.

6   Conclusions and Future Work

We have shown how to build a shell that provides a simple, but powerful strongly typed functional programming language. We were able to do this using only Clean's support for run-time type unification and dynamic linking, albeit syntax transformations and a few low-level functions were necessary. The shell named Esther supports type checking and inference before evaluation. It offers application, lambda abstraction, recursive let, pattern matching, and function definitions: the basics of any functional language.

Additionally, infix operators and support for overloading make the shell easy to use. The support for infix operators and overloading required the storage of additional information in the file system. We have chosen to use file attributes to store the infix information, and instances for an overloaded function f are stored as files named "instance f *Type*".

By combining compiled code, Esther allows the use of any pre-compiled program as a function in the shell. Because Esther stores functions/expressions constructed at the command line as a dynamic, it supports writing compiled programs at the command line. Furthermore, these expressions written at the command line can be used in any pre-compiled Clean program. The evaluation of expressions using recombined compiled code is not as fast as using the Clean compiler. Speed can be improved by introducing less combinators during bracket abstraction, but it seams unfeasible to make Esther perform the same optimizations as the Clean compiler. In practice, we find Esther responsive enough, and more optimizations do not appear worth the effort at this stage. One can always construct a Clean module using the same syntax and use the compiler to generate a dynamic that contains more efficient code.

Further research will be done on a more elaborate typed file system, and support for types and type definitions at the command line. Esther will be incorporated into our ongoing research on the development of a strongly typed functional operating system.

References

1. Rinus Plasmeijer and Marko van Eekelen. *Concurrent Clean Language Report version 2.1*. University of Nijmegen, November 2002. http://cs.kun.nl/~clean.
2. Simon Peyton Jones and John Hughes et al. *Report on the programming language Haskell 98*. University of Yale, 1999. http://www.haskell.org/definition/.
3. Arjen van Weelden and Rinus Plasmeijer. Towards a Strongly Typed Functional Operating System. In R. Peña and T. Arts, editors, *14th International Workshop on the Implementation of Functional Languages, IFL'02*, pages 215–231. Springer, September 2002. LNCS 2670.
4. Martín Abadi, Luca Cardelli, Benjamin Pierce, and Gordon Plotkin. Dynamic Typing in a Statically Typed Language. *ACM Transactions on Programming Languages and Systems*, 13(2):237–268, April 1991.
5. Marco Pil. Dynamic Types and Type Dependent Functions. In K. Hammond, T. Davie, and C. Clack, editors, *10th International Workshop on the Implementation of Functional Languages, IFL '98*, volume 1595 of *LNCS*, pages 169–185, London, 1999. Springer.
6. Martijn Vervoort and Rinus Plasmeijer. Lazy Dynamic Input/Output in the Lazy Functional Language Clean. In R. Peña and T. Arts, editors, *14th International Workshop on the Implementation of Functional Languages, IFL'02*, pages 101–117. Springer, September 2002. LNCS 2670.
7. M. Abadi, L. Cardelli, B. Pierce, G. Plotkin, and D. Rèmy. Dynamic Typing in Polymorphic Languages. In *Proceedings of the ACM SIGPLAN Workshop on ML and its Applications*, San Francisco, June 1992.
8. Simon L. Peyton Jones, Alastair Reid, Fergus Henderson, C. A. R. Hoare, and Simon Marlow. A Semantics for Imprecise Exceptions. In *SIGPLAN Conference on Programming Language Design and Implementation*, pages 25–36, 1999.
9. M. Schönfinkel. Über die Bausteine der mathematischen Logik. In *Mathematische Annalen*, volume 92, pages 305–316. 1924.
10. Haskell B. Curry and Robert Feys. *Combinatory Logic*, volume 1. North-Holland, Amsterdam, 1958.
11. J. Roger Hindley and Jonathan P. Seldin. *Introduction to Combinators and λ-Calculus*. Cambridge University Press, 1986. ISBN 0521268966.
12. Antoni Diller. *Compiling Functional Languages*. John Wiley and Feys Sons Ltd, 1988.
13. Simon L. Peyton Jones. *The Implementation of Functional Programming Languages*. Prentice-Hall, 1987.
14. Paul Haahr and Byron Rakitzis. Es: A Shell with Higher-order Functions. In *Proceedings of the USENIX Winter 1993 Technical Conference*, pages 51–60, 1993.
15. Jim Mattson. The Haskell Shell. http://www.informatik.uni−bonn.de/~ralf/software/examples/Hsh.html.
16. J. K. Ousterhout. Tcl: An Embeddable Command Language. In *Proceedings of the USENIX Winter 1990 Technical Conference*, pages 133–146, Berkeley, CA, 1990. USENIX Association.
17. O. Shivers. A Scheme Shell. Technical Report MIT/LCS/TR-635, 1994.
18. Mark P Jones, Alastair Reid, the Yale Haskell Group, the OGI School of Science, and Engineering at OHSU. *The Hugs 98 User Manual*, 1994–2002. http://cvs.haskell.org/Hugs/.
19. Pat Niemeyer. Beanshell 2.0. http://www.beanshell.org.

Polymorphic Type Reconstruction
Using Type Equations*

Venkatesh Choppella

Indian Institute of Information Technology and Management Kerala
Thiruvananthapuram, Kerala 695 581, India
choppell@iiitmk.ac.in

Abstract. The W algorithm of Milner [Mil78] and its numerous variants [McA98,LY98,YTMW00] implement type reconstruction by building type substitutions. We define an algorithm W^E centered around building type equations rather than substitutions. The design of W^E is motivated by the belief that reasoning with substitutions is awkward. More seriously, substitutions fail to preserve the exact syntactic form of the type equations they solve. This makes analysing the source of type errors more difficult. By replacing substitution composition with unions of sets of type equations and eliminating the application of substitution to environments, we obtain an algorithm for type reconstruction that is simple and also useful for type error reconstruction. We employ a sequentiality principle for unifier composition and a constructive account of mgu-induced variable occurrence relation to design W^E and prove its correctness. We introduce syntax equations as a formal syntax for progam slices. We use a simple constraint generation relation to relate syntax equations with type equations to trace program slices responsible for a type error.

1 Introduction

The Damas-Milner type system [DM82,Dam85], also known as the Hindley-Milner type system, is the basis for type reconstruction in higher-order, polymorphically typed functional languages like ML [MTH90] and Haskell [PJH99]. Type reconstruction in Damas-Milner is implemented using Milner's principal type algorithm W [Mil78]. An important practical concern affecting the usability of these languages has been the issue of intelligent type error diagnosis, that is, locating the elements of the source program that contribute to the type error in an ill-typed program. The problem of type error diagnosis has led to several proposals for modifying W [McA98,LY98,YTMW00].

The W algorithm and the above mentioned variants compute the principal type of an expression by building substitutions, which are maps from type variables to types. Each type variable is a placeholder for the type of a subexpression

---

* Part of this work was done when the author was at Oak Ridge National Laboratory, Oak Ridge TN, USA, managed by UT-Battelle, LLC for the U.S. Department of Energy under contract number DE-AC05-00OR22725.

P. Trinder, G. Michaelson, and R. Peña (Eds.): IFL 2003, LNCS 3145, pp. 53–68, 2004.

of the program expression. It is intuitively appealing, however, to consider dividing the process of building solution substitutions into two phases: an initial phase in which type constraints are constructed and accumulated followed by a second phase in which these constraints are solved to obtain a solution substitution. Such a separation of phases, for example, is the basis of Wand's proof [Wan87] of Hindley's theorem, in which the typability problem for simply-typed lambda calculus is reduced to term unification [CF58,Hin69]. Viewing type assignments as solutions to type equations was encouraged by Milner himself [Mil78], and later by Cardelli [Car87] as well, mainly through examples. In this paper, we present an algorithm W^E that relies on a limited separation of the generation of type equations from their solution. Using the algorithm for unification source-tracking developed earlier [Cho02,CH03], we show how this algorithm may be used for tracking the source of type errors.

The substitutions computed by the Milner W algorithm and others are solutions (*unifiers*) of sets of type equations, yet these equations are never made explicit in these algorithms. Since substitutions lose information about the exact form of the term equations they solve, it is difficult to reconstruct source information from substitutions alone. Therefore, we seek a type reconstruction algorithm centered around the computation of type equations with the following property: The equations should have an mgu that is trivially related to the mgu computed by W. Otherwise, the non-unifiability of these equations, which indicates untypability, should be diagnosable independent of the Damas-Milner type system, using unification source-tracking [CH03], for example.

Separating the generation of type equations from their solution is, however, easier said than done for Damas-Milner type reconstruction. The difficulty may be traced to the non-compositional behavior of the W algorithm and its variants: in the expression let $x = e$ in e', the type of e is required to compute the type of e'. This non-compositional behavior is due to the absence of the principal typing (as opposed to the principal type) property of the Damas-Milner type system [Wel02].

To be sure, separation *is* possible, either by generating type *inequations*, or by unfolding all the let bindings in the original program. But these approaches move the type reconstruction problem outside the realm of unification and the Damas-Milner regime respectively, and are also unsatisfactory from a practical point of view. The solution of type inequations requires semi-unification rather than ordinary unification [Hen93], while the unfolding of let bindings reduces the problem to typability in the Curry-Hindley calculus at the cost of an increase in program size in practice, and an exponential increase in the theoretical worst case [KMM91].

Our approach offers a middleground in which the type equation generation phase is continued until a let expression let $x = e$ in e' is encountered. The type equations for e' refer to the type of e, which is obtained by solving the type equations generated by e. By solving the equations at let boundaries, we avoid both the problem of proliferation of type equations caused by let unfolding and the need to generate type inequations.

1.1   Summary of Contributions and Outline of Paper

The main contributions of this paper are:

1. A sequentiality principle for unifier composition that relates unifier composition with union of term equations (Theorem 1, Section 2).
2. A constructive characterization of variable occurrences in terms computed by applying most general unifiers (Lemmas 1 and 2, Section 2.2). This result relies on the unification path framework developed earlier [CH03]. It is used to provide a formal, constructive interpretation of a common implementation mechanism for identifying non-generic variables. (Section 4.2).
3. A type equation based polymorphic type reconstruction algorithm W^E for Damas-Milner (Section 4).
4. An application of the unification source-tracking algorithm developed in [CH03] to extract type equation slices from the output of W^E (Section 5).
5. A simple framework for error diagnosis in the Damas-Milner type system. The framework consists of *syntax equations* (Section 5.1), which are a formal notation for expressing program slicing information, *type equations*, and a *constraint generation relation* relating syntax equations to type equations (Section 5.2). Type equation slices computed in (4) are mapped back to syntax equation slices generating a type error.

Section 2 presents a constructive view of unification. Section 3 briefly reviews the Milner W algorithm. Section 4 defines W^E and sketches its correctness. Section 5 shows how W^E can be used for tracking type errors. Section 6 compares our approach with published variants of W and other related work. Section 7 concludes with pointers to future work.

Proofs of all the results of this paper are included in an accompanying technical report [Cho03b].

2   A Constructive View of Unification

Term unification is at the heart of Damas-Milner type reconstruction. In this section we first introduce a sequentiality principle for term unification. This principle is used to justify the correctness of replacing substitution operations with generation of term equations. Using examples, we then briefly review the constructive approach to term unification offered by the unification path framework of Choppella and Haynes [CH03]. We use this framework to formulate a constructive account of the occurrence of variables in solutions computed by most general unifiers. We assume familiarity with the basic concepts of term unification, including terms, substitutions, idempotent substitutions, term equations, unifiers, and most general unifiers (mgus).

If E is a system of term equations and s is a substitution, then sE denotes the set of equations $\{s\tau \stackrel{?}{=} s\tau' \mid \tau \stackrel{?}{=} \tau' \in E\}$. $vars(S)$ denotes the set of variables occurring in the syntactic entity S, where S represents a term, substitution, term equation, or aggregates of these objects. If E is a set of term equations and s is a most general unifier (mgu) of E, then $ind(s, E)$ denotes the set of independent variables of s (that is, all variables unchanged by s) also occurring in E.

Our first result relates mgu composition with the union of term equations and forms the basis of our reformulation of W.

Theorem 1 (Sequentiality of unifier composition).

If s_1 is a unifier (mgu) of E_1, and s'_2 is a unifier (respectively mgu) of $s_1 E_2$, then $s'_2 s_1$ is a unifier (respectively mgu) of $E_1 \cup E_2$.

A consequence of the sequentiality of unifier composition is the "left-to-right" bias of W [McA98]. Theorem 1 suggests that a way out of this sequentiality is to replace unifier composition with the symmetric operation of term equation union.

2.1 Unification Paths

A system of term equations E is efficiently represented using a *unification graph* (also denoted E) using structure sharing: variable nodes are shared; constructor nodes may be shared. E is unifiable if and only if the quotient graph $E/\sim$ under the unification closure $\sim$ of E is acyclic and homogenous (Paterson and Wegman [PW78]). Thus, the unifiability of E depends on the connectivity properties of $E/\sim$.

Unification source-tracking consists of witnessing the connectivity in the quotient graph $E/\sim$ in terms of a special connectivity relation in the "source" graph E. This special connectivity relation is defined using the idea of *unification paths* introduced in [Cho02]. Unification paths are defined over the labeled directed graph (LDG) underlying E (also denoted E). The LDG underlying E is obtained by labeling each projection edge from a constructor vertex labeled f to its ith child with the symbol f_i. Equational edges in E are oriented arbitrarily and labeled ϵ, the empty string. The inverse E^{-1} of E is the LDG obtained by reversing the orientation and inverting the label of each edge of E. The inverse of a label f_i is f_i^{-1}; the inverse of ϵ is ϵ. Each inverted projection symbol f_i^{-1} is treated as an open parenthesis symbol whose matching closed parenthesis symbol is f_i. A *unification path over E* is any labeled path p in $E \cup E^{-1}$ whose label $l(p)$ is a suffix of a balanced string over these parenthesis symbols. The formal relation between unification paths in E and paths in $E/\sim$ and an extension of the unification algorithm to compute unification paths is presented in [CH03]. In the rest of this section, we summarize the relation between unification paths, unification closure and non-unifiability.

Let u, v be vertices in the unification graph of a system of term equations E. $E \models p : u \rightsquigarrow v$ ($E \models u \rightsquigarrow v$) denotes that p is a (there is a) unification path from u to v over the unification graph of E, respectively. Thus, $\rightsquigarrow$ is a reachability relation. In the framework of unification paths, unification closure is a special case of unification path reachability: $E \models u \sim v$ if and only if $E \models p : u \rightsquigarrow v$ and $l(p)$ is a balanced parentheses string. Unification failure is also a special case of reachability. For a clash, $E \models u \sim v$, for some constructor vertices u and v

with different labels. For a cycle, $E \models p : u \rightsquigarrow u$, for some variable u in E and path p such that $l(p)$ is an unbalanced suffix of a balanced parentheses string. The following example illustrates the idea of unification paths:

Example 1. Consider the system of (named) term equations E

$$e : t_7 \stackrel{?}{=} t_8 \rightarrow t_6 \qquad f : t_7 \stackrel{?}{=} t_1 \qquad g : t_8 \stackrel{?}{=} t_5$$
$$h : t_{10} \stackrel{?}{=} t_{11} \rightarrow t_9 \qquad j : t_{10} \stackrel{?}{=} t_5 \rightarrow t_6 \qquad k : t_{11} \stackrel{?}{=} t_5 \rightarrow t_6$$

The LDG underlying the unification graph of E is shown in Figure 1. Constructor vertices are identified by circles containing a constructor symbol. Projection edges originate from constructor edges and are identified by solid arrows. Equational edges are named and are identified by open arrows. The names of the left and right projection edges originating from a constructor vertex targeted by an equational edge y are assumed to be y_1 and y_2 respectively. To reduce clutter, these names are omitted. The labels on these edges are also omitted, but are equal to $\rightarrow_1$ and $\rightarrow_2$, respectively. Each $\rightarrow_i$ for $i = 1, 2$ may be thought of as a closed parenthesis symbol whose open parenthesis symbol is $\rightarrow_i^{-1}$. The label ϵ on each equational edges is also omitted. An edge y in E^{-1} corresponds to an edge y^{-1} in E with the direction of y and its label inverted. The thick brush edges highlight specific unification paths of interest. The quotient graph with respect to the unification closure of E is shown in Figure 2. The vertex set of $E/\sim$ is the set of equivalence classes of $\sim$.

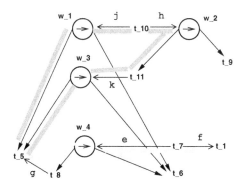

Fig. 1. Unification graph of the set of term equations of Example 1.

The element $t_6 \sim t_9$ of $\sim$ is witnessed by the unification path $j_2^{-1} j^{-1} h h_2$ whose label is $\rightarrow_2^{-1} \epsilon\epsilon \rightarrow_2$, which simplifies to the balanced string $\rightarrow_2^{-1} \rightarrow_2$. E is non-unifiable because the quotient graph $E/\sim$ has a cycle. The cycle in the quotient graph corresponds to the unification cycle $j_1^{-1} j^{-1} h h_1 k k_1$ highlighted in the source graph E. The label of this path is $\rightarrow_1^{-1} \rightarrow_1 \rightarrow_1$ after simplification.

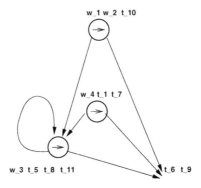

Fig. 2. Quotient graph modulo the unification closure of the unification graph in Figure 1.

2.2 Unification Paths, mgu's and Variable Occurrences

The use of unification paths is not limited to witnessing unification failure. In this section, we show that when a system of equations is unifiable, unification paths may be used as witnesses to the variable occurrence relation imposed by any most general unifier for that system of equations. This witness construction is used in Section 4.2 to track the source of non-generic type variables computed during Damas-Milner type reconstruction.

Lemma 1 (Reachability and mgu-induced occurrence relation).
Let E be a unifiable set of term equations whose mgu is s. If $t' \in vars(E)$ and $t \in ind(s, E)$, then t occurs in $s(t')$ if and only if $E \models t' \rightsquigarrow t$.

Example 2. Continuing Example 1, consider the system E' consisting of the equations $\{e, f, g\}$. The unification graph of E' is a subgraph of E. The following substitution s' is an mgu of E': $\{t_1 \mapsto t_5 \rightarrow t_6, t_7 \mapsto t_5 \rightarrow t_6, t_8 \mapsto t_5\}$. Note that $ind(s', E') = \{t_5, t_6\}$. Both variables t_5 and t_6 occur in $s'(t_1)$. This occurrence is witnessed by the reachability of t_5 and t_6 from t_1 in E' via the unification paths $f^{-1}ee_1g$ and $f^{-1}ee_2$ respectively, highlighted in Figure 1.

It is useful to extend the notion of reachability relative to an arbitrary set of variables. The set of variables *in E reachable from V* is defined as:

$$reachable(E, V) \stackrel{\text{def}}{=} \{t \in vars(E) \mid \exists t' \in V : E \models t' \rightsquigarrow t\}$$

Example 3. Continuing Example 2, let $V = \{t_1\}$. The set $reachable(E', V)$ is $vars(E') = \{t_1, t_5, t_6, t_7, t_8\}$. It is simple to verify that every variable in E' is indeed reachable from t_1 via a unification path.

Lemma 2 (Reachability and variable occurrences). *If E is a set of term equations, s is an idempotent mgu of E, and V is any set of variables, then*

$$vars(sV) \cap ind(s, E) = reachable(E, V) \cap ind(s, E) \qquad (1)$$

Lemma 2 implies that if $t \in E$ is an independent variable of s and occurs in $s(V)$ (lhs of (1)), then this occurrence can be *witnessed* by a unification path over E from some variable in V to t (rhs). This result is used in Section 4.2 to constructively characterize the non-genericity of type variables.

3   The Milner W Algorithm

The syntax of program and type expressions and the Milner W algorithm for computing principal types are shown in Figure 3.

$$x \in Var$$

$$e \in Exp ::= x \mid \lambda x.\, e \mid @\, e\, e \mid \text{let}\, x = e \text{ in } e$$

$$t \in TyVar$$
$$\tau \in Ty \quad ::= t \mid \tau \to \tau$$
$$\sigma \in TySch ::= \tau \mid \forall t.\sigma$$

$$s \in TySubst = TyVar \xrightarrow{\text{fin}} Ty$$
$$A \in TyEnv = Var \xrightarrow{\text{fin}} TySch$$

```
1  W(A, e) =
2  case e of
3     x_i :
4                let ∀ᾱ.τ = A(x)
5                   in ⟨Id, τ[ᾱ/ᾱ']⟩ where ᾱ'  new
6     @_i e_j e_k:
7                let ⟨s_j, τ_j⟩ = W(A, e_j) and ⟨s'_k, τ_k⟩ = W(s_j A, e_k)
8                       and u = mgu{s'_k(τ_j) ≟ τ_k → t}
9                   in ⟨u s'_k s_j, u(t)⟩ where t  new
10    λ_i x_j.e_k:
11               let ⟨s_k, τ_k⟩ = W(A[x : t], e_k)
12                  in ⟨s_k, s_k(t) → τ_k⟩ where t  new
13    let_i x_j = e_k in e_l:
14               let ⟨s_k, τ_k⟩ = W(A, e_k) and ᾱ = vars(τ_k) − FV(s_k A)
15                      and ⟨s'_l, τ_l⟩ = W((s_k A)[x : ∀ᾱ.τ_k], e_l)
16                  in ⟨s'_l s_k, τ_l⟩
```

Note: W fails if the mgu on line 8 does not exist.

Fig. 3. The syntax of program and type expressions and the principal type algorithm W of the Damas-Milner type system DM.

We abbreviate $\forall t_1 \ldots \forall t_n.\tau$ by $\forall t_1, \ldots, t_n.\tau$ and $t_1, \ldots, t_n$ by $\bar{t}$. The set of *free* type variables in a type scheme $\forall \bar{t}.\tau$ is equal to $vars(\tau) - \bar{t}$. The set of free variables $FV(A)$ in a type environment A is the union of all free variables in all type schemes in the range of A. The *closure* $clo(A, \tau)$ of the type τ with respect to the type environment A denotes the type scheme $\forall \overline{\alpha}.\tau$, where $\overline{\alpha} = vars(\tau) - FV(A)$.

The following example of untypability illustrates the well-known restriction of monomorphic types imposed on λ-bound variables.

Example 4. In the core ML expression $\lambda z.$ let $y = \lambda x.$ @zx in @yy, although y is let-bound, y can only be assigned a monomorphic type. This in turn makes the application @yy and hence the expression e untypable. More precisely, since z is λ-bound, the type τ_z of z is monomorphic. This type is assigned to the subexpression $\lambda x.$ @zx as well. The type assigned to the let-bound variable y is the closure $clo([z : \tau_z], \tau_z)$, which is τ_z. This monomorphic type τ_z is in turn assigned to y causing @yy to be untypable.

The use of substitutions (composition and application to terms and type environments) in W is pervasive. In the next section, we reformulate W to minimize the use of substitutions.

4 W^E: Polymorphic Type Reconstruction Using Type Equations

The algorithm W^E (Figures 4 and 5) is based on the construction of type equations rather than substitutions. W^E takes a type environment A and an expression e. It returns a pointed set of type equations $\langle t, E \rangle$ consisting of a type variable t, a placeholder for the type of e, and a set E of type equations generated for e.

```
1  W^E(A, e_i) =
2  case e_i of
3      x_i :
4                      let   ∀ᾱ.τ = A(x)
5                            and  τ_i = τ[ᾱ/ᾱ']
6                            and  d_i = {t_i =? τ_i}
7                            and  E_i = d_i
8                      in  ⟨t_i, E_i⟩
9                            where  t_i, ᾱ'  new
10     @_i e_j e_k :
11                     let   ⟨t_j, E_j⟩ = W^E(A, e_j)
12                           and  ⟨t_k, E_k⟩ = W^E(A, e_k)
13                           and  d_i = {t_j =? t_k → t_i}
14                           and  E_i = E_j ∪ E_k ∪ d_i
15                     in  ⟨t_i, E_i⟩ where   t_i  new
```

Fig. 4. Algorithm W^E: VAR and APP cases.

16	$\lambda_i \, x_j.e_k$:
17	$\mathbf{let} \; \langle t_k, E_k \rangle = W^E(A[x : t_j], e_k)$
18	$\mathbf{and} \; d_i = \{t_i \stackrel{?}{=} t_j \rightarrow t_k\}$
19	$\mathbf{and} \; E_i = E_k \cup d_i$
20	$\mathbf{in} \; \langle t_i, E_i \rangle \; \mathbf{where} \;\; t_i, t_j \;\; \text{new}$
21	$\mathbf{let}_i \, x_j = e_k \; \mathbf{in} \; e_l$:
22	$\mathbf{let} \; \langle t_k, E_k \rangle = W^E(A, e_k)$
23	$\mathbf{and} \; s_k = mgu(E_k)$
24	$\mathbf{and} \; \tau_k = s_k(t_k)$
25	$\mathbf{and} \; \overline{\alpha} = vars(\tau_k) - FV(s_k(A))$
26	$\mathbf{and} \; \langle t_l, E_l \rangle = W^E(A[x : \forall \overline{\alpha}.\tau_k], e_l)$
27	$\mathbf{and} \; d_i = \{t_i \stackrel{?}{=} t_l, t_j \stackrel{?}{=} t_k\}$
28	$\mathbf{and} \; E_i = E_k \cup E_l \cup d_i$
29	$\mathbf{in} \; \langle t_i, E_i \rangle \; \mathbf{where} \; t_i, t_j \;\; \text{new}$

Note: W^E fails if the mgu on line 23 does not exist.

Fig. 5. Algorithm W^E ABS and LET cases.

Unlike in W, the role of substitutions in W^E is greatly diminished: Unifiers are computed only at let boundaries (line 23, Figure 5). Substitution composition is replaced by type equation union. Substitutions are not applied to type environments, except to compute generic variables (line 25, Figure 5). However, this application too can be eliminated (see Section 4.2). W computes the type substitution for the application $@_i \, e_j \, e_k$ in a non-compositional way (line 7, Figure 3). This instance of non-compositionality is eliminated when computing type equations in W^E (lines 11-12, Figure 4). Except at let boundaries, W^E neither computes nor applies substitutions. The relation between W^E and W is formally explored in the next section.

Example 5. Assume the expression e of Example 4 is decorated with locations in the following way: $\lambda_0 \, z_1. \, \mathbf{let}_2 \;\; y_3 \;\; = \;\; \lambda_4 \, x_5. \, @_6 \, z_7 \, x_8 \; \mathbf{in} \;\; @_9 \, y_{10} \, y_{11}$. This allows us to refer to values as *attributes* of these locations. Thus, e_0 refers to the expression e at location 0, $\langle t_0, E_0 \rangle$ to the pointed set of type equations at location 0 etc. $W^E(\emptyset, e_0)$ returns $\langle t_0, E_0 \rangle$, where E_0 is the union of the set E of equations e, f, g, h, j and k of Example 1 and the following equations:

$$a : t_0 \stackrel{?}{=} t_5 \rightarrow t_6 \qquad b : t_2 \stackrel{?}{=} t_9 \qquad c : t_3 \stackrel{?}{=} t_4 \qquad d : t_4 \stackrel{?}{=} t_5 \rightarrow t_6$$

4.1 Correctness of W^E

We consider a hybrid algorithm W^{SE} obtained by splicing together W and W^E. W^{SE} takes an expression e and a type environment A and returns the tuple $\langle t, E, s, \tau \rangle$ consisting of a type variable t, a set E of type equations, a substitution s, and a type τ. The pair $\langle t, E \rangle$ is exactly that returned by W^E. The type τ is equal to the type returned by W and the substitution s is an extension of the substitution returned by W. The algorithm W^{SE} is given in [Cho03b].

Our goal is to show that t, E, s and τ are related in the following manner: if $W^{SE}(A,e) = \langle t, E, s, \tau \rangle$, then t is a variable in E, s is an mgu of E and $\tau = s(t)$. However, this statement needs to be strengthened before it can be proved as an invariant of W^{SE}.

Lemma 3 (W^{SE} invariants). *Let e be an expression and A a type environment. If $W^{SE}(A,e) = \langle t, E, s, \tau \rangle$, then*

1. *$t \in vars(E)$, s is an mgu of E, and $s(t) = \tau$. Furthermore,*
2. *if σ is any idempotent substitution such that $vars(\sigma)$ is disjoint from $vars(E) - FV(A)$, and $W^{SE}(\sigma A, e) = \langle t^\sigma, E^\sigma, s^\sigma, \tau^\sigma \rangle$, then s^σ is an mgu of σE.*

The proof of invariant (2) relies on Theorem 1 (details are in [Cho03b]). The invariants of W^{SE} are used to relate W and W^E:

Theorem 2 (Relation between W and W^E). *Let e be an expression and A a type environment:*

1. *If $W(A,e) = \langle s, \tau \rangle$, then $W^E(A,e) = \langle t, E \rangle$, E is unifiable with an mgu s', s is a restriction of s', and $s'(t) = \tau$.*
2. *If $W^E(A,e) = \langle t, E \rangle$ and E is unifiable with mgu s', then $W(A,e) = \langle s, \tau \rangle$ for some s and τ such that s is a restriction of s' and $s'(t) = \tau$.*

In W, not all locations of a program are decorated with type variables. This is why the substitution s returned by W is a restriction of the substitution s' returned by W^E.

4.2   Constructive Interpretation of Non-genericity

The algorithm W^E still has one instance where a substitution is applied to a type environment (line 25, Figure 5) in order to compute the generic variable set $\overline{\alpha} = vars(\tau_k) - FV(s_k A)$. To eliminate it, we employ the well-known implementation trick of computing $\overline{\alpha}$ as the difference between $vars(\tau_k)$ and the *non-generic* variables $\overline{\beta} = vars(\tau_k) \cap FV(s_k A)$. This trick relies on the following informal observation: a variable β of $vars(\tau)$ is non-generic if it can be reached from some type variable in A in the "currently computed unification closure of the unification graph constructed so far." Using the results of Section 2.2, this statement can be formalized and tightened. Since s_k is an mgu of E_k and $\overline{\beta} \in ind(s_k, E_k)$, by Lemma 2, each non-generic variable $\beta \in \overline{\beta}$ is in $reachable(E_k, FV(A))$. Hence, for each $\beta \in \overline{\beta}$, there is a type variable $t \in FV(A)$ such that $E_k \models t \rightsquigarrow \beta$. This characterization is constructive because there is a unification path witnessing the reachability of β. It also immediately implies that $t \in vars(E_k)$, and thus reveals the following two bounds on the search for the non-generic variables of τ_k:

1. the type equation space in which to determine the reachability is bounded by E_k.
2. the set of type variables in $FV(A)$ from which to search for reachability to variables in τ_k is bounded by $FV(A) \cap vars(E_k)$.

Example 6. Consider the invocation $W^E(A_4, e_4)$ in the computation $W^E(\emptyset, e_0)$ of Example 5. e_4 is the subexpression λ_4 x_5. @$_6$ z_7 x_8 of e_0, and $A_4 = [z : t_1]$. This invocation returns $\langle t_4, E_4 \rangle$ (line 22, Figure 5), where E_4 is the type equation set $\{d, e, f, g\}$. The mgu s_4 of E_4 maps t_1, t_4 and t_7 to $t_5 \rightarrow t_6$, and maps t_8 to t_5. Since both $s_4(t_1)$ and $\tau_4 = s_4(t_4)$ (line 24) are equal to $t_5 \rightarrow t_6$, $vars(\tau_4) - FV(s_4(A_4)) = \emptyset$ (line 25). This means that both t_5 and t_6 occurring in τ_4 are non-generic type variables.

Unification paths from the type variable t_1 of the λ-bound variable z provide a constructive explanation of the non-genericity of t_5 and t_6. These paths were already identified in Example 2. While searching for paths from the free variables of the type environment A_4, due to observation (1), we can limit our search for reachability to E_4. The type environment A_4 contains only $[z : t_1]$. In general, though, the binding of z could be nested arbirtrarily deep, making A_4 much larger. Due to observation (2), the search for source vertices of the unification paths needs to consider only those free variables in the type environment A_4 that occur in E_4.

5   Using W^E for Source-Tracking Type Errors

Any ordinary unification algorithm can be used to compute the mgu (line 23, Figure 5) in W^E. However, when the unification source-tracking algorithm of [CH03] is used, W^E can report type equation slices causing a type error. A type error in Damas-Milner is signaled by non-unifiability of a system of type equations, and the unification source-tracking algorithm is designed to return the equation slices generating the symptom of non-unifiability (clash or cycle).

Example 7. The expression e in Example 5 is untypable because the system of equations E_0 is non-unifiable. When the unification source-tracking algorithm of [CH03] is used as part of W^E, it signals non-unifiability and returns the unification cycle $j_1^{-1} j^{-1} h h_1 k k_1$ witnessing this unification failure (see Example 1). This path may be partitioned into the following type equation slices: $t_{10} \overset{?}{=} t_{11} \rightarrow \Box$, $t_{10} \overset{?}{=} t_5 \rightarrow \Box$, $t_{11} \overset{?}{=} t_5 \rightarrow \Box$. Each slice is obtained by erasing (replacing by $\Box$'s) information not relevant to the type error. The type equation slices obtained by dividing the unification path witnessing the non-genericity of t_5 are $t_1 \overset{?}{=} t_7$, $t_7 \overset{?}{=} t_8 \rightarrow \Box$, $t_8 \overset{?}{=} t_5$. The corresponding slices for t_6 are $t_1 \overset{?}{=} t_7$, $t_7 \overset{?}{=} \Box \rightarrow t_6$.

Type equation slices by themselves are only partly useful for type error diagnosis. We want to be able to identify the slices of the *source program* contributing to the type error. In the next few sections, we present a framework for computing program slices from type equation slices.

5.1   Syntax Equations

We express the syntactic relation between locations of a program expression using a system of *syntax equations*, inspired by the flat system formalism for set equations of Barwise and Moss [BM96]. Syntax equations encode constraints between various locations of a program. They are a more expressive alternative to using locations as units of program slicing information. Syntax equations are either *local*, relating an expression to its immediate subexpressions, or *referential*, in which a variable occurrence refers to its binding location. Each location i with constructor f and children at locations $i_1, \ldots i_n$ is represented by the equation $i = f(i_1, \ldots, i_n)$. Each variable reference at location i to a λ-bound (respectively let-bound) variable at location j is represented by the syntax equation $i = \lambda\mathsf{var}(j)$ (respectively $i = \mathsf{letvar}(j)$).

Example 8. The decorated expression $\lambda_0\ z_1.\ \mathsf{let}_2\ \ y_3\ =\ \lambda_4\ x_5.\ @_6\ z_7\ x_8$ in $@_9\ y_{10}\ y_{11}$ of Example 5 yields the following syntax equations: The lhs of each equation the is the subexpression at which the equation was generated.

$$
\begin{array}{lll}
0 = \lambda(1,2) & 2\ = \mathsf{let}(3,4,9) & 4\ = \lambda(5,6) \\
6 = @(7,8) & 7\ = \lambda\mathsf{var}(1) & 8\ = \lambda\mathsf{var}(5) \\
9 = @(10,11) & 10 = \mathsf{letvar}(3) & 11 = \mathsf{letvar}(3)
\end{array}
$$

5.2   A Simple Constraint Generation Relation

We relate each type equation to its source information by defining a *constraint generation relation* relating the syntax equation at location i of a subexpression to the (new) type equations generated by W^E at i. Each element of the constraint generation relation is of the form "syntax equation $\Longrightarrow$ type equation".

Example 9. The constraint generation relation for the decorated expression e of Example 8 is given below:

$$
\begin{array}{ll}
0\ = \lambda(5,6) \quad \Longrightarrow a : t_0 \overset{?}{=} t_5 \to t_6 & 2\ = \mathsf{let}(3,4,9) \Longrightarrow b : t_2 \overset{?}{=} t_9 \\
2\ = \mathsf{let}(3,4,9) \Longrightarrow c : t_3 \overset{?}{=} t_4 & 4\ = \lambda(5,6) \quad \Longrightarrow d : t_4 \overset{?}{=} t_5 \to t_6 \\
6\ = @(7,8) \quad \Longrightarrow e : t_7 \overset{?}{=} t_8 \to t_6 & 7\ = \lambda\mathsf{var}(1) \quad \Longrightarrow f : t_7 \overset{?}{=} t_1 \\
8\ = \lambda\mathsf{var}(5) \quad \Longrightarrow g : t_8 \overset{?}{=} t_5 & 9\ = @(10,11) \Longrightarrow h : t_{10} \overset{?}{=} t_{11} \to t_9 \\
10 = \mathsf{letvar}(3) \quad \Longrightarrow j : t_{10} \overset{?}{=} t_5 \to t_6 & 11 = \mathsf{letvar}(3) \quad \Longrightarrow k : t_{11} \overset{?}{=} t_5 \to t_6
\end{array}
$$

The type equation slices causing the type error in e and the syntax equation slices deriving them are:

$$
\begin{array}{ll}
\square\ = @(10,11) \Longrightarrow t_{10} \overset{?}{=} t_{11} \to \square & 10 = \mathsf{letvar}(3) \Longrightarrow t_{10} \overset{?}{=} t_5 \to \square \\
11 = \mathsf{letvar}(3) \ \Longrightarrow t_{11} \overset{?}{=} t_5 \to \square &
\end{array}
$$

5.3   Limitations of the Simple Constraint Generation Relation

The $\lambda\mathsf{var}$ and local syntax equations generate type equations that are *linear* (each type variable occurs just once). Furthermore, the type variables in these type equations refer to locations occurring in the corresponding syntax equations. This is, however, not true at let variable references. Consider Example 9 in which the type equations generated at locations 10 and 11 contain variables t_5 and t_6 *not occurring* in the corresponding syntax equations. In general, however, type equations at references to let bindings could contain newly cloned *generic* type variables not occurring anywhere before. The simple generation relation shown here is inadequately equipped to trace the origin of generic type variables. This problem will be addressed in a successor paper [Cho04] where a framework for expressing success proofs (why a type variable is mapped to a certain type by a substitution) will be presented.

6   Related Work

The problem of type error diagnosis has received much attention. A more detailed survey of related work is reported elsewhere [Cho03b].

Lee and Yi [LY98] present a top-down variant of algorithm W that relies on eager application of intermediate substitutions. They prove that this eager application not only generates better error messages, but that their algorithm halts sooner than W for untypable programs. Our algorithm W^E fails *later* than W does, but when used with the unification source-tracking algorithm of [CH03], returns the set of type equations slices that led to the failure. The algorithm U_{AE} of Yang et al. [YTMW00] depends on unifying type assumption environments. McAdam [McA98] uses a special algorithm for unifying substitutions. Our approach of unifying type equations is more natural and simpler. McAdam [McA00] uses an annotated graph structure to directly store program source information with the unification graph. In contrast, our approach separates the extraction of type equation slices (using unification source-tracking) with the extraction of program slices from the type slices (using the constraint generation relation). Haack and Wells [HW03] focus on the generation of minimal program slices which combines the use of a novel unification algorithm with a constraint collecting algorithm due to Damas [Dam85]. Their analysis of type diagnosis is inspired by intersection types, while the recent work of Neubauer and Thiemann [NT03] employs disjoint unions.

Trace-based approaches for type error diagnoses have also been suggested. Early work here is Maruyama et al. [MMA92]. Their trace information is unfortunately too closely dependent on the order of the unifications performed. Recently, Heeren et al. [HHS03] have proposed the use of type inference directives and specialized type rules to control the order of unification and type inference. Our approach, on the other hand, is based on tracing inferences in the connectivity space of the term equation graph rather than the execution sequence of the reconstruction algorithm.

The early work of Wand [Wan86] and Johnson and Walz [JW86,Wal89] correctly identified that the root of the type error problem lay in the source-tracking of unification. Their work focused on retrofitting unification algorithms with source-tracking information, but lacked a formal basis. There has also been a considerable effort in the area of *type explanation*, where the focus is to provide human readable analyses of type errors, often in an interactive environment that sometimes includes visual navigation of the type graph annotated with various entities [BS94,DB96,YM00,Chi01]. Our approach for computing slicing information has a more formal basis: the unification paths used in our framework encode *proofs* in the unification path logic P^U introduced in [CH03]. Other formal approaches for include the unification logics of Le Chenadec [LC89] and the pushdown automata of Cox [Cox87].

Remy [Rém92] proposed an improvement in the search for non-generic variables using a ranked variant of the Damas-Milner based on levels of nesting of let constructs. In our approach, non-genericity is constructively demonstrated using unification paths. The unification path formalism is also simpler and ties in more naturally with our overall framework for type and error reconstruction.

7   Conclusions and Future Work

We have argued that substitution-based type reconstruction algorithms are limited in their ability to effectively track the source of type errors. This is because substitutions fail to preserve the type equations that they solve. We have formalized a sequentiality principle for unifier composition. This formalism sheds light on how to obtain the type equation based type reconstruction algorithm W^E. We believe that W^E is easier to understand and reason with than other algorithms implementing Damas-Milner. We have used the framework of unification paths developed earlier to build a constructive account of the non-genericty of type variables. We have introduced syntax equations as a new syntactic formalism for expressing program slicing. We have introduced a simple constraint generation relation to relate syntax equations to type equations. W^E, the constraint generation framework, and the unification source-tracking algorithm developed earlier together constitute a simple framework for source-tracking type errors. We have implemented this framework in Scheme for a mini-ML prototype [Cho03a].

A central feature of Damas-Milner is the controlled cloning of existing type variables to create generic type. The origin of these generic type variables, cannot, however, be accurately traced by the constraint generation relation described. This problem is addressed in a forthcoming paper [Cho04]. The algorithm W^E is defined on the core subset of ML. Considerable work is needed to extend this algorithm to the large type systems of current day functional programming languages which typically support features like polymorphic recursion, subtyping, type classes, overloading, reference types etc. Also, our program slicing information is currently text-based. A visual front-end for viewing slicing information would be very useful. We are currently developing a graphical front-end for W^E using existing graph displaying packages.

References

[BM96]   J. Barwise and L. Moss. *Vicious Circles*. CSLI, 1996.
[BS94]   M. Beaven and R. Stansifer. Explaining type errors in polymorphic languages. *ACM Letters on Programming Languages*, 1994.

[Car87]   L. Cardelli. Basic polymorphic typechecking. *Science of Computer Programming*, 8:147–172, 1987.

[CF58]   H. B. Curry and R. Feys. *Combinatory Logic*, volume 1. North Holland, 1958.

[CH03]   V. Choppella and C. T. Haynes. Source-tracking Unification. In Franz Baader, editor, *Proceedings of 19th International Conference on Automated Deduction, CADE-19, Miami Beach, USA*, number 2741 in Lecture Notes in Artificial Intelligence, pages 458–472. Springer, 2003.

[Chi01]   Olaf Chitil. Compositional explantion of types and debugging of type errors. In *Sixth ACM SIGPLAN International Conference on Functional Programming (ICFP'01)*. ACM Press, September 2001.

[Cho02]   Venkatesh Choppella. *Unification Source-tracking with Application to Diagnosis of Type Inference*. PhD thesis, Indiana University, August 2002. IUCS Tech Report TR566.

[Cho03a] Venkatesh Choppella. An implementation of algorithm of W^E. http://www.iiitmk.ac.in/hyplan/choppell/WE.tar.gz, October 2003.

[Cho03b] Venkatesh Choppella. Polymorphic Type reconstruction using type equations (full version with proofs). Technical Report SP-06, Indian Institute of Information Technology and Managament, Kerala, Technopark, Thiruvananthapuram, Kerala, October 2003.

[Cho04]   Venkatesh Choppella. Source-tracking Damas-Milner using unification path embeddings. Technical report, Indian Institute of Information Technology and Management, Kerala, Technopark, Thiruvananthapuram, Kerala, 2004. In preparation.

[Cox87]   P. T. Cox. On determining the causes of non-unifiability. *Journal of Logic Programming*, 4(1):33–58, 1987.

[Dam85]   L. Damas. *Type assignment in Programming Languages*. PhD thesis, University of Edinburgh, April 1985.

[DB96]   Dominic Duggan and Frederick Bent. Explaining type inference. *Science of Computer Programming*, 27(1):37–83, July 1996.

[DM82]   L. Damas and R. Milner. Principal type-schemes for functional languages. In *Proc. 9th ACM Symp. on Principles of Programming Languages*, pages 207–212, January 1982.

[Hen93]   F. Henglein. Type inference with polymorphic recursion. *ACM Transactions on Programming Languages and Systems*, 15(2):253–289, April 1993.

[HHS03]   Bastiaan Heeren, Jurriaan Hage, and S. Doaitse Swierstra. Scripting the type inference process. In *Proceedings of the eighth ACM SIGPLAN international conference on Functional programming*, pages 3–13, Uppsala, Sweden, August 2003. ACM Press.

[Hin69]   R. Hindley. The principal type-scheme of an object in combinatory logic. *Transactions of the American Mathematical Society*, 146:29–60, December 1969.

[HW03]   Christian Haack and Joe Wells. Type error slicing in higher order polymorphic languages. In *Proc. of Theory and Practice of Software (TAPAS-2003)*. Springer, 2003.

[JW86]   G. F. Johnson and J. A. Walz. A maximum-flow approach to anomaly isolation in unification-based incremental type inference. In *Proceedings of the 13th ACM Symposium on Programming Languages*, pages 44–57, 1986.

[KMM91]   P. C. Kanellakis, H. G. Mairson, and J. C. Mitchell. Unification and ML type reconstruction. In J.L. Lassez and G. Plotkin, editors, *Computational Logic: Essays in honor of Alan Robinson*, pages 444–478. MIT Press, 1991.

[LC89]   P Le Chenadec. On the logic of unification. *Journal of Symbolic computation*, 8(1):141–199, July 1989.
[LY98]   Oukseh Lee and Kwangkeun Yi. Proofs about a folklore let-polymorphic type inference algorithm. *ACM Transactions on Programming Languages*, 20(4):707–723, July 1998.
[McA98]   Bruce J. McAdam. On the unification of substitutions in type inference. In Kevin Hammond, Anthony J. T. Davie, and Chris Clack, editors, *Implementation of Functional Languages*, volume 1595 of *Lecture Notes in Computer Science*, pages 139–154. Springer-Verlag, September 1998 1998.
[McA00]   B. McAdam. Generalising techniques for type debugging. In Phil Trinder, Greg Michaelson, and Hans-Wolfgang Loidl, editors, *Trends in Functional Programming*, pages 49–57. Intellect, 2000.
[Mil78]   R. Milner. A theory of type polymorphism in programming. *Journal of Computer and System Sciences*, 17:348–375, 1978.
[MMA92]   H. Maruyama, M. Matsuyama, and K. Araki. Support tool and strategy for type error correction with polymorphic types. In *Proceedings of the Sixteenth annual international computer software and applications conference, Chicago*, pages 287–293. IEEE, September 1992.
[MTH90]   R. Milner, M. Tofte, and R. Harper. *The Definition of Standard ML*. MIT Press, 1990.
[NT03]   Matthias Neubauer and Peter Thiemann. Discriminative sum types locate the source of type errors. In *Proceedings of the eighth ACM SIGPLAN international conference on Functional programming*, pages 15–26, Uppsala, Sweden, August 2003. ACM Press.
[PJH99]   S. Peyton-Jones and J. Hughes (Eds.). Haskell 98: A non-strict, purely functional language, February 1999.
           `http://www.haskell.org/onlinereport`.
[PW78]   M. Paterson and M. Wegman. Linear unification. *Journal of Computer and System Sciences*, 16(2):158–167, 1978.
[Rém92]   D. Rémy. Extension of ML type system with a sorted equation theory on types. Technical Report 1766, INRIA, October 1992.
[Wal89]   J. A. Walz. *Extending Attribute Grammars and Type Inference Algorithms*. PhD thesis, Cornell University, February 1989. TR 89-968.
[Wan86]   M. Wand. Finding the source of type errors. In *13th Annual ACM Symp. on Principles of Prog. Languages.*, pages 38–43, January 1986.
[Wan87]   M. Wand. A simple algorithm and proof for type inference. *Fundamenta Informaticae*, 10:115–122, 1987.
[Wel02]   J. B. Wells. The essence of principal typings. In *Proc. 29th Int'l Coll. Automata, Languages, and Programming*, volume 2380 of *LNCS*. Springer-Verlag, 2002.
[YM00]   Jun Yang and G. Michaelson. A visualisation of polymorphic type checking. *Journal of Functional Programming*, 10(1):57–75, January 2000.
[YTMW00]   Jun Yang, Phil Trinder, Greg Michaelson, and Joe Wells. Improved type error reporting. In *Proceeding of Implementation of Functional Languages, 12th International Workshop*, pages 71–86, September 2000.

Correctness of Non-determinism Analyses in a Parallel-Functional Language[*]

Clara Segura and Ricardo Peña

Departamento de Sistemas Informáticos y Programación
Universidad Complutense de Madrid, Spain
{csegura,ricardo}@sip.ucm.es

Abstract. The presence of non-determinism in the parallel-functional language Eden creates some problems. Several non-determinism analyses have been developed to determine when an Eden expression is sure to be deterministic, and when it may be non-deterministic. The correctness of these analyses had not been proved yet. In this paper we define a "maximal" denotational semantics for Eden in the sense that the set of possible values produced by an expression is bigger than the actual one. This semantics is enough to prove the correctness of the analyses. We provide the abstraction and concretisation functions relating the concrete and abstract values so that the determinism property is adequately captured. Finally we prove the correctness of the analyses with respect to the previously defined semantics.

1 Introduction

The presence of non-determinism in the parallel-functional language Eden creates some problems: It affects the referential transparency of programs [11] and invalidates some optimizations done in the Glasgow Haskell Compiler (GHC) [10]. Three non-determinism abstract interpretation based analyses have been defined to determine when an Eden expression is sure to be deterministic, and when it may be non-deterministic [7,8]. They have been formally related and compared with respect to expresiveness and efficiency [5].

However the correctness of these analyses had not been proved yet as there was no appropriate denotational semantics for Eden including non-determinism. Very recently it has been published in our group a complete denotational semantics [3] for Eden based on continuations. There, non-determinism is expressed by the fact that, after evaluating an expression, a process may arrive to *a set* of different states, so that several continuations are possible. Unfortunately this semantics is not still appropriate for our purposes: On the one hand it provides lots of details that would obscure the proof of correctness. On the other, the set of states a process may arrive to do not constitute a mathematical domain and this is essential when abstract interpretation is used.

So, the first contribution of this paper is the definition of an appropriate denotational semantics, in one sense simpler and in another sense more complex than

---

[*] Work partially supported by the Spanish project TIC 2000-0738.

P. Trinder, G. Michaelson, and R. Peña (Eds.): IFL 2003, LNCS 3145, pp. 69–85, 2004.

that of [3]. Moreover, as concurrency and parallelism aspects are abstracted away, the non-determinism analyses would also be correct for any non-deterministic functional language whose semantics is (upper) approximated by this one. It is a *plural* semantics in the style of [12] but with higher order and algebraic types incorporated. The domains of values are defined by means of Hoare powerdomains considering that the behaviour of the non-deterministic operator is near to angelic non-determinism. To our knowledge, this is the first time that a powerdomain-based non-deterministic semantics including higher-order values is defined. It is not the actual semantics of Eden but an upper approximation to it in the sense that, if an Eden expression e may evaluate to value v, then v is included in the set s denoted by e in the semantics, but s may include values that the implementation will never arrive to. However, this semantics is enough to prove the correctness of the analyses.

The second contribution of the paper is the proof of correctness itself. We provide the abstraction and concretisation functions relating the concrete and abstract values so that the determinism property is adequately captured. We prove that they form a Galois connection and then we prove the correctness of the analyses with respect to the semantics. The techniques we use are rather standard in the abstract interpretation area but the problem addressed – non-determinism analysis with functional domains, denotational semantics with Hoare higher-order powerdomain – and the proof itself are new.

The plan of the paper is as follows. In Section 2 we describe Eden and the non-determinism analyses that have been defined for it. In Section 3 we present the denotational semantics including non-determinism. Finally, in Section 4 correctness of the analyses is formally proved.

2   Non-determinism Analyses for Eden

2.1   Eden in a Nutshell

The parallel-functional language Eden extends the lazy functional language Haskell by constructs to explicitly define and communicate processes. The three main new concepts are *process abstractions*, *process instantiations* and the non-deterministic process abstraction `merge`.

A *process abstraction* expression `process x -> e` of type `Process a b` defines the behaviour of a process having the formal parameter `x::a` as input and the expression `e::b` as output. An instantiation is achieved by using the predefined infix operator `(#) :: Process a b -> a -> b`. Process abstractions of type `Process a b` can be compared to functions of type `a -> b`, the main difference being that the former, when instantiated, are executed in parallel. Process instantiations can be compared to function applications: Each time an expression `e1 # e2` is evaluated, a new parallel process is created to evaluate `(e1 e2)`.

The evaluation of an expression `e1 # e2` leads to the dynamic creation of a process together with its interconnecting communication channels. The instantiating or *parent process* will be responsible for evaluating and sending `e2` via an implicitly generated channel, while the new *child process* will evaluate first the expression e1 until a process abstraction process x -> e is obtained and then the application (\ x -> e) e2, returning the result via another implicitly generated channel. The instantiation protocol deserves some attention: (1) Closure e1 together with the closures of all the free variables referenced there (its whole environment) are *copied*, in the current evaluation state (possibly unevaluated), to a new processor, and the child process is created there to evaluate the expression (\ x -> e) e2, where e2 must be remotely received. (2) Expression e2 is eagerly evaluated in the parent process to normal form. The result is communicated to the child process as its input argument. (3) The normal form of the value (\ x -> e) e2 is sent back to the parent. Normal forms are full, except for lambdas where they are weak ones. For input or output tuples, independent concurrent threads are created to evaluate each component.

Processes communicate via *unidirectional channels* which connect one writer to exactly one reader. Once a process is running, only fully evaluated data objects are communicated. The only exceptions are lists, which are transmitted in a *stream*-like fashion, i.e. element by element. Each list element is first evaluated to full normal form and then transmitted. Concurrent threads trying to access input which is not available yet, are temporarily suspended. This is the only way in which Eden processes synchronize.

Lazy evaluation is changed to eager evaluation in two cases: Processes are eagerly instantiated, and instantiated processes produce their output even if it is not demanded. These modifications aim at increasing the parallelism degree and at speeding up the distribution of the computation. The rest of the language is as lazy as Haskell is. In general, a process is implemented by several threads concurrently running in the same processor, so that different values can be produced independently. The concept of a virtually shared global graph does not exist. Each process evaluates its outputs autonomously.

Non-determinism is introduced in Eden by means of a predefined process abstraction merge :: Process [[a]] [a] which *fairly* interleaves a set of input lists, to produce a single non-deterministic list. Its implementation immediately copies to the output list any value appearing at any of the input lists. So, merge can profitably be used to quickly react to requests coming in an unpredictable order from a set of processes. This feature is essential in reactive systems and very useful in some deterministic parallel algorithms. Eden is aimed at both types of applications.

2.2   A Simplified Language

In the next section a denotational semantics is defined for a simplified version of Eden, see Figure 1, in order to prove the correctness of several non-determinism analyses. The language is an extended simplification of Core-Haskell [9], a simple functional language with second-order polymorphism. As Eden is an extension of Haskell, it is obviously polymorphic. But in order to simplify the rest of the paper, we have removed this aspect of the language. So there are neither type abstractions nor type applications.

$$
\begin{array}{lll}
prog & \rightarrow & bind_1;\ldots;bind_m \\
bind & \rightarrow & v = expr & \{\text{non-recursive binding}\} \\
 & | & \textbf{rec } v_1 = expr_1;\ldots;v_m = expr_m & \{\text{recursive binding}\} \\
expr & \rightarrow & expr\ x & \{\text{application to an atom}\} \\
 & | & \lambda v.expr & \{\text{lambda abstraction}\} \\
 & | & \textbf{case } expr \textbf{ of } alts & \{case \text{ expression}\} \\
 & | & \textbf{let } bind \textbf{ in } expr & \{let \text{ expression}\} \\
 & | & (x_1,\ldots,x_m) & \{\text{tuple}\} \\
 & | & C\ x_1 \ldots x_m & \{\text{saturated constructor application}\} \\
 & | & x & \{\text{atom: variable } v \text{ or literal } k\} \\
 & | & merge_t & \{\text{non-determinism operator}\} \\
alts & \rightarrow & Calt_1;\ldots;Calt_m;\quad m \geq 0 \\
 & | & TAlt \\
TAlt & \rightarrow & (v_1,\ldots,v_m) \rightarrow expr & \quad m \geq 0\ \{\text{tuple alternative}\} \\
Calt & \rightarrow & C\ v_1 \ldots v_m \rightarrow expr & \quad m \geq 0\ \{\text{algebraic alternative}\}
\end{array}
$$

Fig. 1. A simplified version of a parallel functional language.

The variables contain type information, so we will not write it explicitly in the expressions. When necessary, we will write $e :: t$ to make explicit the type of an expression. A type may be a basic type K, a tuple type $(t_1,\ldots,t_m)$, an algebraic (sum) type T^1, or a functional type $t_1 \rightarrow t_2$.

Process abstractions **process** $v \rightarrow e$ and process instantiations $e\ \#\ x$ do not appear in the language. This simplification is motivated by an approximation to the semantics explained in Section 3.2. When an unevaluated non-deterministic free variable is duplicated in two different processes, it may happen that the actual value computed by each process is different. However, within the same process, a variable is evaluated at most once and its value is shared thereafter. Consequently this means that variables are *definite* (each occurrence denotes the same single value) within the same process and are not definite (different occurrences may denote different values) within different processes. In general, in Eden the *unfoldability* property does not hold (a variable cannot be replaced by its definition, i.e. $[\![(\lambda x.e)\ e']\!]\ \rho \neq [\![e[e'/x]]\!]\ \rho$), except in the case that the unfolded expression is deterministic. This is a consequence of having definite variables within a process.

So, there are some occurrences that surely have the same value but others may have different values. The following example illustrates this situation. Assume ne is a non-deterministic expression in

$$\textbf{let } v = ne \textbf{ in } (p_1\ v)\#v + (p_2\ v)\#v$$

The second and fourth occurrences of v necessarily have the same value as they are evaluated in the parent process. However the first and third occurrences may have different values as v is copied twice and evaluated in two children processes. So, an upper approximation is obtained by considering that

---

[1] Defined by **data** $T = C_1\ t_{11} \ldots t_{1n_1}\ |\ldots|\ C_m\ t_{m1} \ldots t_{mn_m}$.

- All the occurrences of each variable may have a different value, i.e. all the variables are non-definite.
- All functions behave as processes, and all function applications behave as process instantiations. Consequently, we will only have syntactical lambda abstractions and function applications with the semantics of process abstractions and process instantiations.

The semantics defined in Section 3.2 will make these assumptions.

As polymorphism is omitted, the merge operator is monomorphic, so we consider the existence of an instance $merge_t$ for every type t. Additionally we simplify this operator so that it merges just two lists of values: $merge_t : [t] \to [t] \to [t]$. Eden's merge is more convenient since it may receive as arguments any finite number of lists, but it can be simulated by the simplified one, $merge_t$.

2.3 Motivation for the Analyses

The non-deterministic process merge may be used to create non-deterministic expressions and to define non-deterministic functions. Subsection 2.4 introduces several analyses to detect at compile time these non-deterministic expressions. The analyses annotate the expressions with a mark which, in the simplest case is just d or n. The first one means that the expression is *sure* to be deterministic, while the second one means that it *may be* non-deterministic. So, a possible better name for these analyses would be *determinism* analyses because the sure value is the deterministic one. We found at least three motivations for developing these analyses.

On the one hand, to annotate the places in the text where equational reasoning may be lost due to the presence of non-determinism. This is important in an optimizing compiler such as that of Eden built on top of GHC [9]. A lot of internal transformations such as *inlining* or *full laziness* are done on the assumption that it is always possible to replace equals by equals. This is not true when the expressions involved are non-deterministic. For instance, the full laziness transformation moves a binding out of a lambda when it does not depend on the lambda argument. So, the expression

$$\textbf{let } f = \lambda x. \textbf{ let } y = e_1 \textbf{ in } e_2$$
$$\textbf{in } e_3$$

when e_1 does not depend on x is transformed to

$$\textbf{let } y = e_1$$
$$\textbf{in let } f = \lambda x.e_2 \textbf{ in } e_3$$

If e_1 is non-deterministic, this transformation restricts the set of values the expression may evaluate to, as now expression e_1 is evaluated only once instead of many times.

A second motivation is to be able to implement in the future a semantics for Eden, different from the currently implemented one, in which all variables will be guaranteed to be definite, i.e. they will denote the same value in all the processes. To this aim, when a non-deterministic binding is to be copied to a newly instantiated process, the runtime system will take care of previously evaluating the binding to normal form. Doing this evaluation for all bindings would make Eden more eager than needed and would decrease the amount of parallelism as more work would be done in parent processes. So, it is important to do this evaluation only when it is known that the binding is possibly non-deterministic.

A third motivation could be to be able to inform the programmer of the deterministic expressions of the program. In this way, the part of the program where equational reasoning is still possible would be clearly determined. A first step towards this aim is doing the analysis at the core language level. A translation of the annotations to source level would also be required in order to provide the programmer with meaningful information. For the moment we have not implemented this translation.

2.4   A Hierarchy of Analyses

Three non-determinism analyses have been developed to determine when an Eden expression is sure to be deterministic and when it may be non-deterministic. In [7], two different abstract interpretation based analyses were presented and compared with respect to expressiveness and efficiency. The first one $[\![\cdot]\!]_1$ was efficient (linear) but not very powerful, and the second one $[\![\cdot]\!]_2$ was powerful but less efficient (exponential). In [8] an intermediate analysis $[\![\cdot]\!]_3$ and its implementation (written in Haskell) were described. Such analysis is a compromise between power and efficiency (cubic). Its definition is based on the second analysis $[\![\cdot]\!]_2$. The improvement in efficiency is obtained by speeding up the fixpoint calculation by means of a widening operator wop, and by using an easily comparable representation of functions. By choosing different operators we obtain different variants of the analysis $[\![\cdot]\!]_3^{wop}$. That paper described one particular variant $[\![\cdot]\!]_3^{W}$ in detail.

In [5], the three analyses were formally related so that they become totally ordered by increasing cost and precision. It was shown that all variants of the third analysis are safe approximations to the second analysis and that the first analysis is only a safe aproximation to those variants of the third analysis satisfying a particular property. An example was given to show the differences in precision between $[\![\cdot]\!]_1$, $[\![\cdot]\!]_2$ and $[\![\cdot]\!]_3^{W}$. In Figure 2 we show the relation between the first and second analyses, and some variants of the third one.

In this paper we only summarize the second analysis as we are going to prove its correctness with respect to the Eden semantics. The previous results lead us to correctness of the whole hierarchy of analyses with respect to it.

In Figure 3 the abstract domains for $[\![\cdot]\!]_2$ are shown. There is a domain *Basic* with two values: d represents *determinism* and n *possible non-determinism*, with the ordering $d \sqsubseteq n$. This is the abstract domain corresponding to basic types and algebraic types. The abstract domains corresponding to a tuple type and a function/process type are respectively the cartesian product of the components'

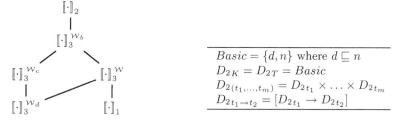

Fig. 2. A hierarchy of analyses.

$$Basic = \{d, n\} \text{ where } d \sqsubseteq n$$
$$D_{2K} = D_{2T} = Basic$$
$$D_{2(t_1,\dots,t_m)} = D_{2t_1} \times \dots \times D_{2t_m}$$
$$D_{2t_1 \to t_2} = [D_{2t_1} \to D_{2t_2}]$$

Fig. 3. Abstract domains for the second analysis.

$$[\![v]\!]_2 \, \rho_2 = \rho_2(v)$$
$$[\![k]\!]_2 \, \rho_2 = d$$
$$[\![(x_1,\dots,x_m)]\!]_2 \, \rho_2 = ([\![x_1]\!]_2 \, \rho_2, \dots, [\![x_m]\!]_2 \, \rho_2)$$
$$[\![C \, x_1 \dots x_m]\!]_2 \, \rho_2 = \bigsqcup_i \phi_{t_i}([\![x_i]\!]_2 \, \rho_2) \text{ where } x_i :: t_i$$
$$[\![e \, x]\!]_2 \, \rho_2 = ([\![e]\!]_2 \, \rho_2) \, ([\![x]\!]_2 \, \rho_2)$$
$$[\![\lambda v.e]\!]_2 \, \rho_2 = \lambda z \in D_{2t_v}.[\![e]\!]_2 \, \rho_2 \, [v \mapsto z] \text{ where } v :: t_v$$
$$[\![merge_t]\!]_2 \, \rho_2 = \lambda z_1 \in Basic.\lambda z_2 \in Basic.n$$
$$[\![\text{let } v = e \text{ in } e']\!]_2 \, \rho_2 = [\![e']\!]_2 \, \rho_2 \, [v \mapsto [\![e]\!]_2 \, \rho_2]$$
$$[\![\text{let rec } \overline{\{v_i = e_i\}} \text{ in } e']\!]_2 \, \rho_2 = [\![e']\!]_2 \, (\text{fix } (\lambda \rho_2'.\rho_2 \, \overline{[v_i \mapsto [\![e_i]\!]_2 \, \rho_2']}))$$
$$[\![\text{case } e \text{ of } (v_1,\dots,v_m) \to e']\!]_2 \, \rho_2 = [\![e']\!]_2 \, \rho_2 \, \overline{[v_i \mapsto \pi_i([\![e]\!]_2 \, \rho_2)]}$$
$$[\![\text{case } e \text{ of } \overline{C_i \, \overline{v_{ij}} \to e_i;}]\!]_2 \, \rho_2 = \begin{cases} \mu_t(n) \text{ if } [\![e]\!]_2 \, \rho_2 = n \\ \bigsqcup_i [\![e_i]\!]_2 \, \rho_{2i} \text{ otherwise} \end{cases}$$
$$\text{where } \rho_{2i} = \rho_2 \, \overline{[v_{ij} \mapsto \mu_{t_{ij}}(d)]}, v_{ij} :: t_{ij}, e_i :: t$$

Fig. 4. Abstract interpretation $[\![\cdot]\!]_2$.

domains and the domain of continuous functions between the domains of the argument and the result. In [7] polymorphism was also included, but in this paper we do not treat it.

In Figure 4 the analysis is shown. It is an abstract interpretation based analysis in the style of [1]. We outline here only some cases. The interpretation of a tuple is the tuple of the abstract values of the components. Functions are interpreted as abstract functions. So, applications are interpreted as abstract functions applications. The interpretation of a constructor application belongs to *Basic*, obtained as the least upper bound (lub) of the components' abstract values. But each component $x_i :: t_i$ has an abstract value belonging to D_{2t_i}, that must be first *flattened* to a basic abstract value. This is done by a function called the *flattening function* $\phi_t : D_{2t} \to Basic$, defined in Figure 5. The idea is to flatten the tuples (by applying the lub operator) and to apply the functions to deterministic arguments.

In a recursive **let** expression the fixpoint can be calculated by using Kleene's ascending chain. We have two different kinds of *case* expressions (for tuple and algebraic types). The more complex one is the algebraic *case*. Its abstract value is non-deterministic if either the discriminant or any of the expressions in the alternatives is non-deterministic. Note that the abstract value of the discriminant e, let us call it b, belongs to *Basic*. That is, when it was interpreted, the

$$\phi_t : D_{2t} \rightarrow Basic$$
$$\phi_K = \phi_T = id_{Basic}$$
$$\phi_{(t_1,\ldots,t_m)}(e_1,\ldots,e_m) = \bigsqcup_i \phi_{t_i}(e_i)$$
$$\phi_{t_1 \rightarrow t_2}(f) = \phi_{t_2}(f(\mu_{t_1}(d)))$$

$$\mu_t : Basic \rightarrow D_{2t}$$
$$\mu_K = \mu_T = id_{Basic}$$
$$\mu_{(t_1,\ldots,t_m)}(b) = (\mu_{t_1}(b),\ldots,\mu_{t_m}(b))$$
$$\mu_{t_1 \rightarrow t_2}(b) = \begin{cases} \lambda z \in D_{2t_1}.\mu_{t_2}(n) \text{ if } b = n \\ \lambda z \in D_{2t_1}.\mu_{t_2}(\phi_{t_1}(z)) \text{ if } b = d \end{cases}$$

Fig. 5. Functions ϕ_t and μ_t.

$$A_K = \mathcal{P}(\llbracket K \rrbracket) \quad \text{where } \llbracket Int \rrbracket = \mathbb{Z}_\perp$$
$$A_{(t_1,\ldots,t_m)} = A_{t_1} \times \ldots \times A_{t_m}$$
$$A_T = \mathcal{P}(\llbracket T \rrbracket)$$
$$\quad \text{where } \llbracket T \rrbracket = \oplus_{i=1}^m (C_i \times \times_{j=1}^{n_i} A_{t_{ij}})_\perp, \quad \textbf{data } T = C_1\, t_{11}\ldots t_{1n_1}\mid\ldots\mid C_m\, t_{m1}\ldots t_{mn_m}$$
$$A_{t_1 \rightarrow t_2} = [A_{t_1} \rightarrow A_{t_2}]$$

Fig. 6. Domain of values.

information about the components was lost. We want now to interpret each alternative's right hand side in an extended environment with abstract values for the variables $v_{ij} :: t_{ij}$ in the left hand side of the alternative. We do not have such information, but we can safely approximate it by using the *unflattening function* $\mu_t : Basic \rightarrow D_{2t}$ defined in Figure 5. Given a type t, it *unflattens* a basic abstract value and produces an abstract value in D_{2t}. The idea is to obtain the best safe approximation both to d and n in a given domain. The flattening and unflattening functions are mutually recursive. In [7] they were explained in detail and an example was given to illustrate their definitions. They have some interesting properties (e.g. they are a Galois insertion pair [2]), studied in [5]. Tuples are treated separately from algebraic types because we want the analysis to be more precise here due to the use of tuples in Eden as input or output channels of processes.

3   A Denotational Semantics for Non-determinism

3.1   The Domain of Values

To capture the idea of a non-deterministic value, the traditional approach is to make an expression to denote a *set* of values. This is obvious for basic types such as integers, but things get more complex when we move to structured types such as functions or tuples. Should a functional expression denote a set of functions or a function from sets to sets? Should a tuple expression denote a set of tuples or a tuple of sets? Additionally, the denoted values should constitute a domain. In the literature, three powerdomains with different properties have been proposed: Hoare, Smyth and Plotkin powerdomains [12]. The first one models *angelic* or bottom-avoiding nondeterminism (in which bottom is never chosen unless it is the only option), the second one models *demonic* non-determinism (it chooses bottom whenever it is a possible option) and the third one models *erratic* non-determinism (in which bottom is an option as the other ones).

Regarding structured domains we have chosen a functional expression to denote a single function from sets to sets. In this sense, the following two bindings

$$f_1 = head(merge_{Int \to Int}[\lambda x.0][\lambda x.1])$$
$$f_2 = \lambda x.head(merge_{Int}[0][1])$$

will both denote the function $\lambda x.\{0, 1, \perp\}$. That is, the information whether the non-deterministic decision is taken at binding evaluation time or at function application time is lost. Non-deterministic decisions are deferred as much as possible; in this example to function application time. This is consistent with the plural semantics we have adopted for our language in Section 3.2: Several occurrences of the same variable (let us say f_1) may represent different values.

Regarding the selection of powerdomain, we have decided to use Hoare's one. This is consistent with the implementation of merge in Eden: If one of the input lists is blocked (i.e., it denotes $\perp$), merge will still produce an output list by copying values from the non-blocked list. Only if both lists are blocked will the output list be blocked. Nevertheless, merge will terminate only when both input lists terminate. This behaviour is very near to angelic non-determinism. If D is a domain, $\mathcal{P}(D)$ will denote the Hoare powerdomain of D. First, a preorder relation is defined in $P(D)$ (all subsets of D) as follows:

$$A \sqsubseteq_{P(D)} B \quad iff \quad \forall a \in A. \exists b \in B.a \sqsubseteq_D b$$

This preorder relation induces an equivalence relation $\equiv \overset{\text{def}}{=} \sqsubseteq \cap \sqsupseteq$ identifying sets such as $\{0, 1, \perp\}$ and $\{0, 1\}$. The Hoare powerdomain is the quotient $\mathcal{P}(D) \overset{\text{def}}{=} (P(D) - \emptyset)/\equiv$. A property enjoyed by all elements of a Hoare powerdomain is that they are downwards closed, i.e. $\forall x \in A.y \sqsubseteq_D x \Rightarrow y \in A$.

In Figure 6, the domains of semantic values for every type are defined. Notice that, for basic and constructed types, the domains consist of sets of values while for tuples and functions, the domains consist of single values. In the definition for constructed types, $\oplus$ denotes the coalesced sum of (lifted) domains. Sets of values are needed for the constructed types because non-deterministic values of such types may contain several different constructors. However, those with only one constructor could be treated as tuples.

If the constructed type is recursive, notice that the recursive occurrences denote sets of values. For instance, a non-deterministic list would consist of a set of lists. A non-empty list of this set would consist of a head value and a tail value formed by a set of lists. Note also that the domain allows the existence of infinite values as limits of their finite approximations.

3.2   A Maximal Semantics: Non-definite Variables

In Figure 7 a denotational semantics for Eden is given. There $\{v\}^*$ denotes the downwards closure of a value, i.e. a set of values containing all values below v. The environment ρ maps variables of type t to values of their corresponding non-deterministic domains A_t. The semantic function $[\![.]\!]$ maps an expression of

$$\llbracket v \rrbracket\ \rho = \rho(v)$$
$$\llbracket k \rrbracket\ \rho = \{k\}^*$$
$$\llbracket (x_1, \ldots, x_m) \rrbracket\ \rho = (\llbracket x_1 \rrbracket\ \rho, \ldots, \llbracket x_m \rrbracket\ \rho)$$
$$\llbracket C\ x_1 \ldots x_m \rrbracket\ \rho = \{C\ \llbracket x_1 \rrbracket\ \rho \ldots \llbracket x_m \rrbracket\ \rho\}^*$$
$$\llbracket \lambda v.e \rrbracket_2\ \rho = \lambda s \in A_{t_v}.\llbracket e \rrbracket\ \rho\ [v \mapsto s]\ \text{where } v :: t_v$$
$$\llbracket e\ x \rrbracket\ \rho = (\llbracket e \rrbracket\ \rho)\ (\llbracket x \rrbracket\ \rho)$$
$$\llbracket merge_t \rrbracket\ \rho = \lambda s_1 \in A_{[t]}.\lambda s_2 \in A_{[t]}.\bigcup\{mergeS\ l_1\ l_2 \mid l_1 \in s_1, l_2 \in s_2\}$$
$$\llbracket \textbf{let}\ v = e\ \textbf{in}\ e' \rrbracket\ \rho = \llbracket e' \rrbracket\ \rho\ [v \mapsto \llbracket e \rrbracket\ \rho]$$
$$\llbracket \textbf{let rec}\ \{v_i = e_i\}\ \textbf{in}\ e' \rrbracket\ \rho = \llbracket e' \rrbracket\ (fix\ (\lambda \rho'.\rho\ \overline{[v_i \mapsto \llbracket e_i \rrbracket\ \rho']}))$$
$$\llbracket \textbf{case}\ e\ \textbf{of}\ (v_1, \ldots, v_m) \to e' \rrbracket\ \rho = \llbracket e' \rrbracket\ \rho\ \overline{[v_i \mapsto \pi_i(\llbracket e \rrbracket\ \rho)]}$$
$$\llbracket \textbf{case}\ e\ \textbf{of}\ \overline{C_i\ \overline{v_{ij}} \to e_i;} \rrbracket\ \rho = \begin{cases} \bot_{A_t} \text{ if } \llbracket e \rrbracket\ \rho = \bot_{A_T} \\ \bigsqcup_{A_t}\{\overline{\llbracket e_k \rrbracket\ \rho[v_{kj} \mapsto s_{kj}]}^{m_k} \mid C_k\ \overline{s_{kj}}^{m_k} \in \llbracket e \rrbracket\ \rho\} \text{ otherwise} \end{cases}$$

Fig. 7. A denotational semantics for Eden.

$$mergeS\ \bot\ \bot = \{\bot\} \qquad mergeS\ \bot\ l_2 = \{l_2 +\!\!+ \bot\}^* \qquad mergeS\ l_1\ \bot = \{l_1 +\!\!+ \bot\}^*$$
$$mergeS\ [\,]\ [\,] = \{[\,]\}^* \qquad mergeS\ [\,]\ l_2 = \{l_2\}^* \qquad mergeS\ l_1\ [\,] = \{l_1\}^*$$
$$mergeS\ (s_1 : ls_1)\ (s_2 : ls_2) = \{s_1 : (\bigcup_{l' \in ls_1} mergeS\ l'\ (s_2 : ls_2)), s_2 : (\bigcup_{l' \in ls_2} mergeS\ (s_1 : ls_1)\ l')\}^*$$
$$\text{where } \bot +\!\!+ \bot = \bot$$
$$[\,] +\!\!+ \bot = \bot$$
$$(xs : xss) +\!\!+ \bot = xs : \{xss' +\!\!+ \bot \mid xss' \in xss\}$$

Fig. 8. Non-determinism semantics.

type t and an environment ρ to a value in A_t. The only expression introducing sets of values is $merge_t$. Its behaviour is that of a lambda abstraction returning all the possible interleavings of all pairs of input lists. The detail of the auxiliary function $mergeS$ is given in Figure 8.

These decisions configure a plural semantics for Eden as every occurrence of the same variable within an expression is mapped to *all* possible values for that variable (see definitions for **let** and lambda in Figure 7). This is not the actual semantics of Eden, but just a safe upper approximation to it in the sense that the set of possible values denoted by an expression is bigger than the actual one. As an example, the expression **let** $f = head(merge_{Int \to Int}[\lambda x.0]\ [\lambda x.1])$ **in** $(f\ 3) + (f\ 4)$ in fact may only produce the values 0 or 2 while the approximated semantics will say that it may also produce the value 1. It is *maximal* in the sense that all variables are considered non definite, while in the actual semantics only those variables duplicated in different processes may be non definite if they are non-deterministic. Notice that with this approximated semantics unfoldability holds although in the actual semantics this is not true. The denotation given to $merge_t$ is also an upper approximation as the actual one only produces fair interleavings.

The reason for this maximal semantics is that, if we are able to show the correctness of the analysis with respect to it, then the analysis will be correct with respect to the actual semantics. We remind the reader that the sure value is the deterministic one. If the analysis detects an expression as deterministic then it should be semantically deterministic.

An exception is the algebraic **case** expression where the variables in the right hand side of the alternatives are definite. The discriminant's value is a set that may contain different constructors, so we have to take the lub of all the alternatives' values that match them. As the discriminant is immediately evaluated, the non-deterministic decision is immediately taken so that all the occurrences of the same variable in the right hand side have the chosen value.

For example, let a type **data** $Fool = C\ Int \mid C'\ Int$ and the values $s_1 = \{\bot, C\{0, \bot\}, C'\{0, \bot\}\}$, $s_2 = \{\bot, C\{1, \bot\}, C\{0, \bot\}\}$ and $s'_2 = \{\bot, C\{1, \bot\}, C\{0, \bot\}, C\{0, 1, \bot\}\}$. Let an expression $e' = \mathbf{case}\ e\ \mathbf{of}\ C\ v \rightarrow v + v; C'\ v' \rightarrow v' + 4$. If $[\![e]\!]$ $\rho = s_1$, then $[\![e']\!]\ \rho = \{0, 4, \bot\}$. Notice that s_2 and s'_2 are different: If $[\![e]\!]\ \rho = s_2$ then $[\![e']\!]\ \rho = \{0, 2, \bot\}$, but if $[\![e]\!]\ \rho = s'_2$, then $[\![e']\!]\ \rho = \{0, 1, 2, \bot\}$. This is because the variables in the right hand side of a **case** alternative are definite. We could have chosen another option when building the environments for the right hand sides (see [6]) but this is nearer to the actual semantics. The rest of the rules are self-explanatory.

4   Capturing the Determinism Meaning

4.1   Deterministic Values

In this section we are proving that $[\![\cdot]\!]_2$ is correct with respect to the denotational semantics presented in the previous section (see Theorem 1). In order to establish the correctness predicate we need first to define the semantic property we want to capture, that is the determinism of an expression. In Figure 9 the boolean functions det_t are defined. Given $s \in A_t$, $det_t(s)$ tells us whether s is a deterministic value or not. A value of type K is deterministic if it is a set with at most one element different from $\bot$ (as $\bot$ belongs to each $s \in A_K$), which is established by the function $unit$. A tuple is deterministic if each component is deterministic. A constructed value $s \in A_T$ is deterministic if its elements different from $\bot$ (again $\bot$ belongs to each $s \in A_T$) have the same constructor, which is established by the function one, and additionally the least upper bound of the values in each component is deterministic. For example, values s_1, s_2 and s'_2 defined in Section 3.2 are non-deterministic: The first one because it has two different constructors, and the other two because the least upper bound of the first component, $\{0, 1, \bot\}$, is non-deterministic. The definition of det_t in Figure 9 and the propositions below assume that there are not algebraic infinite values. This is not a severe restriction as processes communicating infinite values will not terminate and Hoare powerdomains ignores non-termination ($\bot$ is included in all values).

Finally, a function is deterministic if given a deterministic argument it produces a deterministic result.

Let us note that this semantical definition of determinism characterizes a possibly non-terminating single value expression as being deterministic. This is in accordance with the Hoare powerdomain semantics we have adopted producing Scott-closed sets: Where the actual semantics produces a single value, our approximate semantics produces a non-singleton set because it always includes $\bot$. That is, predicate det_t characterizes determinism up to non-termination. Notice also that, if we eliminate $\bot$ in the definitions of $unit$ and one, then predicate

$det_K(s) = unit(s)$
    where $unit(\{\bot\}) = true$ $unit(\{z, \bot\}) = true$ $unit_- = false$
$det_{(t_1,\ldots,t_m)}((s_1,\ldots,s_m)) = \bigwedge_{i=1}^m det_{t_i}(s_i)$
$det_T(s) = \begin{cases} \bigwedge_{i=1}^m det_{t_i}(\bigsqcup\{s_i \mid C\ s_1\ldots s_m \in s, s_i :: t_i\}) & \text{if } one(s) \\ false & \text{otherwise} \end{cases}$
    where $one(s) = (s = \{\bot\}) \vee (\exists C.\forall s' \in s.s' \neq \bot \Rightarrow s' = C\ s_1\ldots s_m)$
$det_{t_1 \to t_2}(f) = \forall s \in A_{t_1}.det_{t_1}(s) \Rightarrow det_{t_2}(f(s))$

Fig. 9. Semantic definition of determinism.

$\alpha_t : A_t \to D_{2t}$
$\alpha_K(s) = \begin{cases} d & \text{if } det_K(s) \\ n & \text{otherwise} \end{cases}$
$\alpha_{(t_1,\ldots,t_m)}((s_1,\ldots,s_m)) = (\alpha_{t_1}(s_1),\ldots,\alpha_{t_m}(s_m))$
$\alpha_T(s) = \begin{cases} d & \text{if } det_T(s) \\ n & \text{otherwise} \end{cases}$
$\alpha_{t_1 \to t_2}(f) = \lambda z \in D_{2t_1}.\bigsqcup_{s_1 \in \Gamma_{t_1}(z)} \alpha_{t_2}(f(s_1))$

$\Lambda_t : \mathcal{P}(A_t) \to D_{2t}$
$\Lambda_t(S) = \bigsqcup_{s \in S} \alpha_t(s)$

Fig. 10. Abstraction function.

det_t characterizes real singleton sets in the basic type, tuples and algebraic type cases, and functions mapping single values into single values in the functional type case. Predicates det_t have some properties (see [6]) we do not show here.

4.2   Abstraction and Concretisation Functions

In this section we define the abstraction Λ_t and concretisation Γ_t functions that relate the abstract and concrete domains, following the ideas in [1]. We will prove that they are a Galois connection, a crucial property in the correctness proof.

The function Λ_t is just an extension of a function α_t to Hoare sets by applying it to each element of the set and taking the lub. So α_t will also be called abstraction function. With this function, defined in Figure 10, we want to abstract the determinism behaviour of the concrete values. It loses information, i.e. several concrete values may have the same abstract value. In Figure 11 function Γ_t is defined. For each abstract value, it returns all the concrete values that can be approximated by that abstract value. They are mutually recursive.

A value of type K or T is abstracted to d only if it is deterministic. The abstraction of a tuple is the tuple of the abstractions. The abstraction of a function f of type $t_1 \to t_2$ is a little more involved. It is an abstract function taking an argument $z \in D_{2t_1}$. Such z represents several concrete values $s_1 \in \Gamma_t(z)$ whose abstract images are $\alpha_{t_2}(f(s_1))$. So the abstraction of the result is the lub of these abstract images.

$$\Gamma_t : D_{2t} \to \mathcal{P}(A_t)$$

$$\Gamma_K(b) = \begin{cases} \{s \in A_K \mid unit(s)\} & \text{if } b = d \\ \mathcal{P}(A_K) & \text{if } b = n \end{cases}$$

$$\Gamma_{(t_1,\ldots,t_m)}((z_1,\ldots,z_m)) = \{(s_1,\ldots,s_m) \mid \alpha_{t_i}(s_i) \sqsubseteq z_i \forall i \in \{1..m\}\}$$

$$\Gamma_T(b) = \begin{cases} \{s \in A_T \mid det_T(s)\} & \text{if } b = d \\ \mathcal{P}(A_T) & \text{if } b = n \end{cases}$$

$$\Gamma_{t_1 \to t_2}(f^\#) = \{f \in A_{t_1 \to t_2} \mid \forall s \in A_{t_1}.\alpha_{t_2}(f(v)) \sqsubseteq f^\#(\alpha_{t_1}(s))\}$$

Fig. 11. Concretisation function.

The concretisation function is defined so that it builds a Galois connection with Λ_t, which implies that for each concrete value there may be several abstract approximations but there exists only one best (least) approximation.

It can easily be proved that Γ_t is well defined, i.e. it produces downwards closed sets of concrete values. It can also be proved that for each type t, functions α_t, Λ_t and Γ_t are continuous. Both things are shown in [6].

The most important result in this section is that Λ_t and Γ_t are a Galois connection (i.e. $\Lambda_t \cdot \Gamma_t \sqsubseteq id_{D_{2t}}$ and $\Gamma_t \cdot \Lambda_t \sqsupseteq id_{\mathcal{P}(A_t)}$), which is equivalent to the following proposition, that will be intensively used in the correctness proof.

Proposition 1 *For each type t, $z \in D_{2t}$, and $s \in A_t$: $s \in \Gamma_t(z) \Leftrightarrow \alpha_t(s) \sqsubseteq z$.*

This proposition can be proved by structural induction on t (see [6]).

Finally we present an interesting property that only holds when the concrete domains of basic and algebraic types have at least two elements different from $\perp$. In the following proposition we show that α_t is surjective, i.e. each abstract value is the abstraction of a concrete value, which in particular belongs to the concretisation of that abstract value. This means that Λ_t and Γ_t are a Galois insertion ($\Lambda_t \cdot \Gamma_t = id_{D_{2t}}$).

Proposition 2 *If all $[\![K]\!]$ and $[\![T]\!]$ have at least two elements different from $\perp$, then for each type t and $z \in D_{2t}$, there exists $s \in \Gamma_t(z)$ such that $\alpha_t(s) = z$.*

This can be proved by structural induction on t (see [6]). If the proposition hypothesis about $[\![K]\!]$ and $[\![T]\!]$ does not hold then it is easy to see that all the concrete values are abstracted to d and none to n. In fact we are avoiding the *Unit* type. However this property is not necessary in the correctness proof.

4.3   A Proof of Partial Correctness

In this subsection we prove that $[\![\cdot]\!]_2$ is correct with respect to the denotational semantics: When the analysis tells that an expression is deterministic, then the concrete value produced by the denotational semantics is semantically deterministic. Otherwise we do not know anything about it. We have to formally describe this intuition. On the one hand, we said in Section 2.4 that $\mu_t(d)$ is the best safe approximation to d in a given domain, so the analysis tells us that an expression is deterministic when its abstract value is less than or equal to $\mu_t(d)$. On the other hand the semantical determinism of a concrete value is established by the predicate det_t. So, the main correctness result is expressed as follows.

Theorem 1. *Let ρ and ρ_2 be two environments, such that for each variable $x :: t_x$, $\alpha_{t_x}(\rho(x)) \sqsubseteq \rho_2(x)$. Then for each $e :: t$: $[\![e]\!]_2\ \rho_2 \sqsubseteq \mu_t(d) \Rightarrow det_t([\![e]\!]\ \rho)$.*

Notice that this only proves the partial correctness of the analysis with respect to the actual semantics of Eden. This (not formally defined) semantics only produces non-singleton sets when the expression e contains at least one occurrence of `merge`. If expression e completely terminates, then we can ignore the undefined values in $[\![e]\!]\ \rho$ and then $det_t([\![e]\!]\ \rho)$ amounts to saying that $[\![e]\!]\ \rho$ consists of a single value, i.e. e is deterministic in the actual semantics sense.

The theorem is proved in two parts written as Propositions 3 and 4, shown below. The first one tells us that all the values whose abstraction is below $\mu_t(d)$ are semantically deterministic. The second one asserts that the analysis is an upper approximation to the abstraction of the concrete semantics. The proofs use intensively some properties of ϕ_t and μ_t already shown in [5].

Proposition 3 *For each type t, and $s \in A_t$: $\alpha_t(s) \sqsubseteq \mu_t(d) \Leftrightarrow det_t(s)$.*

Proof 1 *We use structural induction on t. The interesting case is the function type, $t = t_1 \rightarrow t_2$. The rest are straightforward.*

- $(\Rightarrow)$. *We have to prove that $\forall s \in A_{t_1}.det_{t_1}(s) \Rightarrow det_{t_2}(f(s))$. So, let $s \in A_{t_1}$ such that $det_{t_1}(s)$. We have that*

$$
\begin{aligned}
\alpha_{t_2}(f(s)) &\sqsubseteq \bigsqcup\nolimits_{s_1 \in \Gamma_{t_1}(\alpha_{t_1}(s))} \alpha_{t_2}(f(s_1)) && \{s \in \Gamma_{t_1}(\alpha_{t_1}(s))\} \\
&\sqsubseteq \mu_{t_2}(\phi_{t_1}(\alpha_{t_1}(s))) && \{\alpha_t(f) \sqsubseteq \mu_t(d)\} \\
&\sqsubseteq \mu_{t_2}(\phi_{t_1}(\mu_{t_1}(d))) && \{\text{by i.h. on } t_1 \text{ and monotonicity}\} \\
&= \mu_{t_2}(d) && \{\phi_t \cdot \mu_t = id_{Basic}, \text{ by Prop. 2(b) in [5]}\}
\end{aligned}
$$

  Consequently, by i.h. on t_2 we have $det_{t_2}(f(s))$.
- $(\Leftarrow)$. *We have to prove that $\forall z \in D_{2t_1}.\bigsqcup\nolimits_{s_1 \in \Gamma_{t_1}(z)} \alpha_{t_2}(f(s_1)) \sqsubseteq \mu_{t_2}(\phi_{t_1}(z))$. Let $z \in D_{2t_1}$. We distinguish two cases.*
  - $z \sqsubseteq \mu_{t_1}(d)$. *Then*

$$
\begin{aligned}
s_1 &\in \Gamma_{t_1}(z) \\
&\Rightarrow \alpha_{t_1}(s_1) \sqsubseteq z && \{\text{by Proposition 1}\} \\
&\Rightarrow \alpha_{t_1}(s_1) \sqsubseteq \mu_{t_1}(d) && \{z \sqsubseteq \mu_{t_1}(d)\} \\
&\Rightarrow det_{t_2}(f(s_1)) && \{\text{by i.h. on } t_1 \text{ and } det_t(f)\} \\
&\Rightarrow \alpha_{t_2}(f(s_1)) \sqsubseteq \mu_{t_2}(d) && \{\text{by i.h. on } t_2\} \\
&\Rightarrow \alpha_{t_2}(f(s_1)) \sqsubseteq \mu_{t_2}(\phi_{t_1}(z)) && \{z \sqsubseteq \mu_{t_1}(d) \text{ and } \phi_t \cdot \mu_t = id_{Basic}\}
\end{aligned}
$$

  - $z \not\sqsubseteq \mu_{t_1}(d)$. *In this case $\phi_{t_1}(z) = n$ (by Proposition 3 in [5]). The proposition holds trivially as $\mu_{t_2}(n)$ is the top element in D_{2t_2} (by Proposition 2(d) in [5]).*

□

Proposition 4 *Let ρ and ρ_2 be two environments, such that for each variable $x :: t_x$, $\alpha_{t_x}(\rho(x)) \sqsubseteq \rho_2(x)$. Then for each expression $e :: t$: $\alpha_t(\llbracket e \rrbracket) \, \rho \sqsubseteq \llbracket e \rrbracket_2 \, \rho_2$.*

Proof 2 *We use structural induction on e. We show here only two interesting cases. In the* **letrec** *case a double induction is necessary (see [6]).*

- $e = C \; x_1 \ldots x_m :: T$. *We distinguish two cases. If $\alpha_T(\llbracket C \; x_1 \ldots x_m \rrbracket \, \rho) = d$ then it is trivial, as d is the bottom element in Basic.*
  If $\alpha_T(\llbracket C \; x_1 \ldots x_m \rrbracket \, \rho) = n$, then $\neg det_T(\{C \; (\llbracket x_1 \rrbracket \, \rho) \ldots (\llbracket x_m \rrbracket \, \rho)\}^*)$ by definition of α_t and $\llbracket \cdot \rrbracket$. In $\{C \; (\llbracket x_1 \rrbracket \, \rho) \ldots (\llbracket x_m \rrbracket \, \rho)\}^*$ there is just one constructor, so the only possibility for it to be non-deterministic, is that there exists $i \in \{1..m\}$ such that $\neg det_{t_i}(\sqcup\{s_j \mid C \; s_1 \ldots s_m \in \{C \; (\llbracket x_1 \rrbracket \, \rho) \ldots (\llbracket x_m \rrbracket \, \rho)\}^*\})$, i.e. such that $\neg det_{t_i}(\llbracket x_i \rrbracket \, \rho)$. By Proposition 1, this implies that $\alpha_{t_i}(\llbracket x_i \rrbracket \, \rho) \not\sqsubseteq \mu_{t_i}(d)$ and consequently $\phi_{t_i}(\alpha_{t_i}(\llbracket x_i \rrbracket \, \rho)) = n$ (by Proposition 3 in [5]), so

$$\llbracket C \; x_1 \ldots x_m \rrbracket_2 \, \rho_2 = \bigsqcup\nolimits_{j=1}^{m} \phi_{t_j}(\llbracket x_j \rrbracket_2 \, \rho_2) \quad \{\text{by definition of } \llbracket \cdot \rrbracket_2\}$$
$$\sqsupseteq \bigsqcup\nolimits_{j=1}^{m} \phi_{t_j}(\alpha_{t_j}(\llbracket x_j \rrbracket \, \rho)) \quad \{\text{by i.h. on } t_j \text{ and monotonicity}\}$$
$$= n \qquad\qquad \{\phi_{t_i}(\alpha_{t_i}(\llbracket x_i \rrbracket \, \rho)) = n\}$$

- $e = \lambda v.e' :: t_1 \to t_2$. *By definition of $\llbracket \cdot \rrbracket$ and α_t we have to prove that $\bigsqcup_{s_1 \in \Gamma_{t_1}(z)} \alpha_{t_2}(\llbracket e' \rrbracket \, \rho[v \mapsto s_1]) \sqsubseteq \llbracket e' \rrbracket_2 \, \rho_2[v \mapsto z]$.*
  If $s_1 \in \Gamma_{t_1}(z)$ then $\alpha_{t_1}(s_1) \sqsubseteq z$ by Proposition 1, so $\rho[x \mapsto s_1]$ and $\rho_2[v \mapsto z]$ satisfy the theorem hypothesis about the environments. We can then apply induction hypothesis on e' and obtain $\alpha_{t_2}(\llbracket e' \rrbracket \, \rho[v \mapsto s_1]) \sqsubseteq \llbracket e' \rrbracket_2 \, \rho_2[v \mapsto z]$.
  $\square$

5 Conclusions and Future Work

We have proved the correctness of a whole hierarchy of non-determinism analyses for the parallel-functional language Eden. In order to do this, we have defined first a denotational semantics for Eden where non-determinism is represented. We have chosen to use a plural semantics in which non-deterministic choices for variables are deferred as much as possible. A semantics nearer to the actual one (within a single process) would have been a singular one in which environments map variables to single values. This would reflect the fact that non-deterministic choices are done at binding evaluation time instead of at each variable occurrence. For instance, a let-bound variable will get its value the first time it is evaluated and this value will be shared thereafter by all its occurrences. In order to consider all the possible values the variable can have, we build one environment for each of them:

$$\llbracket \text{let } v = e \text{ in } e' \rrbracket \, \rho = \bigsqcup_{z \in \llbracket e \rrbracket \, \rho} \llbracket e' \rrbracket \, \rho[v \mapsto z]$$

The same would be true for case-bound and lambda-bound variables. We have tried to define this singular semantics and things go wrong when trying to give semantics to mutually recursive definitions. The traditional fixpoint computation by using Kleene's ascending chain gives a semantics more plural than expected. For instance, in the definition

$$\textbf{letrec} \quad f = head(merge_{Int \to Int} \ [g] \ [\lambda x.0])$$
$$g = head(merge_{Int \to Int} \ [f] \ [\lambda x.1])$$
$$\textbf{in} \ (f, g)$$

Kleene's ascending chain will compute the following set of possible environments:

$$\overline{\rho} = \{ \ \{f \mapsto \lambda x.\{\bot\}, \ g \mapsto \lambda x.\{\bot\}\}, \quad \{f \mapsto \lambda x.\{0\}^*, \ g \mapsto \lambda x.\{1\}^*\},$$
$$\{f \mapsto \lambda x.\{0\}^*, \ g \mapsto \lambda x.\{0\}^*\}, \quad \{f \mapsto \lambda x.\{1\}^*, \ g \mapsto \lambda x.\{1\}^*\},$$
$$\{f \mapsto \lambda x.\{1\}^*, \ g \mapsto \lambda x.\{0\}^*\} \ \}$$

However, the lazy evaluation of the expression will never produce the fifth possibility. In [12] a singular semantics for a small non-deterministic recursive functional language was defined. The problem with fixpoints did not arise there because the language was extremely simple: Only one recursive binding was allowed in the program and this had to be a lambda abstraction. Additionally, the language was only first-order. The problem arises when there are at least two mutually recursive bindings to non normal-form expressions. In order to define a real singular semantics, we think that an operational approach should be taken, similar to that of [4]. In this way, the actual lazy evaluation with its updating of closures and sharing of expressions could be appropriately modeled. We forsee to do it as future work.

Another extension of the present work is to include polymorphism in the language, in the semantics and in the proof of correctness. The analyses originally presented in [7, 8] already included this aspect.

References

1. G. L. Burn, C. L. Hankin, and S. Abramsky. The Theory of Strictness Analysis for Higher Order Functions. In *Programs as Data Objects*, volume 217 of *LNCS*, pages 42–62. Springer-Verlag, 1986.
2. P. Cousot and R. Cousot. Systematic design of program analysis frameworks. In *POPL'79*, pages 269–282. ACM, 1979.
3. M. Hidalgo and Y. Ortega. Continuation Semantics for Parallel Haskell Dialects. In *APLAS'03*, volume 2895 of *LNCS*, pages 303–321. Springer-Verlag, 2003.
4. J. Hughes and A. Moran. Making Choices Lazily. In *FPCA'95*, pages 108–119. ACM Press, 1995.
5. R. Peña and C. Segura. Three Non-determinism Analyses in a Parallel-Functional Language. Technical Report 117-01, Univ. Complutense de Madrid, Spain, 2001. (http://dalila.sip.ucm.es/miembros/clara/publications.html).
6. R. Peña and C. Segura. Correctness of Non-determinism Analyses in a Parallel-Functional Language. Technical Report 131-03, Univ. Complutense de Madrid, Spain, 2003. (http://dalila.sip.ucm.es/miembros/clara/publications.html).
7. R. Peña and C. Segura. Non-Determinism Analysis in a Parallel-Functional Language. In *IFL'00*, volume 2011 of *LNCS*, pages 1–18. Springer-Verlag, 2001.

8. R. Peña and C. Segura. A Polynomial Cost Non-Determinism Analysis. In *IFL'01*, volume 2312 of *LNCS*, pages 121–137. Springer-Verlag, 2002.

9. S. L. Peyton Jones, C. V. Hall, K. Hammond, W. D. Partain, and P. L. Wadler. The Glasgow Haskell Compiler: A Technical Overview. In *Joint Framework for Inf. Technology, Keele, DTI/SERC*, pages 249–257, 1993.

10. S. L. Peyton Jones and A. L. M. Santos. A Transformation-based Optimiser for Haskell. *Science of Computer Programming 32(1-3):3-47*, September 1998.

11. H. Søndergaard and P. Sestoft. Referential Transparency, Definiteness and Unfoldability. *Acta Informatica*, 27(6):505–517, May 1990.

12. H. Søndergaard and P. Sestoft. Non-Determinism in Functional Languages. *Computer Journal*, 35(5):514–523, October 1992.

Inferring Cost Equations
for Recursive, Polymorphic
and Higher-Order Functional Programs

Pedro B. Vasconcelos* and Kevin Hammond

School of Computer Science, University of St Andrews, St Andrews, KY16 9SS, UK
Tel.: +44 (0)1334 463253, Fax: +44 (0)1334 463278
{pv,kh}@dcs.st-and.ac.uk

Abstract. This paper presents a type-based analysis for inferring size- and cost-equations for recursive, higher-order and polymorphic functional programs without requiring user annotations or unusual syntax. Our type reconstruction algorithm is capable of inferring first-order cost equations for a non-trivial subset of higher-order, recursive and polymorphic functions. We illustrate the approach with reference to some standard examples of recursive programs.

1 Introduction

Obtaining good-quality information concerning runtime costs (whether space or time) is important to many systems engineering activities, including compiler or database optimization, parallel computing, and real-time systems. Many of these activities require predictive information, acquired automatically at compile-time. Although there has been some success in predicting costs for applicative languages in restricted settings [17, 14, 13, 2], the problem of automatically analyzing costs of languages with recursion, higher-order functions and parametric polymorphism remains an open one. These properties are key characteristics of recent statically typed functional language designs such as Standard ML or Haskell.

This paper presents a type-based analysis to automatically infer *upper bound evaluation costs* for a simple, but representative, functional language with parametric polymorphism, higher-order functions and recursion. Our aim is to produce a practical analysis that can deal with these essential languages features without resorting to artificially restrictive syntactic forms. We use a *type and effect system* [11] approach in which a standard Hindley-Milner type system [10] and the associated Damas-Milner inference algorithm [4] are extended by "effects" describing evaluation cost. Our analysis derives first-order cost equations with finite solutions for a non-trivial subset of higher-order, polymorphic and recursive functions. It is *fully automatic* in producing cost equations without requiring any user intervention, even in the form of type annotations. However, obtaining closed-form solutions to these equations currently requires the use of an external solver.

---

* On leave from DCC-FC & LIACC, University of Porto, Portugal.

P. Trinder, G. Michaelson, and R. Peña (Eds.): IFL 2003, LNCS 3145, pp. 86–101, 2004.
© Springer-Verlag Berlin Heidelberg 2004

2   Language Notation and Cost Semantics

$\mathcal{L}$ is a very simple functional language, intended solely as a vehicle to explore static analysis for cost determination. $\mathcal{L}$ is strict, polymorphic, and higher-order, with lists as its only compound data type. The terms e of $\mathcal{L}$ are defined by the following grammar, where x, n, b and p are the syntactic categories for variables, natural numbers, booleans and primitive operations, respectively.

$$e ::= x \mid n \mid b \mid [] \mid e_1 {::} e_2 \mid p(e) \mid \lambda x.e \mid \mathsf{fix}\ x.e \mid e_1\ e_2$$
$$\mid\ \mathsf{if}\ e_1\ \mathsf{then}\ e_2\ \mathsf{else}\ e_3 \mid \mathsf{let}\ x = e_1\ \mathsf{in}\ e_2$$

$\mathcal{L}$ has a conventional structure. The term $\lambda x.e$ is a function abstraction, while $\mathsf{fix}\ x.e$ is a recursive function satisfying the equation $x = e$ (i.e. a least fixed point under a suitable domain). Let-bindings introduce polymorphic local variable definitions as in the standard Hindley-Milner system [10]. Constructors and primitive operations (arithmetic on naturals and lists projections) are restricted to the correct number of arguments; partial applications can be obtained for these forms, if required, using λ-abstractions. To simplify our presentation (and without loss of generality), we consider here only unary primitives. The terms '$\lambda x.e$', '$\mathsf{fix}\ x.e$' and '$\mathsf{let}\ x = e'$ in e' bind the variable x in the sub-term e. We follow the usual definitions of *free variables* and *closed terms*.

2.1   A Cost Model for $\mathcal{L}$

We consider a *call-by-value reduction semantics* for $\mathcal{L}$ (a formal presentation of this semantics can be found elsewhere [16]). Rather than assigning distinct costs to primitive operations, conditionals, etc. we will define the cost of an $\mathcal{L}$-expression solely in terms of the *number of β-reduction steps*, $(\lambda x.e)\ e' \rightarrow_\beta e[e'/x]$ and assign zero cost other reduction rules for primitives, constructors, etc. This cost metric has the advantages of being both easily understood and of capturing the asymptotic costs for recursive definitions. Our effect system could easily be extended to alternative metrics if required. Runtime errors have been modeled by the *absence* of a reduction, e.g. $\mathsf{head}([]) \not\rightarrow$, and so have zero cost. In our model, divergent reductions thus have infinite cost, whereas both confluent *and* erroneous reduction sequences have finite cost.

3   A Type and Effect System for Sizes and Costs

This section presents the type and effect system that will form the basis for our analysis. We have already proven that this type and effect system correctly expresses upper bound cost information for recursive, higher-order and polymorphic programs [16]. This paper builds on that earlier work by developing the corresponding type reconstruction (cost inference) algorithm.

$z + \epsilon = \epsilon + z = \epsilon$	$z \times \epsilon = \epsilon \times z = \epsilon$
$n + \omega = \omega + n = \omega$	$n \times \omega = \omega \times n = \omega$, if $n > 0$
$\epsilon - n = \epsilon$	$0 \times \omega = \omega \times 0 = 0$
$\omega - n = \omega$	$\epsilon \times \omega = \omega \times \epsilon = \epsilon$
$n_1 - n_2 = \epsilon$, if $n_2 > n_1$	

Fig. 1. Extending arithmetic to $\overline{\mathbb{N}}$.

3.1   Cost Expressions

We represent both *sizes* of data types and *costs* for reductions uniformly using terms from a *cost algebra*. The basic values for this algebra are elements of the set $\overline{\mathbb{N}} = \mathbb{N} \cup \{\epsilon, \omega\}$. Natural numbers represent finite sizes and costs, ϵ represents the *undefined* value and ω represents the *unbounded* value. The usual ordering $\leq$ on naturals extends to $\overline{\mathbb{N}}$ by setting $x \leq \omega$ and $\epsilon \leq x$ for all $x \in \overline{\mathbb{N}}$, i.e. ϵ and ω are, respectively, the bottom and top elements of $(\overline{\mathbb{N}}, \leq)$. Let $\ell \in \mathbf{ZVar}$ be the syntactical category of *effect variables* and $\{f_0, f_1, \ldots\}$ be a countable set of *function names* (used to construct recurrence equations for recursive definitions — Section 4.4). The set $\mathbf{ZExp}$ of *cost expressions* is generated by the grammar:

$$z ::= \ell \mid n \mid \epsilon \mid \omega \mid z_1 + z_2 \mid z - n \mid z_1 \times z_2 \mid \max(z_1, z_2) \mid f_i(z) .$$

Note that we only allow subtraction of constant values; this suffices for our development and ensures that cost expressions are *monotone*, i.e. costs can only increase when any variable increases. This property is desirable for obtaining an inference algorithm for our type system (Section 4.5). We write cost expressions following the usual associativity and precedence rules for $+$, $-$ and $\times$.

3.2   Semantics for Cost Expressions

A *valuation* ρ is a total mapping from effect variables to cost values $\rho : \mathbf{ZVar} \to \overline{\mathbb{N}}$. Given a valuation ρ, the semantics of a cost expression is defined by the *evaluation function* $[\![\cdot]\!] \rho : \mathbf{ZExp} \to \overline{\mathbb{N}}$. Evaluation is defined by extending arithmetic from $\mathbb{N}$ to $\overline{\mathbb{N}}$ (cf. Figure 1). This evaluation semantics allows us to define extensional equality on cost expressions: $z = z'$ iff $[\![z]\!] \rho = [\![z']\!] \rho$ for all valuations ρ. Similarly, we lift the ordering $\leq$ from $\overline{\mathbb{N}}$ to a (partial) order on cost expressions.

3.3   Sized Types

Our effect system uses *sized types* [6], a small extension to standard Hindley-Milner polymorphic types: each type, other than function and boolean types, carries a superscript specifying an upper bound for its *size*. For function types, a *latent cost* [13] is attached to the function arrow. This latent cost is an upper bound on the *cost* of evaluating the function body.

Let α be the syntactical category for type variables $\mathbf{TVar}$; the *sized types* τ are defined inductively by the following grammar:

$$\tau ::= \alpha \mid \mathsf{Bool} \mid \mathsf{Nat}^z \mid \mathsf{List}^z \tau \mid \tau_1 \xrightarrow{z} \tau_2 .$$

Sized types allow us to describe the sizes of the elements of a structure as well as the structure itself, e.g.: $\mathsf{List}^5\left(\mathsf{Nat}^{10}\right)$ denotes a list whose length is at most 5 with natural numbers no larger than 10 as elements.

In order to represent polymorphic types we allow universal quantification over type or effect variables, yielding a *sized type scheme* as in [13]. We will write type schemes with a single outermost quantifier and a sequence of variables, i.e. $\forall\boldsymbol{\gamma}.\tau \equiv \forall\gamma_1\ldots.\forall\gamma_n.\tau$, where $\gamma_i \in \mathbf{TVar}\cup\mathbf{ZVar}$ are type or effect variables. Polymorphism allows size dependencies to be expressed for function types; for example, the type scheme for a function to double its argument (a natural number) might be $\forall n.\mathsf{Nat}^n \xrightarrow{0} \mathsf{Nat}^{2\times n}$, where we assume zero cost for the operation. The variables $\gamma_1,\ldots,\gamma_n$ are *bound* in the type scheme $\forall\gamma_1\ldots\gamma_n.\tau$. A variable that is not bound is said to be *free*.

We use a number of standard notational conventions: given a sized type τ, we denote the *sequences* of type and effect variables occurring in τ by $\mathrm{TV}(\tau)$ and $\mathrm{ZV}(\tau)$, respectively. We use $+\!\!+$ for *sequence concatenation*; when the ordering among elements is not relevant, we treat sequences as *sets* and combine them using set operations $\cup,\cap,\backslash$. Finally, we use θ for substitutions from type variables to sized types and ϕ for substitutions from effect variables to cost expressions.

3.4   Type and Effect System

Figure 2 presents type system rules for core $\mathcal{L}$ expressions. The system derives judgements of the form $\Gamma \vdash e : \sigma \,\&\, z$ which can be informally read as "under type assumptions Γ, expression e admits type scheme σ and z is an upper bound for the cost of e". A *type environment* Γ is a sequence of assumptions $[x : \sigma]$

$$\frac{}{\Gamma \vdash x : \Gamma(x) \,\&\, 0}\;[\text{var}_{st}] \qquad \frac{}{\Gamma \vdash n : \mathsf{Nat}^n \,\&\, 0}\;[\text{nat}_{st}] \qquad \frac{}{\Gamma \vdash b : \mathsf{Bool}\,\&\, 0}\;[\text{bool}_{st}]$$

$$\frac{\Gamma[x:\tau_1] \vdash e : \tau_2 \,\&\, z}{\Gamma \vdash \lambda x.e : \tau_1 \xrightarrow{z} \tau_2 \,\&\, 0}\;[\text{abs}_{st}] \qquad \frac{\Gamma \vdash e_1 : \tau_1 \xrightarrow{z_3} \tau_2 \,\&\, z_1 \quad \Gamma \vdash e_2 : \tau_1 \,\&\, z_2}{\Gamma \vdash e_1\, e_2 : \tau_2 \,\&\, 1+z_1+z_2+z_3}\;[\text{app}_{st}]$$

$$\frac{\Gamma \vdash e_0 : \mathsf{Bool}\,\&\, z \quad \Gamma \vdash e_1 : \tau \,\&\, z' \quad \Gamma \vdash e_2 : \tau \,\&\, z'}{\Gamma \vdash \mathsf{if}\, e_0 \;\mathsf{then}\; e_1 \;\mathsf{else}\; e_2 : \tau \,\&\, z+z'}\;[\text{if}_{st}]$$

$$\frac{\Gamma[x : \forall\boldsymbol{\ell}.\tau] \vdash e : \tau \,\&\, 0 \quad \{\boldsymbol{\ell}\}\cap\mathrm{FV}(\Gamma) = \emptyset}{\Gamma \vdash \blacksquare\mathsf{x}\, x.e : \tau \,\&\, 0}\;[\blacksquare\mathsf{x}_{st}]$$

$$\frac{\Gamma \vdash e_1 : \sigma_1 \,\&\, z_1 \quad \Gamma[x : \sigma_1] \vdash e_2 : \tau_2 \,\&\, z_2}{\Gamma \vdash \mathsf{let}\, x = e_1 \;\mathsf{in}\; e_2 : \tau_2 \,\&\, z_1+z_2}\;[\text{let}_{st}] \qquad \frac{\Gamma \vdash e : \tau \,\&\, z \quad \tau \mathrel{\underline{\lhd}} \tau' \quad z \leq z'}{\Gamma \vdash e : \tau' \,\&\, z'}\;[\text{weak}_{st}]$$

$$\frac{\Gamma \vdash e : \tau \,\&\, z \quad \{\boldsymbol{\gamma}\}\cap\mathrm{FV}(\Gamma) = \emptyset}{\Gamma \vdash e : \forall\boldsymbol{\gamma}.\tau \,\&\, z}\;[\text{gen}_{st}] \qquad \frac{\Gamma \vdash e : \forall\boldsymbol{\gamma}.\tau \,\&\, z \quad \mathrm{dom}(\theta)\cup\mathrm{dom}(\phi)\subseteq\{\boldsymbol{\gamma}\}}{\Gamma \vdash e : \phi(\theta\tau) \,\&\, z}\;[\text{ins}_{st}]$$

Fig. 2. Typing Rules for the Core $\mathcal{L}$ Expressions.

$$\frac{\tau = \tau'}{\tau \trianglelefteq \tau'} \ [\text{reflex}_{\trianglelefteq}] \qquad \frac{\tau_1 \trianglelefteq \tau_2 \quad \tau_2 \trianglelefteq \tau_3}{\tau_1 \trianglelefteq \tau_3} \ [\text{trans}_{\trianglelefteq}] \qquad \frac{\tau_1 \trianglelefteq \tau_1' \quad \tau_2' \trianglelefteq \tau_2 \quad z' \le z}{\tau_1' \xrightarrow{z'} \tau_2' \trianglelefteq \tau_1 \xrightarrow{z} \tau_2} \ [\text{abs}_{\trianglelefteq}]$$

$$\frac{z_1 \le z_2}{\text{Nat}^{z_1} \trianglelefteq \text{Nat}^{z_2}} \ [\text{nat}_{\trianglelefteq}] \qquad \frac{z_1 \le z_2 \quad \tau_1 \trianglelefteq \tau_2}{\text{List}^{z_1}\tau_1 \trianglelefteq \text{List}^{z_2}\tau_2} \ [\text{list}_{\trianglelefteq}]$$

Fig. 3. Subtyping Relation.

mapping $\mathcal{L}$ variables to type schemes. An environment can be seen as a partial finite mapping by defining $\Gamma(x) = \sigma$ if the rightmost occurrence of $[x : \cdots]$ in Γ is $[x : \sigma]$. The set of all *free type and effect variables* in Γ is represented by $\text{FV}(\Gamma)$. With the exception of the $[\text{weak}_{st}]$ and $[\text{fix}_{st}]$ rules, this represents a straightforward extension of the standard Hindley-Milner rules. Note that:

- The $[\text{weak}_{st}]$ rule allows *weakening*, i.e. relaxing the upper bounds on sizes or cost. It uses a subtyping relation $\trianglelefteq$ (Figure 3), which is *structural*, i.e. if $\tau \trianglelefteq \tau'$ then τ and τ' have the same type constructor.
- In the $[\text{abs}_{st}]$ rule, the latent cost for the arrow type is the cost of evaluating the body of the abstraction, while the cost for the actual abstraction is zero; this is because our reduction semantics evaluates only to *weak normal forms*.
- The $[\text{app}_{st}]$ rule adds the latent cost of the function to the costs of obtaining both function and argument, plus one to count for the β-reduction (this is the only rule where a positive cost is added).
- The $[\text{if}_{st}]$ rule requires that both branches admit the same type and cost, which may necessitate weakening judgements for one or both branches.
- The $[\text{let}_{st}]$ rule implements polymorphism by allowing a quantified type for the locally defined variable; let is *not* costed as a β-reduction.
- The $[\text{ins}_{st}]$ and $[\text{gen}_{st}]$ rules are straightforward extensions of the Hindley-Milner forms to allow for polymorphism on both *type* variables and *effect* variables. Note that unlike [6], our system does not require a side-condition for ω-instantiation in the $[\text{ins}_{st}]$ rule[1].
- The $[\text{fix}_{st}]$ rule allows the body of the recursive function to be typed using *polymorphic recursion restricted to size and cost variables*. The idea is to allow capturing the recursive uses of the function through instantiation.

Unlike elementary strong functional programming [15] and the sized type system of [6], our system does not reject divergent computations. For example, the term

$$loop \equiv \text{fix } f.\lambda x.f \ x$$

admits the type judgement $\vdash loop : \forall \alpha \beta.\alpha \xrightarrow{\omega} \beta \ \& \ 0$. As a consequence, *all types are inhabited* (for example, by the term '*loop* true'). Note that the non-termination is still captured by the latent cost ω in our sized type for *loop*. The

---

[1] Although we have not yet constructed a formal semantics for our sized types, we conjecture that this is because, unlike Hughes, Pareto and Sabry [6], our intended semantics for sized types includes *divergent values*.

reciprocal, however, is not true — i.e. there exist terminating terms that admit only an ω cost:

$$M \equiv \text{if false then } loop \text{ true else false}.$$

Clearly M is terminating but all type judgements $\vdash M : \text{Bool } \& z$ must derive an unbounded cost $z = \omega$ because of the application of $loop$ in one of the branches of the conditional.

In general, our system can only assign finite costs to recursions when the size of some component of an argument decreases strictly in each iteration (i.e. when a single argument-derived size induces a well-founded ordering). It follows that we can infer cost equations with finite solutions for many *primitive recursive* definitions (subject to the limitations of expressibility in the cost algebra), plus some more general forms as shown in Section 5.

4 Inference Algorithm

This section describes a type reconstruction algorithm for our system that is an extension of Damas-Milner algorithm W [4]. The algorithm takes an unannotated $\mathcal{L}$ expression and yields a sized type and a cost effect, together with a set of constraints and recurrence equations.

4.1 Flat Sized Types and Constraints

As is done in other analysis based on type and effect inference (e.g. [1]), we restrict annotations in the types to variables (yielding *flat sized types*) and separately collect *effect constraints*. This allows us to employ standard unification to solve type equations and deal with the more complex cost algebra only in the constraints. Our constraints express *lower bounds* for the effect variables (as in [13]) and *recurrence equations* collected from recursive definitions (discussed in Section 4.4):

$$c ::= \ell \geq z \mid f_i(\boldsymbol{\ell}) = z \qquad (1)$$
$$C ::= \emptyset \mid \{c\} \cup C$$

4.2 Flat Sized Type Schemes

In order to represent polymorphic types, our *flat sized type schemes* $\forall \boldsymbol{\gamma}.(\tau, C)$ quantify over both a flat type and a constraint set. The constraint set C is chosen to capture the subtyping relation allowed by the *weakening rule*. For example, the type scheme $\forall m.\text{Nat}^m \xrightarrow{1} \text{Nat}^{m+1}$ can be translated to the flat form,

$$\forall m, n, k.(\text{Nat}^m \xrightarrow{k} \text{Nat}^n, \{n \geq m + 1, \ k \geq 1\}).$$

Because of the restriction to the form of constraints, we cannot represent sized types expressing *functions with partial domains*. For example, $\text{Nat}^{10} \xrightarrow{z} \text{Bool}$

should be translated to ($\mathsf{Nat}^n \xrightarrow{k} \mathsf{Bool}, \{n \leq 10, k \geq z\}$) but the constraint $n \leq 10$ is not in the form of equation (1).

However, allowing type assumptions with partial domain such as $f : \mathsf{Nat}^{10} \xrightarrow{z}$ Bool would cause us to *reject* an application like $f\ 11$ that is typeable in the underlying Hindley-Milner system. By restricting the constraints to the form of equation (1) and cost expressions to be monotone (cf. Section 3.2), we guarantee not to reject terms that admit a Hindley-Milner type.

4.3   Type Reconstruction Rules

The type reconstruction algorithm is presented in Figure 4, in the same inference-rule style used for the type system (cf. Figure 2). The reconstruction rules, however, are *structural*, i.e. exactly one rule applies for each $\mathcal{L}$ syntax form. In particular, we no longer have separate rules for *generalization* and *instantiation* of polymorphic types and *weakening* (i.e. relaxation of sizes or costs). Instead, generalization and instantiation are applied at let-bindings and at the use of identifiers, respectively (as in Damas-Milner algorithm W). Weakening is applied in two distinct situations:

1. in conditionals, to obtain a super-type of the types of both branches [6] and an upper bound on the costs of the branches; and
2. in function applications, to construct a correct sub-typing relation between the type of a concrete argument to a function and the function's domain.

Type reconstruction yields judgements of the form $\Gamma \vdash e : \langle \tau, \theta, z, C \rangle$, where the inputs are a list of well-formed assumptions Γ and an $\mathcal{L}$ expression e, and the output is the tuple $\langle \tau, \theta, z, C \rangle$ consisting of a flat sized type τ, a *unifying substitution* θ, a *cost expression* z and a *constraint set* C.

Our algorithm separates the inference of the *type structure* from the inference of the *effects*. Note that:

- The *unification algorithm* of Figure 5 is used to solve equations on flat sized types: it yields a substitution making two types equal up to annotations and uses an auxiliary *freshening* function ν to avoid unwanted capturing of variables.
- The *domain matching* function of Figure 5 yields a set of constraints imposing a sub-typing relation between two Hindley-Milner identical types (this is possible because our sub-typing relation is structural).
- The $[\mathsf{nat}_{ra}]$ rule captures the size of the natural as a constraint, illustrating that the algorithm manipulates only flat sized types.
- The $[\mathsf{app}_{ra}]$ rule uses domain matching to impose a sub-typing relation between the *argument type* and the *function's domain type*.
- The $[\mathsf{if}_{ra}]$ rule uses unification to obtain the type structure, and domain matching to constrain the result to be a super-type of the types of the branches.
- The $[\mathsf{let}_{ra}]$ rule generalizes not only over free type- and effect-variables in the *type*, but also over variables in the *constraint set* to ensure proper capture of dependencies in constraint chains.

$$\frac{}{\Gamma \vdash b : \langle \mathtt{Bool}, [], 0, \emptyset \rangle} \; [\mathtt{bool}_{ra}] \qquad\qquad \frac{}{\Gamma \vdash n : \langle \mathtt{Nat}^\ell, [], 0, \{\ell \geq n\} \rangle} \; [\mathtt{nat}_{ra}] \qquad \text{fresh } \ell$$

$$\frac{\theta = [\alpha'/\alpha] \quad \phi = [\ell'/\ell]}{\Gamma[x : \forall \alpha \ell.(\tau, C)] \vdash x : \langle \theta\phi\tau, \theta, 0, \phi C \rangle} \; [\mathtt{var}_{ra}] \quad \text{fresh } \alpha', \ell'$$

$$\frac{\Gamma[x : (\alpha, \emptyset)] \vdash e : \langle \tau, \theta, z, C \rangle}{\Gamma \vdash \lambda x.e : \langle \theta\alpha \xrightarrow{\ell} \tau, \theta, 0, \{\ell \geq z\} \cup C \rangle} \; [\mathtt{abs}_{ra}] \quad \text{fresh } \alpha, \ell$$

$$\frac{\begin{array}{c} \Gamma \vdash e_1 : \langle \tau_1, \theta_1, z_1, C_1 \rangle \qquad \theta_1 \Gamma \vdash e_2 : \langle \tau_2, \theta_2, z_2, C_2 \rangle \\ \theta_3 = \mathcal{U}(\theta_2 \tau_1, \tau_2 \xrightarrow{\ell} \alpha) \qquad C_3 = \mathcal{D}(\theta_3 \theta_2 \tau_1, \theta_3(\tau_2 \xrightarrow{\ell} \alpha)) \end{array}}{\Gamma \vdash e_1\, e_2 : \langle \theta_3 \alpha, \theta_3 \theta_2 \theta_1, 1 + \ell + z_1 + z_2, C_1 \cup C_2 \cup C_3 \rangle} \; [\mathtt{app}_{ra}] \qquad \text{fresh } \alpha, \ell$$

$$\frac{\begin{array}{c} \Gamma \vdash e_1 : \langle \tau_1, \theta_1, z_1, C_1 \rangle \quad \theta_1 \Gamma \vdash e_2 : \langle \tau_2, \theta_2, z_2, C_2 \rangle \quad \theta_2 \theta_1 \Gamma \vdash e_3 : \langle \tau_3, \theta_3, z_3, C_3 \rangle \\ \theta_4 = \mathcal{U}(\theta_3 \theta_2 \tau_1, \mathtt{Bool}) \qquad \theta_5 = \mathcal{U}(\theta_4 \theta_3 \tau_2, \theta_4 \tau_3) \\ \tau = \nu(\theta_5 \theta_4 \theta_2 \tau_1) \qquad C = C_1 \cup C_2 \cup C_3 \cup \mathcal{D}(\theta_5 \theta_4 \theta_3 \tau_2, \tau) \cup \mathcal{D}(\theta_5 \theta_4 \tau_3, \tau) \end{array}}{\Gamma \vdash \mathtt{if}\, e_1 \,\mathtt{then}\, e_2 \,\mathtt{else}\, e_3 : \langle \tau, \theta_5 \theta_4 \theta_3 \theta_2 \theta_1, z_1 + \max(z_2, z_3), C \rangle} \; [\mathtt{if}_{ra}]$$

$$\frac{\begin{array}{c} \Gamma \vdash e_1 : \langle \tau_1, \theta_1, z_1, C_1 \rangle \qquad \{\gamma\} = (\mathrm{TV}(\tau_1) \cup \mathrm{ZV}(\tau_1) \cup \mathrm{ZV}(C_1)) \setminus \mathrm{FV}(\theta_1 \Gamma) \\ \theta_1 \Gamma[x : \forall \gamma.(\tau_1, C_1)] \vdash e_2 : \langle \tau_2, \theta_2, z_2, C_2 \rangle \end{array}}{\Gamma \vdash \mathtt{let}\, x = e_1 \,\mathtt{in}\, e_2 : \langle \tau_2, \theta_2 \theta_1, z_1 + z_2, C_1 \cup C_2 \rangle} \; [\mathtt{let}_{ra}]$$

$$\frac{\begin{array}{c} \Gamma[x : (\alpha, \emptyset)] \vdash e : \langle \tau_1, \theta_1, \ldots, \ldots \rangle \\ \theta_1' = \mathcal{U}(\theta_1 \alpha, \tau_1) \qquad \tau = \theta_1' \theta_1 \alpha \qquad \tau' = \nu(\tau) \\ X = \mathrm{FZV}(\theta_1' \theta_1 \Gamma) \quad \{\ell\} = \mathrm{ZV}(\tau') \setminus X \\ C_1 = \mathcal{L}(\tau, X, 1) \qquad C' = \mathcal{L}(\tau', X, 1) \\ \theta_1' \theta_1 \Gamma[x : \forall \ell.(\tau', C')] \vdash e : \langle \tau_2, \theta_2, \ldots, C_2 \rangle \\ \mathcal{E} = \mathcal{R}(\tau_2, X, 1) \end{array}}{\Gamma \vdash \blacksquare\mathtt{x}\, x.e : \langle \theta_2 \tau, \theta_2 \theta_1' \theta_1, 0, C_1 \cup C_2 \cup \mathcal{E} \rangle} \; [\blacksquare\mathtt{x}_{ra}] \qquad \begin{array}{l} \text{fresh } \alpha \\ \text{fresh } f_1, f_2, \ldots, f_n, \\ \text{where } n = |C_1| = |C'| = |\mathcal{E}| \end{array}$$

Fig. 4. Type Reconstruction Rules for the Core $\mathcal{L}$ Expressions.

4.4   Inference for Recursive Definitions

We describe in detail the inference rule for recursive definitions 'fix $x.e$':

- We first infer a type for the function body e under a generic assumption α for the recursive function x. By unifying the result type with the assumed variable α, we obtain *the Hindley-Milner type structure* τ for the function. The cost and constraints obtained from this step are discarded.
- Next we use an auxiliary *recurrence labelling* function $\mathcal{L}$ (Figure 6) to traverse the type and yield a *skeleton of the cost and size effects dependencies*, i.e. a set of constraints relating the type annotations to *fresh cost function symbols* $f_1, \ldots, f_n$. As we want to infer *functional dependencies* for sizes and

$$\mathcal{U} : \tau \times \tau \to \theta$$
$$\mathcal{U}(\alpha, \alpha') = [\alpha'/\alpha]$$
$$\mathcal{U}(\alpha, \tau) = \mathcal{U}(\tau, \alpha) = [\nu(\tau)/\alpha],$$
$$\text{if } \alpha \text{ does not occur in } \tau$$
$$\mathcal{U}(\text{Bool}, \text{Bool}) = []$$
$$\mathcal{U}(\text{Nat}^{\ell_1}, \text{Nat}^{\ell_2}) = []$$
$$\mathcal{U}(\text{List}^{\ell_1}\tau_1, \text{List}^{\ell_2}\tau_2) = \mathcal{U}(\tau_1, \tau_2)$$
$$\mathcal{U}(\tau_1 \xrightarrow{\ell} \tau_2, \tau_1' \xrightarrow{\ell'} \tau_2') = \mathcal{U}(\theta_1\tau_2, \theta_1\tau_2')\theta_1$$
$$\text{where } \theta_1 = \mathcal{U}(\tau_1, \tau_1')$$
otherwise, unification fails

$$\nu : \tau \to \tau$$
$$\nu(\alpha) = \alpha$$
$$\nu(\text{Bool}) = \text{Bool}$$
$$\nu(\text{Nat}^{\ell}) = \text{Nat}^{\ell'}, \qquad \text{fresh } \ell'$$
$$\nu(\text{List}^{\ell}\tau) = \text{List}^{\ell'}\nu(\tau), \qquad \text{fresh } \ell'$$
$$\nu(\tau_1 \xrightarrow{\ell} \tau_2) = \nu(\tau_1) \xrightarrow{\ell'} \nu(\tau_2), \qquad \text{fresh } \ell'$$

$$\mathcal{D} : \tau \times \tau \to C$$
$$\mathcal{D}(\alpha, \alpha) = \emptyset$$
$$\mathcal{D}(\text{Bool}, \text{Bool}) = \emptyset$$
$$\mathcal{D}(\text{Nat}^{\ell_1}, \text{Nat}^{\ell_2}) = \{\ell_2 \geq \ell_1\}$$
$$\mathcal{D}(\text{List}^{\ell_1}\tau_1, \text{List}^{\ell_2}\tau_2) = \{\ell_2 \geq \ell_1\} \cup \mathcal{D}(\tau_1, \tau_2)$$
$$\mathcal{D}(\tau_1 \xrightarrow{\ell} \tau_2, \tau_1' \xrightarrow{\ell'} \tau_2') = \{\ell' \geq \ell\} \cup \mathcal{D}(\tau_1', \tau_1) \cup \mathcal{D}(\tau_2, \tau_2')$$

Fig. 5. Unification, Annotation Freshening & Domain Matching Functions.

$$\mathcal{L} : \tau \times \ell \times n \to C$$
$$\mathcal{L}(\alpha, \boldsymbol{x}, i) = \emptyset$$
$$\mathcal{L}(\text{Bool}, \boldsymbol{x}, i) = \emptyset$$
$$\mathcal{L}(\text{Nat}^{\ell}, \boldsymbol{x}, i) = \{\ell \geq f_i(\boldsymbol{x})\}$$
$$\mathcal{L}(\text{List}^{\ell}\tau, \boldsymbol{x}, i) =$$
$$\{\ell \geq f_i(\boldsymbol{x})\} \cup \mathcal{L}(\tau, \boldsymbol{x}, i+1)$$
$$\mathcal{L}(\tau \xrightarrow{\ell} \tau', \boldsymbol{x}, i) =$$
$$\{\ell \geq f_i(\boldsymbol{x}')\} \cup \mathcal{L}(\tau', \boldsymbol{x}', i+1)$$
$$\text{where } \boldsymbol{x}' = \boldsymbol{x} +\!\!+ \text{ZV}(\tau)$$

$$\mathcal{R} : \tau \times \ell \times n \to \mathcal{E}$$
$$\mathcal{R}(\alpha, \boldsymbol{x}, i) = \emptyset$$
$$\mathcal{R}(\text{Bool}, \boldsymbol{x}, i) = \emptyset$$
$$\mathcal{R}(\text{Nat}^{\ell}, \boldsymbol{x}, i) = \{f_i(\boldsymbol{x}) = \ell\}$$
$$\mathcal{R}(\text{List}^{\ell}\tau, \boldsymbol{x}, i) =$$
$$\{f_i(\boldsymbol{x}) = \ell\} \cup \mathcal{R}(\tau, \boldsymbol{x}, i+1)$$
$$\mathcal{R}(\tau \xrightarrow{\ell} \tau', \boldsymbol{x}, i) =$$
$$\{f_i(\boldsymbol{x}') = \ell\} \cup \mathcal{R}(\tau', \boldsymbol{x}', i+1)$$
$$\text{where } \boldsymbol{x}' = \boldsymbol{x} +\!\!+ \text{ZV}(\tau)$$

Fig. 6. Recurrence Labelling and Collection.

costs, whenever we encounter a type $\tau \xrightarrow{z} \tau'$ we make the annotations in τ *parameters* of the cost functions synthesized for τ' and the latent cost z.

- Finally, we infer a type for the body e again, this time with a polymorphic assumption quantifying over all free annotations in the type. This yields a flat type τ_2 and set of constraints C_2 capturing a *single-step unfolding* of the recursive function. The auxiliary function $\mathcal{R}$ of Figure 6 collects the relations on costs and sizes for this unfolding as a set of *recurrence equations* involving the cost functions $f_1, \ldots, f_n$.

In order to make the presentation self-contained, we use the type inference algorithm *twice* for the body of the recursive function: firstly to obtain the type structure and secondly to obtain the recurrence relations. We could, however, avoid this extra work by requiring Hindley-Milner type signatures for fixpoint terms (this information might be available, for example, from compile-time type-inference prior to the analysis). Alternatively, we could employ a standard Hindley-Milner type inference (rather than our sized-type inference) and avoid unnecessary constraint bookkeeping.

4.5   Solving the Constraint Sets

We now address the issue of solving the *effect constraints* collected during type inference; the *recurrence equations* are left unsolved. (see Section 7 for a discussion on recurrence solving techniques). Our algorithm is presented in Figure 7 and is based on that of Reistad and Gifford [13] and on the *worklist iteration* algorithms for solving dataflow analysis constraints (e.g. [11]).

Initial variable assignment: $\rho(\ell) := \epsilon$, $\forall \ell$.
Iterate over strongly connected components in topological ordering.
For each SCC $C = \{(\ell_i \geq z_i)_{i=1}^n\}$:
    For $j = 1, 2 \ldots n$ or until $\rho \models C$:
        For $i = 1, 2 \ldots n$:
            set $\rho(\ell_i) := \max(\rho(\ell_i), [\![z_i]\!]\rho)$
    If $\rho \not\models C$, then for $i = 1, 2 \ldots n$: set $\rho(\ell_i) := \omega$

Fig. 7. Constraint Solving Algorithm.

We say that an assignment ρ *validates* a constraint set C (and write $\rho \models C$) iff $\rho(\ell) \geq [\![z]\!]\rho$ for all $(\ell \geq z) \in C$. Clearly $\rho(\ell) = \omega$, $\forall \ell$ is always a solution, but we are interested in obtaining the *minimal* solution. Because our cost algebra is monotone, this solution can be computed as a *least fixpoint* of the associated equations [13]. This fixpoint could be reached by assigning ϵ to all variables and iterating through the constraints, updating variable values.[2] However, this procedure will not terminate if the least solution of a variable is ω.

To circumvent this problem, we first decompose the constraint set into *strongly connected components* according to constraint dependencies and solve each component separately. For an SCC with n constraints, a finite solution to the variables (if it exists) must be reached within n iterations (because the largest cyclic dependency will involve at most n constraints). If after n iterations we fail to obtain a solution, then the least solution must be ω.

The algorithm is complete with complexity which is quadratic on the size of the largest SCC. We believe this size will remain small and bounded with larger program sizes. The complexity could be further reduced (at the expense of losing completeness) by limiting the outer j-loop to a fixed limit. We have

---

[2] The *monotonicity* of cost expressions allows variable assignment to be extended incrementally, since if $\rho \models C$ then $\rho' \models C$ for any $\rho' \geq \rho$.

implemented a modified version of this algorithm that computes *symbolic solutions* by starting with an initial assignment where relevant variables are bound to *symbolic parameters*, and subsequently using symbolic evaluation for costs.

5   Examples from Our Prototype Implementation

We have implemented our type reconstruction algorithm and successfully used it to derive good cost information for a variety of sample programs, including simple numeric recursive functions (e.g. *factorial, naïve Fibonacci* and *power*) and a representative subset of the Haskell standard Prelude list functions (e.g. *length, append, map, iterate, filter, foldl/r, reverse, drop, take, zipWith* and an insertion sort algorithm). The prototype implementation has proved to be acceptably efficient in all the examples we have tested. A web implementation of the algorithm, together with several of these examples, is available at `http://www.dcs.st-and.ac.uk/~pv/cost.html`. We present three examples chosen to illustrate the inference process for recursion in the presence of higher-order functions and polymorphism, and to be representative of the scope of our analysis.

5.1   A Worked Example: Map

Our first example is a worked type reconstruction for *map*, the standard higher-order function that applies an argument function to each element in a list:

$$map \equiv \lambda f.\mathsf{fix}\ map'.\lambda xs.\mathsf{if}\ \mathsf{null}(xs)\ \mathsf{then}\ []\ \mathsf{else}\ f\ \mathsf{head}(xs){::}map'\ \mathsf{tail}(xs)$$

This example illustrates how the sized type inference captures the dependency on the argument function cost and how recurrence equations are obtained. We present only the major inference steps for *map*, omitting intermediate results.

1. *Infer function body type under generic assumption*
   $\Gamma = [f : (\alpha_1, \emptyset)]$
   $\Gamma[map' : (\alpha_2, \emptyset)] \vdash \lambda xs.\mathsf{if}\ \mathsf{null}(xs)\ \mathsf{then}\ []\ \mathsf{else}\ \ldots : \langle \tau_1, \theta_1, \ldots, \ldots \rangle,$
   $\tau_1 = \mathsf{List}^{\ell_5}\alpha_3 \xrightarrow{\ell_6} \mathsf{List}^{\ell_7}\alpha_4$
   $\theta_1 = [\alpha_3 \xrightarrow{\ell_1} \alpha_4/\alpha_1,\ \mathsf{List}^{\ell_2}\alpha_3 \xrightarrow{\ell_3} \mathsf{List}^{\ell_4}\alpha_4/\alpha_2]$
2. *Unify to get the type structure*
   $\theta'_1 = \mathcal{U}(\tau_1, \theta_1\alpha_2) = []$
   $\tau = \mathsf{List}^{\ell_2}\alpha_3 \xrightarrow{\ell_3} \mathsf{List}^{\ell_4}\alpha_4$
   $\tau' = \nu(\tau) = \mathsf{List}^{\ell_8}\alpha_3 \xrightarrow{\ell_9} \mathsf{List}^{\ell_{10}}\alpha_4$
3. *Collect free effect variables in environment*
   $X = \mathrm{FZV}(\theta'_1\theta_1\Gamma) = \{\ell_1\}$
4. *Recurrence labelling*
   $C_1 = \mathcal{L}(\tau, \{\ell_1\}, 1) = \{\ell_3 \geq f_1(\ell_1, \ell_2),\ \ell_4 \geq f_2(\ell_1, \ell_2)\}$
   $C' = \{\ell_9 \geq f_1(\ell_1, \ell_8),\ \ell_{10} \geq f_2(\ell_1, \ell_8)\}$

5. *Second inference under polymorphic assumption*

$$\Gamma' = [f : (\alpha_3 \xrightarrow{\ell_1} \alpha_4, \emptyset)]$$

$$\Gamma'[map' : \forall \ell_8 \ell_9 \ell_{10}.(\tau', C')] \vdash \lambda xs.\text{if null}(xs) \text{ then } [] \text{ else } \ldots : \langle \tau_2, \ldots, \ldots, C_2 \rangle$$

$$\tau_2 = \text{List}^{\ell_{11}} \alpha_3 \xrightarrow{\ell_{12}} \text{List}^{\ell_{13}} \alpha_4$$

$$C_2 \simeq \{\ell_{12} \geq \max(2 + \ell_1 + f_1(\ell_1, \ell_{11} - 1), 0), \ell_{13} \geq \max(1 + f_2(\ell_1, \ell_{11} - 1), 0)\}$$

6. *Recurrence collection*

$$\mathcal{E} = \mathcal{R}(\tau_2, \{\ell_1\}, 1) = \{f_1(\ell_1, \ell_{11}) = \max(2 + \ell_1 + f_1(\ell_1, \ell_{11} - 1), 0),$$
$$f_2(\ell_1, \ell_{11}) = \max(1 + f_2(\ell_1, \ell_{11} - 1), 0)\}$$

Note that to make the inference process easier to understand, we have presented the constraint set C_2 after symbolic simplification, and substituted the solutions in the right-hand sides of the recurrence equations in $\mathcal{E}$. Both these steps are done automatically by our implementation of the algorithm.

The result of type inference for *map* is then:

$$map : (\alpha_3 \xrightarrow{\ell_1} \alpha_4) \xrightarrow{\ell_{12}} \text{List}^{\ell_2} \alpha_3 \xrightarrow{\ell_3} \text{List}^{\ell_4} \alpha_4, \ \{\ell_{12} \geq 0, \ell_3 \geq f_1(\ell_1, \ell_2), \ell_4 \geq f_2(\ell_1, \ell_2)\}$$

where the recurrence functions f_1 and f_2 express the cost for the map and the size of the result list, respectively.

The upper-bound for costs of the *base* and *recursive* cases are represented by a single equation in the recurrences: for the empty list, we have $\ell_{11} = 0$ and the base cost is $f_1(\ell_1, 0) = \max(2 + \ell_1 + f_1(\ell_1, \epsilon), 0) = \max(\epsilon, 0) = 0$. Note that ϵ represents the *undefined cost* corresponding to an erroneous computation path (in this example, taking the tail of an empty list).

We can obtain closed-form solutions to the recurrences either by inspection or using computer algebra software: $f_1(\ell_1, \ell_{11}) = (2 + \ell_1) \times \ell_{11}$ and $f_2(\ell_1, \ell_{11}) = \ell_{11}$, i.e. map maintains the list size and its cost is proportional to the list size and function latent cost. Note that these are the best estimates expressible in our cost algebra.

5.2 List Reverse

The next example illustrates analysis for a two-parameter recursion (list reversal) using an accumulating parameter:

$$rev \equiv \text{fix } rev'.\lambda x.\lambda y.\text{if null}(x) \text{ then } y \text{ else } rev' \text{ tail}(x) \text{ (head}(x)::y)$$

We obtain the following sized type and constraints solution:

$$\tau_{rev} = \text{List}^n \alpha \xrightarrow{\ell_1} \text{List}^m \alpha \xrightarrow{\ell_2} \text{List}^k \alpha$$

$$\ell_1 = f_1(n), \ \ell_2 = f_2(n, m), \ k = f_3(n, m)$$

$$f_1(n) = 0$$

$$f_2(n, m) = \max(2 + f_1(n - 1) + f_2(n - 1, 1 + m), 0)$$

$$f_3(n, m) = \max(f_3(n - 1, 1 + m), m)$$

Simplifying the recurrence equations yields the *exact* cost and size,

$$f_2(n, m) = 2 \times n, \quad f_3(n, m) = n + m$$

i.e. the result size is the sum of the two lists sizes and the cost is proportional to the size of the of the first argument. Note that type inference automatically handles the two-parameter recursion. There is no need for the programmer to indicate which parameter is reducing in size or to rewrite the program into an explicitly primitive recursive form.

5.3   List Union

Our final example is a function that constructs the set union of two lists. We first define a higher-order function *any* that tests a predicate for some element of a list. Using *any*, we define *union* for a generic equality function *eq* given as a higher-order parameter. This example generalizes the first-order case presented by both Wegbreit [17] and Rosendahl [14].

let $any = \lambda p.$ fix $any'.\lambda xs.$ if null(xs) then false
  else if p head(xs) then true else any' tail(xs)
let $union = \lambda eq.\lambda xs.$ fix $union'.\lambda ys.$ if null(ys) then xs
  else if any $(eq$ head$(ys))$ xs then $union'$ tail(ys)
  else head(ys)::$union'$ tail(ys)

The types inferred from the definitions above, after substitution of the constraint solutions, are:

$$\tau_{any} = (\alpha \xrightarrow{\ell_1} \mathsf{Bool}) \xrightarrow{0} \mathsf{List}^k \alpha \xrightarrow{\ell_2} \mathsf{Bool}$$

$$\tau_{union} = (\alpha \xrightarrow{\ell_3} \alpha \xrightarrow{\ell_4} \mathsf{Bool}) \xrightarrow{0} \mathsf{List}^n \alpha \xrightarrow{0} \mathsf{List}^m \alpha \xrightarrow{\ell_5} \mathsf{List}^p \alpha$$

where $\ell_2 = f_1(\ell_1, k)$, $\ell_5 = f_2(\ell_3, \ell_4, n, m)$, $p = f_3(\ell_3, \ell_4, n, m)$
    $f_1(\ell_1, k) = \max(1 + \ell_1 + \max(1 + f_1(\ell_1, k-1), 0), 0)$
    $f_2(\ell_3, \ell_4, n, m) = \max(4 + \ell_3 + f_1(\ell_4, n) + f_2(\ell_3, \ell_4, n, m-1), 0)$
    $f_3(\ell_3, \ell_4, n, m) = \max(1 + f_3(\ell_3, \ell_4, n, m-1), n)$

and the recurrences admit the following solutions:

$$f_1(\ell_1, k) = (2 + \ell_1) \times k$$
$$f_2(\ell_3, \ell_4, n, m) = (4 + \ell_3 + (2 + \ell_4) \times n) \times m$$
$$f_3(\ell_3, \ell_4, n, m) = n + m$$

Observe that the costs and sizes are widened to the worst-case when there are no common elements in the two lists: *any* traverses the complete list and the size the of *union* is the sum of the sizes of the two lists.

Because of the partial application of equality, the cost inferred for *union* depends on the two latent costs of the equality function: ℓ_3 is added m times (one for each invocation of *union'*), whereas ℓ_4 is added $n \times m$ times (one for each invocation of *any'*). The particular case where equality is a primitive corresponds to setting $\ell_3 = \ell_4 = 0$ and the cost for *union* is then $(4 + 2 \times n) \times m$, which is asymptotically identical to the non-generic solution presented in [14]. *It follows that our analysis can still obtain good bounds for first-order instances even when deriving costs from a higher-order definition.*

6   Related Work

To the best of our knowledge, there is no comparable analysis capable of automatically inferring costs for recursive, higher-order and polymorphic functional programs. Previous approaches have, however, considered aspects of this problem. The approach described here extends our own earlier work on inference for sized time systems [9, 12] by covering recursive as well as non-recursive language forms. Our sized type system is directly influenced by that of Hughes, Pareto and Sabry [6], who have developed a type checking algorithm for sized types in a higher-order, recursive, and non-strict functional language. While the system of Hughes at al., can be used to prove *termination* for recursion and *productivity* for streams, it does not consider execution costs and does not infer sizes. Chin and Khoo [3] have extended this work to yield an inference algorithm for such sized types. Their system does not, however, infer *costs* and deals only with *monomorphic* definitions and limited forms of higher-order functions. Finally, Chin and Khoo's use of a Presburger arithmetic solver limits the expressiveness of sizes to *affine functions* over size variables, whereas our system allows for general monotone functions, including polynomials.

Most closely related to our analysis is the system by Reistad and Gifford [13] for the cost analysis of Lisp expressions. This system handles higher-order functions through "latent costs" as we have done here, and is partially based on the "time system" by Dornic et al. [5], Rather than trying to infer costs for user-defined recursive functions, however, Reistad and Gifford require the use of fixed higher-order skeletons with known latent costs.

Pioneering work on *automatic complexity analysis* was undertaken by Wegbreit [17]. Wegbreit's METRIC system derived probabilistic complexity measures of a limited range of first-order Lisp programs by solving the difference equations that occur as an intermediate step in the complexity analysis. The analysis, however, is not guaranteed to be sound as the system assumes statistical independence of tests in conditionals. Consequently, the programmer must confirm the validity of the analysis against the semantics of the program.

Le Métayer [7] uses *program transformation* via a set of rewrite rules to derive complexity functions for FP programs. A database of known recurrences is used to produce closed forms for some recursive functions. However, like Reistad and Gifford's approach, recursive definitions must be given in terms of a particular set of skeletons. Moreover, the analysis is not *modular* as the transformation can only be applied to a complete programs. Rosendahl [14] also uses *program transformation*; in this case to obtain a step counting version of first-order Lisp programs. This is followed by abstract interpretation to obtain a program giving an upper bound on the cost. Again this abstract interpretation requires a complete program, limiting both its scalability and its applicability to systems with e.g. compiled libraries. Finally, Benzinger [2] obtains worst-case complexity analysis for NuPrl-synthesized programs by "*symbolic execution*" followed by recurrence solving. The system supports first-order functions and lazy lists but requires higher-order functions to be annotated with complexity information. Moreover, only a restricted primitive recursion syntax is supported. These limitations are justified by Benzinger's objective, which is to aid resource analysis for automatically synthesized programs, rather than to analyze hand-written functions, as in our case.

7   Conclusions and Further Work

The main contribution of this paper is a type reconstruction algorithm to estimate sizes and costs for a simple functional language with recursive, higher-order and polymorphic functions Our algorithm is an extension of the standard Hindley-Milner type inference and as such we achieve full *modularity* of the analysis. The results obtained for recursion by our analysis are determined solely by the *deconstruction of inductive types* (i.e. naturals or lists) and not by any conditionals in the source program. Although this might lead to over-estimation of costs in some cases, it has the advantage of placing no syntactical restrictions on the forms of recursion we can analyze.

We have found that our approach produces accurate cost equations for a representative subset of the Haskell standard Prelude functions, suggesting it should yield useful information in a more practical setting. Although we have not yet analyzed the complexity of the inference algorithm, our experience with the prototype implementations suggests that its execution time is comparable to ordinary type inference.

A number of issues remain to be studied. Firstly, we need to extend our notion of sized types and inference to handle *full integer arithmetic* and a richer set of data-types including *user-defined recursive structures*. This will ultimately allow us to address real languages such as our resource-bounded language *Hume*. Secondly, since this is not the primary focus of our research, we have not addressed the problem of automatically obtaining closed forms for the recurrence equations; for some subclasses of these equations there are mechanical methods that yield closed forms [8]. All general-purpose computer algebra systems (e.g. Maple, Mathematica and MuPAD) provide some functionally to solve these equations. The new Mathematica Version 5 is also able to solve recurrence equations in *multiple variables*[3]. All recurrences obtained for the examples in Section 5 can be solved by Mathematica 5 with only slight human intervention to eliminate the max terms. We intend to automate this step in due course. Thirdly, although we conjecture that a notion of principal type should hold for our system, we have not yet addressed this issue. Since our analysis will derive *an* upper bound sized type, but not necessarily the *least* one, this is, of course, purely a *quality* rather than *soundness* issue. Finally, we have not yet constructed *soundness* or *completeness* proofs relating our inference algorithm to the type system. We believe, however, that these should be analogous to proofs for other type and effect systems [1].

We are grateful to Álvaro J. Rebón Portillo, Clara Segura Díaz, Roy Dyckhoff, Hans-Wolfgang Loidl, Greg Michaelson and the anonymous referees for

---

[3] In practice, the authors have encountered simple recurrences for which Mathematica yields a wrong solution — a bug that has been reported to the software publisher!

their helpful comments on earlier drafts of this paper. This work is generously sponsored by EPSRC grant GR/R 70545/01.

References

1. T. Amtoft, F. Nielson, and H.R. Nielson. *Type and Effect Systems: Behaviours for Concurrency.* Imperial College Press, 1999.
2. R. Benzinger. Automated Complexity Analysis of Nuprl Extracted Programs. *Journal of Functional Programming*, 11(1):3–31, 2001.
3. W.-N. Chin and S.-C. Khoo. Calculating Sized Types. *Higher-Order and Symbolic Computing*, 14(2,3), 2001.
4. L. Damas and A.J.R.G. Milner. Principal Type-Schemes for Functional Programs. In *Proc. 1982 ACM Symp. on Principles of Prog. Langs. – POPL '82*, pages 207–212, 1982.
5. V. Dornic, P. Jouvelot, and D.K. Gifford. Polymorphic Time Systems for Estimating Program Complexity. *ACM Letters on Prog. Lang. and Systems*, 1(1):33–45, March 1992.
6. R.J.M. Hughes, L. Pareto, and A. Sabry. Proving the Correctness of Reactive Systems using Sized Types. In *Proc 1996 ACM Symposium on Principles of Programming Languages – POPL '96*, St Petersburg, FL, January 1996.
7. D. Le Métayer. ACE: An Automatic Complexity Evaluator. *ACM Transactions on Programming Languages and Systems*, 10(2), April 1988.
8. H. Levy and F. Lessman. *Finite Difference Equations.* Macmillan, 1961.
9. H-W. Loidl and K. Hammond. A Sized Time System for a Parallel Functional Language. In *Glasgow Workshop on Functional Programming*, Ullapool, July 1996.
10. A.J.R.G. Milner. A Theory of Type Polymorphism in Programming. *J. Computer System Sciences*, 17(3):348–375, 1976.
11. F. Nielson, H. Nielson, and C. Hankin. *Principles of Program Analysis.* Springer-Verlag, 1999.
12. Á. Rebón Portillo, K. Hammond, H.-W. Loidl, and P.B. Vasconcelos. Cost Analysis using Automatic Size and Time Inference. In *Proc. IFL 2002 – Implementation of Functional Languages, Madrid, Spain*, LNCS 2670. Springer-Verlag, 2003.
13. B. Reistad and D.K. Gifford. Static Dependent Costs for Estimating Execution Time. In *Proc. 1994 ACM Conference on Lisp and Functional Programming – LFP '94*, pages 65–78, Orlando, FL, June 1994.
14. M. Rosendahl. Automatic Complexity Analysis. In *Proc. 1989 Intl. Conf. on Functional Prog. Langs. and Comp. Arch. – FPCA '89*, pages 144–156, 1989.
15. D.A. Turner. Elementary Strong Functional Programming. In *Proc. Symp. on Funct. Prog. Langs. in Education — FPLE '95*, LNCS. Springer-Verlag, Dec. 1995.
16. P.B. Vasconcelos and K. Hammond. A Type and Effect System for Costing Recursive, Higher-Order and Polymorphic Functional Programs. In preparation, 2004.
17. B. Wegbreit. Mechanical Program Analysis. *Comm. of the ACM*, 18(9), 1975.

Dynamic Chunking in Eden

Jost Berthold

Philipps-Universität Marburg, Fachbereich Mathematik und Informatik
Hans Meerwein Straße, D-35032 Marburg, Germany
berthold@informatik.uni-marburg.de

Abstract. Parallel programming generally requires awareness of the granularity and communication requirements of parallel subtasks, since without precaution, the overhead for parameter and result communication may outweigh the gain of parallel processing. While this problem is often solved explicitly at the language level, it can also be alleviated by optimising message passing mechanisms in the runtime environment. We describe how a simple buffering mechanism introduces dynamic list chunking in the runtime environment of the parallel functional language Eden. We discuss design and implementation aspects of dynamic chunking and compare its effects to the original version in a set of measurements. Our optimisation is justified by a simple cost model, measurements analyse the overhead and illustrate the impact of the changed message passing mechanism.

1 Introduction

A major issue in parallel programming is to consider the granularity and communication need of parallel algorithms [6]. Regardless of the underlying language paradigm, communication latency in parallel algorithms may limit the achievable speedup. On the other hand, sending more data at a time can spoil the parallel system's synchronisation and lead to distributed sequential execution. In the field of lazy functional languages, a second obstacle is the conflict between demand-driven evaluation and parallelism [18]. Parallelism control in the coordination language generally has to balance between lazy evaluation and fast parallel startup.

The parallel functional language Eden [3] offers means to define parallel processes and control their execution and granularity explicitly at the language level. As investigated in [9], ingenious programming with respect to the particular language semantics of Eden coordination constructs leads to significantly better speedup, but such optimisations force the programmer to write far from obvious code and thus fail to meet the main intention of the functional paradigm in parallel programming: *"[to] eliminate [...] unpleasant burdens of parallel programming..."* ([8], foreword) by high abstraction. Benchmark programs often use a chunking technique to increase the size of messages between two processes; which we would like to call the *message granularity*, as opposed to the *task granularity*, which refers to the complexity of processes (as a general term, granularity of computation units is reciprocal to their number). However, the data

P. Trinder, G. Michaelson, and R. Peña (Eds.): IFL 2003, LNCS 3145, pp. 102–117, 2004.
© Springer-Verlag Berlin Heidelberg 2004

communication of a parallel program is strongly influenced by the particular hardware and network setup. A common issue for benchmarking programs is to first experiment with different granularities in order to balance communication latency against synchronisation lacks, and then hand-tune the explicitly controlled (message) granularity from the experimental pre-results. The hand-tuning of programs involves severe program restructuring which decreases readability and maintainability. Simple lists are e.g. replaced by lists of lists, which requires complex and error-prone conversions. These problems could however be avoided by optimising the message passing mechanism in the runtime environment.

Such an optimisation should be located at a very low level in the communication facilities of the runtime system, thereby making it completely independent of the language semantics. The main idea in the optimisation is to save communication cost by automatically gathering successive messages to the same receiver. Several messages will thus be *dynamically chunked* in one single big message; as opposed to explicit static chunking of the *data* itself in the program's granularity control.

In this paper, we describe the implementation and the effects of this simple buffering mechanism in the runtime environment of the parallel functional language Eden. The paper is organised as follows: After a short introduction to the language Eden and its implementation in Section 2, we describe the aim of the optimisation as well as some design and implementation aspects in Section 3. The effect of our optimisation is described by a simple cost model in Section 4. Finally, we show measurements which analyse the overhead and the impact of the changed message passing mechanism. Section 5 concludes.

2   Parallel Processing with Eden

2.1   Language Description

Eden extends Haskell [14] with syntactic constructs for *explicitly* defining processes, providing direct control over process granularity, data distribution and communication topology [3, 10]. Its two main coordination constructs are process abstraction and instantiation.

```
process::(Trans a, Trans b)=> (a -> b) -> Process a b
```

embeds functions of type a->b into *process abstractions* of type Process a b where the context (Trans a, Trans b) states that both types a and b belong to the type class Trans of transmissible values. A *process abstraction* process (\x -> e) defines the behavior of a process with parameter x as input and expression e as output.

A *process instantiation* uses the predefined infix operator

```
( # )::(Trans a,Trans b)=> Process a b -> (a -> b)
```

to provide a process abstraction with actual input parameters. The evaluation of an expression (process (\ x -> e1)) # e2 leads to the dynamic creation of a process together with its interconnecting communication channels. The instantiating or *parent process* is responsible for evaluating and sending e2, while the new *child process* evaluates the expression e1[x->e2] and sends the result back to the parent. The (denotational) meaning of the above expression is identical to that of the ordinary function application ((\ x -> e1) e2).

Both input and output of a process can be a tuple, in which case one concurrent thread for each output channel is created, so that different values can be produced independently. Whenever one of their outputs is needed in the overall evaluation, the whole process will be instantiated and will evaluate and send all its outputs eagerly. This deviation from lazy evaluation aims at increasing the parallelism degree and at speeding up the distribution of the computation. Local garbage collection detects unnecessary results and stops the evaluating remote threads. In general, Eden processes do not share data among each other and are encapsulated units of computation. All data is communicated eagerly via (internal) channels, avoiding global memory management and data request messages, but possibly duplicating data.

2.2   Stream and List Processing

Data communicated between Eden processes is generally evaluated to normal form by the sender. Lists are communicated as streams, i.e. each element is sent immediately after its evaluation. This special communication property can be utilised to profit from lazy evaluation, namely by using infinite structures and by reusing the output recursively, as e.g. in the *workpool* skeleton [10]. Another obvious effect is the increased responsiveness of remote processes and the interleaving of parameter supply and parallel computation. Processing long lists of data is a prime example for functional parallel programs, e.g. in a simple parallel sorting program:

Example: The following function sorts a list of values in parallel by distributing it to child processes, which sort the sublists using a sequential sorting algorithm. Finally, the sorted sublists are merged together by the parent.

```
parsort :: (Trans a, Ord a) => ([a] -> [a]) -> [a] -> [a]
parsort _ [] = []
parsort seqsort xs = lmerge [(process seqsort) # sublist |
                    sublist <- unshuffleN noPe xs ] 'using' spine
```

The sublists are created by a split function unshuffleN :: Int -> [a] -> [[a]] which uses the system value noPe to determine the number of available PEs in the parallel setup. The function lmerge merges the returned sorted sublists sequentially in a tree-shape manner. The evaluation strategy spine [16] is applied in order to start all processes simultaneously as soon as the result is needed. ◁

In the child processes, work is done essentially by comparing several inputs. The Eden sending policy leads to a large number of very small messages between the parent and the sorting processes and slows them down (note that the message passing latency also affects the evaluation in Eden, since values are sent eagerly after evaluation, whereas with lazy communication and global memory, data transmission does not affect the evaluation). If the program does not exploit stream communication, it is favourable to send more data together, ideally without disturbing the interleaving between parameter supply and evaluation.

We could modify the parallel sorting function, so that the sorter processes receive their input in bigger chunks instead of element per element:

Example:(cont.d)

```
parsortchunk :: (Trans a, Ord a) => Int -> ([a] -> [a]) -> [a] -> [a]
parsortchunk size seqsort xs =
      lmerge [ process (seqsort . concat) # (chunk size sublist) |
                    sublist <- unshuffleN noPE xs ] 'using' spine
-- simple list chunking
chunk :: Int -> [a] -> [[a]]
chunk _ [] = []
chunk k xs = (take k xs) : chunk k (drop k xs)
```

The chunking function aggregates every size elements to a sub-sublist, which is deconstructed by the receiver, so we reduce the number of messages. But this second version is much less intuitive, and it is far from obvious which parameter for size would be best. Another, even more obscure variant restructures the parallel sorting algorithm and chunks the output as well:

```
parsortchunk2 size seqsort xs =
      lmerge [ lmerge (process (map seqsort) # (chunk size sublist) |
                    sublist <- unshuffleN noPE xs ] 'using' spine
```

In this version, each child process sorts several smaller lists, and the caller merges both each child's results *and* the final result. This overhead for the caller is the price for less communication and a much better overlap of parallel evaluation and communication. We cannot tell the best size parameter for either variant without excessive tests, but it is clear that both variants perform better by saving communication.   ◁

An improvement to this enigmatic optimised code is to use special *skeletons* for specific tasks as e.g. mapping a function to a huge list in parallel. Skeletons are generic patterns of parallelism which take the specific working functions as arguments, as described and discussed for Eden in [10]. Since a skeleton is implemented in a predefined library, it can do chunking implicitly and hidden from the programmer. Programs using skeletons are often easier to read, but skeletons are always restricted to their respective pattern of parallelism. In our example, a map-fold skeleton could do the work, but we are still free to spoil the performance by choosing an inappropriate chunk size, unless the skeleton developer has chosen one for us. Anyway, the chunk size would always be statically fixed.

The idea of this paper is to investigate the effects of an automatic chunking mechanism *inside the runtime system* of Eden, i.e. modifying the communication layer to send data messages in a packet. Such a feature in the runtime system apparently makes programming much easier and chooses the right chunking amount automatically, but will of course introduce a considerable overhead.

3   Dynamic Chunking in the Eden Runtime Environment

Eden's implementation extends the Glasgow-Haskell-Compiler (GHC, [13]) by a parallel runtime environment, which is explicitly controlled by a small number of primitive operations. Using these primitives, high-level process coordination is specified in a functional module. The runtime system itself provides means to instantiate new remote processes and to create and use the (now explicit) channels between them. Apart from that, it synchronises computations and controls process termination. The Eden runtime system as a whole has been described in the past (e.g. in [2, 1]) and will thus be omitted in this paper, the Eden message protocol being the only detail of topical interest, together with the more general properties of its message passing mechanisms shared with GUM [17].

3.1   Eden Message Protocol and Its Penalties

Message Protocol. Eden processes communicate via 1:1 channels, which are represented by a link from an outport to an inport, structures which the RTS uses to address messages correctly. As a general rule, every message between processes contains these two ports. Eden processes send the following message types:

Msg.-Type	Sender (Port)	Receiver(Port)	[Data]

Create Process instantiates a process at the receiver PE.
Terminate stops a remote thread which sends data to a closed inport.
Value sends a single value as a subgraph in normal form.
Head sends an element (subgraph in normal form) of a list.

In addition, we also have messages to and from the system manager program *SysMan.c*, a stand-alone C + PVM program which controls the startup and shutdown of all PEs. Those messages do not belong to the Eden protocol, but to the system's communication as a whole, since they are sent between the PEs and not between processes.

Ready Announces a PE to *SysMan* (no data)
Task-Ids From *SysMan*. Contains the addresses of all PEs started (in PVM) for the parallel computation.
Finish From *SysMan*: Stops the parallel system. (no data)
From one of the PEs to *SysMan*: initiate system stop.

The message **Create Process** is sent by a thread in the generator (parent) process as an effect of the primitive operation `createProcess#`. The receiver unpacks the included subgraph into its heap and starts a new process by creating a thread to evaluate the subgraph.

Terminate is sent by the runtime system after garbage collection (and not by a process), when the marking of a garbage collection does not reach a synchronisation node which represents data evaluated remotely.

Messages **Value** and **Head** are the interesting ones for the work presented here. They both transmit evaluated data (as single values or as stream data) between processes. The included subgraph in normal form replaces a synchronisation node in the receiver's heap, which is linked to the receiving inport. This is a direct replacement for single values, while for stream data, a new Cons closure is created and its references filled with the received subgraph and a new synchronisation node for the rest of the stream/list.

Simple Cost Analysis. Following the concept of stream communication in the language specification, if a child process receives or sends back a very long list, every element is sent in a separate **Head** message. Since data transmission is eager in Eden, the amount of messages is not limited by the demand-driven evaluation (as it would be in GUM, the GpH runtime environment). Sending a message always implies a certain penalty for the required actions in the underlying communication middleware. This penalty has been quantified by using special test primitives in a debug runtime system.

In the test program, we extract the time for all actions directly related to the message passing subsystem by repeatedly linearising a graph structure of variable size and either sending it or not – the difference indicates time spent for sending actions. The test program does not care about receiving those linearised subgraphs, so network latency is not involved. To quantify the influence of data sizes sent, we use a simple linear model, where sending time is estimated as basic time λ for each message plus variable time linearly growing with the message size in words, weighted by a factor β.

Fig. 1 show results of the measurements and the time estimation obtained by linear regression. The obtained values are $\lambda = 63.34\,\mu sec$ and $\beta = 0.1\,\mu sec$, showing that the amount of data has only a small impact on the time needed to

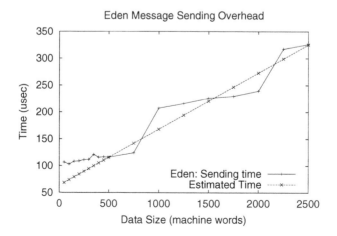

Fig. 1. Message sending penalty measurement and linear model: $time = \lambda + \beta \cdot datasize$.

send a message to another PE, compared to the basic sending action itself. We see that the linear model is not completely correct (influence of a step function, due to properties of the underlying message-passing middleware PVM and TCP/IP), but this deviation is not relevant to what we want to show.

3.2   Concept of Dynamic Low-Level Chunking

Summing up, dynamic chunking aims at decreasing the defacto number of stream data messages between the PEs automatically by collecting "messages" sent by one process to another one in a send buffer. Messages in the buffer are then sent together in a "packet"[1]. This drastically reduces the amount of packets, while their data size increases. As explained, reducing the number of messages should be transparent to the language design and thus have no effect on language properties. It is obtained by introducing a new low-level layer of communication in the runtime system, whose particular functionality is explained in this section.

Collecting messages in the runtime system needs send buffers of sufficient size in every PE of the parallel system. Their size is at least the maximum size of one message plus additional room for administrative fields. We maintain one send buffer per communication partner, which is every PE in the system. Alternatives would be to have either only one send buffer or one buffer per channel (i.e. sending thread). Both solutions have obvious disadvantages, either in the administration of the buffers or in the achievable effects.

As well as the sender, the receiver of a packet must buffer it for processing to make the change transparent to the next layer of abstraction, the message processing unit of the runtime environment. We would in fact only need one single buffer to receive packets, if we processed the whole packet at once. On the other hand, having an own receive buffer for each PE makes it very easy to implement a fair processing manner, since we can choose between several buffers without losing data. The receive buffers are simply processed in a round robin manner and one message at a time, realising a fair PE communication.

Buffering other messages than the **Head** message would slow down the computation globally by artificial latency, which is absolutely clear for **Create Process** and **Terminate**, but also valid for **Value** messages, since no other message will follow a single value. To prevent deadlock situations (two PEs holding back each other's messages), the scheduler must as well force packets to be sent when there are no runnable threads.

In total, the criteria to send a packet are:

- if the packet contains an urgent message.
- before adding a message, if this message is bigger than the remaining space in the packet.
- immediately after adding a message, if no other message can fit into the packet any more. The minimum message size in Eden is two ports.

---

[1] In the following, we refer to "message" and "packet" in the sense that a packet is sent by the MP-System and contains several messages, where (virtually) "sending a message" means to add it to the packet.

– during scheduling, if the packet age is more than a given timeout value. The maximum age is a runtime system parameter accessible to the user.
– when the whole PE does not have any runnable threads (send all packets).

As well as the specific timeout value for packets (adjustable in milliseconds), information about all actions related to sending packets can be collected for statistical purpose. The methods which decide about sending packets are the place where all information about the buffering mechanism is brought together, e.g. average and maximum packet sizes, no. of timeouts, packets forced etc.

3.3 Implementation Remarks

The existing runtime system for GpH and Eden provides two communication layers (files *HLComms* and *LLComms*), but in the current implementation, this separation only structures the code and differentiates between the high-level message protocol of the virtual machine and the concrete message passing. As depicted in Fig. 2, *HLComms* defines methods to send, receive and process messages conforming to the described message protocol (different for GUM and Eden), while *LLComms* provides basic methods to map these abstract sending and receiving operations to the message passing system (MP-System), currently PVM [15]. So we find a 1:1 relation between (abstract) messages sent by a process and (concrete) messages in the MP-System, which had to be given up for our modification.

	Layer	Communication	Messages	Module
System Communication (Start, Stop)	Process-Comm.	Process::Outport ↓↑ Process::Inport	Process instantiation , Data , Termination	HLComms.c
	PE-/PVM Comm.	PEs 1-n/ PVM-PEs	PVM-Messages	LLComms.c

Fig. 2. Two Layers Model of the Communication modules.

The message buffering system is implemented in a changed module *LLComms* which provides a slightly modified interface. All methods in the interface of *LLComms* do not access the MP-System itself any more, but new internal functions. The former behaviour remains unchanged to keep the new layer transparent with respect to communication routines, which are shared with the GUM system. Message buffering could be used for GUM without any changes, but data is only sent on demand in GUM, and GpH does not use any concepts comparable to the stream channel communication in Eden, so there is no need for dynamic chunking in GUM at all. On the contrary, Hammond/Loidl dismiss message buffering for GUM entirely in [11], since each additional latency would definitely lead to a slow-down.

Functionality provided by *HLComms* sends and processes messages according to the Eden protocol and uses the MP-System only by the interface of *LLComms*. Therefore, only a slight modification was necessary to force urgent messages immediately.

Receiving message packets only requires changes in internal methods of *LL-Comms* in order to work on the receive buffers instead of with the MP-System. Modifications have been made to the receiving routine, to the selector for sender and message type and to the unpacking method. Furthermore, we had to implement a separate method for a blocking receive. *Sending* messages has been discussed above in the concept. As explained, we need an additional method to force packet sending and have to administer the send buffers in the low-level module.

We shall not digress too much on this low-level implementation, but need to say some words about the startup and system messages, which, of course, must be adapted to message buffering, too. The system messages (**Ready, Finish, Task-Ids**) are sent and processed by the same methods as data messages, but the startup messages should be sent and processed *before* the other message buffers are completely set up. Furthermore, message buffering allows us to receive system messages from *SysMan* with priority. We therefore introduced a special handling for system messages to and from *SysMan*.

As already mentioned, the message buffering mechanism introduces a middle-layer into the communication subsystem of GUM and Eden. This also has an architectural aspect: Fig. 3 shows the modified communication system, which now abstracts from the concrete underlying message-passing system (currently PVM[2]). Internal functions inside *LLComms* still use PVM, but they have been moved away from the interface and concentrated in the internals. As they are completely independent of the GHC runtime system as a whole, this section can easily be placed in an additional module, thereby facilitating the port to other MP-systems.

	Layer	Communication	Messages	Module
System-Communication (Start, Stop)	Process-Comm.	Process::Outport ↓↑ Process::Inport	Process instantiation, Data, Termination	HLComms.c
	PE-Comm.	(virtual) PEs 1-n	Eden-Packets	LLComms.c
PVM-Comm.		(virtual/real) PEs (pvm_tids)	Simple data (C-Integer)	LLComms.c

Fig. 3. New Three-Layer-Model of Communication in the runtime system.

The dependencies in every other file than *LLComms* have been eliminated, so that the layer concept in the shared communication system is consequently implemented. The system management by *SysMan* is an exception, since it uses more specific functionality from the MP system, e.g. notification of errors on child PEs and PE placement on the physical machines. It is reasonable to keep the system management closely associated with the concrete MP-system, since a generic version could never anticipate needed functions for particular platforms and will always provide only a reduced functionality.

---

[2] GUM has recently been ported to MPI, but in a different version and manner than what we describe here[19].

4 Results

4.1 Expected Effects of Dynamic Chunking

As already motivated in Section 3.1, we can expect considerably decreased run-time particularly when the measured program sends small elements of a long list. The effect depends on the size of the sent data and might be consumed by the additional overhead for the buffer administration. In the following simplifying model, we estimate the runtime change for message buffering in dependency of the global data size and number of messages.

As explained in Section 3.1, all sending operations of a parallel algorithm (put together in one formula) require the constant cost λ per message (assume N_{msg} messages) and a factor β for cost related to the total data $size$ (taken over all messages, number of copy operations not taken into account). Without message buffering, we get the following estimation:

$$T_{unbuf.d} = \lambda \cdot N_{msg} + \beta \cdot size \tag{1}$$

By dynamic chunking, we collect the messages in N_{packet} packets and send those packets instead of single messages. This requires an additional copy operation when sending a packet (depending roughly on $size$, since the amount of data is the same, but the operation copies much more data in one call). Simplifying in this way, we get:

$$T_{buf.d} = \lambda \cdot N_{packet} + (\beta + T_{copy}) \cdot size + Overhead \tag{2}$$

where the *Overhead* describes additional actions required for our buffering mechanism. It consists of a constant part for the administration of the buffers on startup and variable cost for preparing the buffer and checking it every time we add a new message to it. The check as well as the preparation are very simple and will be estimated by an upper bound. As we cannot argue about the scheduling loop, where this check is also needed, we postulate a constant number of passes per message (since sending must always be preceded by an evaluation). In all, we get:

$$Overhead \leq \overbrace{N_{PEs} \cdot T_{alloc}}^{\text{startup}} + \overbrace{N_{msg} \cdot (const' \cdot T_{check} + T_{prepare})}^{\text{Buffer operations}} \tag{3}$$

$$= const + N_{msg} \cdot T_{var} \tag{4}$$

where the additional cost T_{var} indicates variable cost per message.

Assuming we save $N = N_{msg} - N_{packet}$ messages by dynamic chunking, we decrease the time for sending messages by:

$$T_{unbuf.d} - T_{buf.d} \geq \lambda \cdot N - (T_{var} \cdot N_{msg} + T_{copy} \cdot size + const)$$

or, considering $N = N_{msg} - N_{packet}$:

$$T_{unbuf.d} - T_{buf.d} \geq (\lambda - T_{var}) \cdot N - T_{var} \cdot N_{packet} - T_{copy} \cdot size - const \tag{5}$$

We see that savings of $(\lambda - T_{var}) \cdot N$ stand vis-à-vis to additional costs which depend on the amount of data ($size$) and the number of packets (N_{packet}) (neglecting the constant). As per definition, $T_{var} \cdot N_{packet}$ decreases in the same way as N increases. Postulating an optimal use of the message buffers, the remaining cost is $size \cdot T_{copy}$. It must be said that T_{copy} only gives a rough estimation of the real cost, since the number of copy operations is considerably smaller than for the unbuffered variant, at least reduced by $N = N_{msg} - N_{packet}$. Therefore, we can expect that dynamic chunking has a strong impact when messages are small enough and the program optimally synchronised, while for bigger messages, runtime will increase in a moderate way with bigger amounts of data.

Determining N in practice is a different matter, since it does not only depend on known factors as buffer size and timeout, but also on the global synchronisation, i.e. data dependencies in the computation and speed differences between different machines. And it is even harder to talk about the overhead introduced for *receiving* packets.

4.2   Measurements

Overhead Test. Fig. 4 shows results of the test setup described in Section 3.1, applied to the Eden implementation which uses dynamic chunking. In this test, the sending operations simulate single-value transmission. Messages are never buffered, but sent immediately using the implemented buffering mechanism, so we get a good estimate of the overhead variables in 5. A linear regression yields a constant $\lambda' = 99.6$ μsec and a variable $\beta' = 0.12$ μsec, resulting in $T_{copy} = 0.02$ μsec and $T_{var} = 36.26$ μsec for the cost model we sketched.

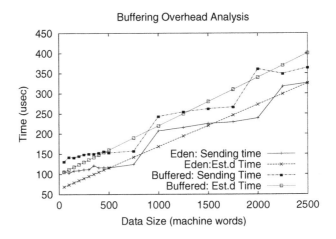

Fig. 4. Overhead measurement corresponding to Fig. 1.

System Test. The pure effect of dynamic chunking can be observed with a simple system test which does not perform *any* remote evaluation, but only echoes its input list.

```
echo :: Trans a => Process [a] [a]
echo = process id
```

Fig. 5 shows the runtime for echoing a list of 10000 items of the determined size (in machine words, 32 bit). As expected, runtime is much faster with small messages, but not excessively longer for big ones. A characteristic value for this system setup and program is around 300 words per message, where overhead and savings are equal. This size may vary, according to different machine and network setup and to the time spent on computation (zero for `echo`).

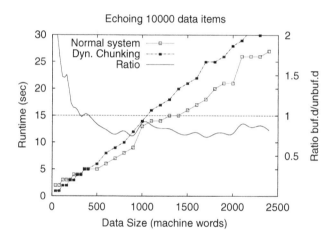

Fig. 5. Measurement with echo process, 10000 messages of variable data size. (2 non-dedicated Linux PCs, PC-Pool, Univ. of Marburg)

A variable parameter, besides buffer size, is the buffer timeout for packets, which can be adjusted by a runtime parameter. The system test with `echo` cannot give results for this parameter, since it does not perform any computation on child side and only depends on network speed and synchronisation effects. In all, it is clear that a high buffer timeout may increase the charge of the packets, but it introduces an additional message latency. Only by experiments, the complex dependencies between process synchronisation and message latency can be optimised using this parameter. The implemented runtime statistics on dynamic chunking can help to find the right runtime parameters.

Benchmark Programs. Dynamic chunking has been tested with the simple sorting functions shown in Section 2.2, as well as with different other benchmark programs: a simple ray-tracer and a Mandelbrot Set visualisation. We used up to eight nodes of a Beowulf Cluster connected through 100MBit Ethernet.

Program	Problem size	Normal	Dyn. Chunking
parsort (8 PEs)	100K Integers	37.9 sec	13.7 sec
mandelbrot (8 PEs)	300x300 pixels	38.3 sec	20.3 sec
raytracer (8 PEs)	huge scene	27.3 sec	26.9 sec

The differences between dynamic chunking and the previous runtime environment are evident. Dynamic chunking applied to a straight-forwardly expressed parallel algorithm, as e.g. the parsort program, can speed up runtimes massively (e.g by factor 3 for the sorting program with 100K Integers as input). The Mandelbrot Set visualisation runs up to 40 % faster with dynamic chunking, while the ray-tracer, which is highly hand-optimised and already chunks pixels to lines, has nearly equivalent runtimes.

Unsurprisingly, the sorting program exhibits a rather poor speedup curve, which is due to the sequential start and end phase of the algorithm and to the fast sequential merge sort used. A slower sorting function such as insertion sort would show better speedups by totally degrading the overall performance. The Mandelbrot Set visualisation and the raytracer both use predefined implementation skeletons for map and show better speedups.

For a fair comparison, we also have to consider hand-tuned variants with static chunking. Fig. 6 shows the impact of these modifications for selected chunk sizes. Apparently, the program runs much faster with the appropriate chunking parameter. Additionally, since the hand-tuning has modified (and improved) the structure of the parallel algorithm, the version parsortchunk2 outperforms the other one by far.

Measuring programs with static chunking and a runtime system which supports dynamic chunking mixes two effects. The results show that the dynamic chunking mechanism does not replace explicit optimisations, but it does not disturb them either. Hand-tuned programs may run faster with dynamic chunking if their parameters are not optimally chosen. Another interesting point is that the version parsortchunk, where only the input to child processes is chunked, exposes rather unstable behaviour when run without dynamic chunking. Since the input arrives much faster, the child processes start working earlier and flood the caller with their results (each element in single message) resulting in high network traffic and affecting other actions on the network. Dynamic chunking reduces the number of replies and leads to a much better synchronisation, which is why the runtime is considerably smaller, whereas for the second version, dynamic chunking has almost no effects when bigger static chunk sizes are chosen.

5 Related Work and Conclusion

We have introduced a message buffering mechanism into the runtime environment for the language Eden, which performs list chunking dynamically and

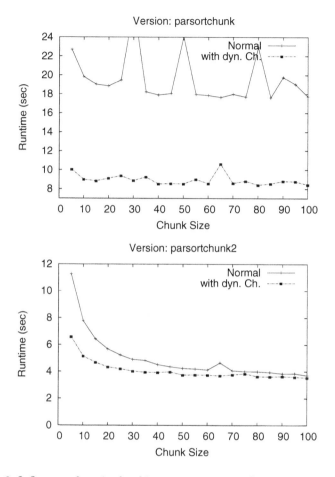

Fig. 6. Influence of static chunking on runtimes in the sorting program.
(Beowulf Cluster, Heriot Watt University, Edinburgh, 8 nodes)

adapts itself to the respective program behaviour. Although dynamic chunking is tailored precisely to a specific property of Eden's semantics, the buffering mechanism is generic and can easily be exploited for other parallel Haskell dialects.

Coordination languages and implementations which would profit from using message buffering are those in which PEs communicate much, but often exchange only small data. Necessarily, the impact is limited to languages with (at least partly) explicit communication. When data is only transmitted on demand and separated from evaluation, the implementation can freely choose different strategies, and performance will degrade by message buffering, since it introduces an artificial latency into the communication subsystem. The problem of dynamic chunking for Eden is rather specific and message buffering is usually a concern for more basic software such as message-passing middleware and alike [15, 12, 7], where it is commonly used with success. We are not aware of comparable work in parallel functional languages, but partly related topics are the discussion of different data fetching strategies for GUM in [11] and the SCL subsystem for the data-parallel Nepal [5, 4], which implements a customised library for generic space-efficient vector transmission.

Our measurements show that dynamic buffering massively improves straightforward parallelised Eden programs, while hand-optimised programs do not profit as much, due to the (nevertheless acceptable) overhead of buffer administration. For programs which are already highly hand-optimised, dynamic chunking affects program performance only in a moderate way. In particular, dynamic chunking performs well for parallel computations with few processors, where the administrative overhead is smaller. The measurements show that dynamic chunking does not completely replace optimisation by static chunking on the language level, but it produces much better results for intuitive straight-forward parallelisations. Programs can remain unchanged, and runtime statistics can give the programmer hints to suitable chunking parameters.

An additional advantage of message buffering in the Eden runtime environment is the new modularity of the communication subsystem. This independence of the concrete MP-system should be exploited for future ports to new platforms and advanced middleware, as well as the general idea of modularity and aspect orientation in the parallel runtime system can be extended to the design of a generic and flexible platform for parallel languages using Haskell as a sequential base.

Acknowledgements

We would like to thank the colleagues from Heriot-Watt University, Edinburgh, for the opportunity to use their Beowulf Cluster and especially Phil Trinder for reviewing a document on the same subject. We also thank Rita Loogen and the IFL workshop attendants for fruitful discussions and suggestions.

References

1. J. Berthold, U. Klusik, R. Loogen, S. Priebe, and N. Weskamp. High-level Process Control in Eden. In H. K. et al., editor, *EuroPar 2003 – Intl. Conf. on Parallel and Distributed Computing*, volume 2790 of *LNCS*, Klagenfurt, Austria, 2003.
2. S. Breitinger, U. Klusik, and R. Loogen. From (Sequential) Haskell to (Parallel) Eden: An Implementation Point of View. In *PLILP'98*, LNCS 1490, pages 318–334. Springer, 1998.
3. S. Breitinger, R. Loogen, Y. Ortega Mallén, and R. Peña Marí. The Eden Coordination Model for Distributed Memory Systems. In *HIPS'97 – Workshop on High-level Parallel Progr. Models*, pages 120–124. IEEE Comp. Science Press, 1997.
4. M. Chakravarty and G. Keller. How Portable is Nested Data Parallelism ? In W. Cheng and A. Sajeev, editors, *PART'99*, Melbourne, Australia, 1999. RMIT University, Springer-Verlag. Available at
http://www.cse.unsw.edu.au/˜chak/papers/CK99.html.

5. M. Chakravarty, G. Keller, R. Lechtchinsky, and W. Pfannenstiel. Nepal – Nested Data-Parallelism in Haskell. Technical report, University of New South Wales, 2000. *http://www.cse.unsw.edu.au/~chak/papers/ndp-haskell.ps.gz*.

6. I. Foster. *Designing and Building Parallel Programs*. Addison-Wesley, 1995. *http://www.mcs.anl.gov/dbpp/*.

7. G. Geist, J. Kohl, and P. Papadopoulos. PVM and MPI: a Comparison of Features. *Calculateurs Paralleles Vol. 8 No. 2 (1996)*, 8(2), May 1996.

8. K. Hammond and G. Michaelson, editors. *Research Directions in Parallel Functional Programming*. Springer-Verlag, 1999.

9. U. Klusik, R. Loogen, and S. Priebe. Controlling Parallelism and Data Distribution in Eden. In *SFP'00*, Trends in Functional Programming, pages 53–64, Univ of St. Andrews, Scotland, July 2000. Intellect.

10. U. Klusik, R. Loogen, S. Priebe, and F. Rubio. Implementation Skeletons in Eden – Low-Effort Parallel Programming. In *IFL'00*, volume 2011 of *LNCS*, pages 71–88, Aachen, Germany, Sept. 2000. Springer.

11. H.-W. Loidl and K. Hammond. Making a Packet: Cost-Effective Communication for a Parallel Graph Reducer. In *IFL'96*, volume 1268 of *LNCS*, pages 184–199, Bad Godesberg, Germany, September 1996. Springer.
   http://www.cee.hw.ac.uk/~dsg/gph/papers/ps/packet.ps.gz.

12. MPI-2: Extensions to the Message-Passing Interface. Technical report, University of Tennessee, Knoxville, July 1997.

13. S. Peyton Jones, C. Hall, K. Hammond, W. Partain, and P. Wadler. The Glasgow Haskell Compiler: a Technical Overview. In *JFIT'93*, pages 249–257, March 1993.

14. S. Peyton Jones and J. Hughes. Haskell 98: A Non-strict, Purely Functional Language, 1999. Available at *http://www.haskell.org/*.

15. *Parallel Virtual Machine Reference Manual, Version 3.2*. University of Tennessee, August 1993.

16. P. Trinder, K. Hammond, H.-W. Loidl, and S. Peyton Jones. Algorithm + Strategy = Parallelism. *J. of Functional Programming*, 8(1):23–60, 1998.

17. P. Trinder, K. Hammond, J. Mattson Jr., A. Partridge, and S. Peyton Jones. GUM: a Portable Parallel Implementation of Haskell. In *PLDI'96*, pages 78–88. ACM Press, May 1996.

18. P. W. Trinder, H.-W. Loidl, and R. F. Pointon. Parallel and Distributed Haskells. *J. of Functional Programming*, 12(4&5):469–510, 2002.

19. A. A. Zain. Heriot-Watt University, Edinburgh. personal contact, July 2003.

With-Loop Scalarization –
Merging Nested Array Operations

Clemens Grelck[1], Sven-Bodo Scholz[2], and Kai Trojahner[1]

[1] University of Lübeck
Institute of Software Technology and Programming Languages
{grelck,trojahne}@isp.uni-luebeck.de
[2] University of Kiel
Institute of Computer Science and Applied Mathematics
sbs@informatik.uni-kiel.de

Abstract. Construction of complex array operations by composition of more basic ones allows for abstract and concise specifications of algorithms. Unfortunately, naïve compilation of such specifications leads to creation of many temporary arrays at runtime and, consequently, to poor performance characteristics.

This paper elaborates on a new compiler optimization, named WITH-LOOP-SCALARIZATION, which aims at eliminating temporary arrays in the context of nested array operations. It is based on WITH-loops, a versatile array comprehension construct used by the functional array language SaC both for specification as well as for internal representation of array operations.

The impact of WITH-LOOP-SCALARIZATION on the runtime performance of compiled SaC code is demonstrated by several experiments involving support for arithmetic on arrays of complex numbers and the application kernel FT from the NAS benchmark suite.

1 Introduction

Dedicated array languages like APL [19], J [20], or NIAL [21] allow for very abstract and concise specifications when processing large amounts of data homogeneously structured along multiple orthogonal axes. They provide large sets of built-in operations, which are universally applicable to arrays of any rank (number of axes) and of any shape (extent along individual axes). These basic operations form the building blocks for construction of entire application programs in a step-wise and layered process.

The advantages of this programming style are manifold. Arrays are treated as conceptual entities with certain algebraic properties rather than as loosely coupled collections of elements. Operations handle entire arrays in a homogeneous way; explicit indexing, which may be considered the most error-prone property of conventional array processing, is almost completely avoided.

However, this specificational advantage does not come for free. Compilation of such specifications turns out to be rather difficult as soon as runtime performance matters. Besides the challenge of compiling the basic array operations

P. Trinder, G. Michaelson, and R. Peña (Eds.): IFL 2003, LNCS 3145, pp. 118–134, 2004.

into efficiently executable code [1, 7, 4, 26] the main problem is the compositional nature of programs in general. Separate compilation of individual basic array operations requires all intermediate results of a complex operation to be explicitly created. While in a scalar language such values can be held in registers, in an array language entire arrays have to be created. As this incurs substantial overhead, one of the key challenges is to develop techniques which avoid actual creation of such intermediate arrays at runtime.

Different sources of intermediate arrays may be distinguished. The most prominent source are array operations that are defined as sequences of basic operations where, in a pipelined fashion, the result of one basic operation directly serves as argument of the subsequent one. As a simple example, consider the selection of the inner elements of an array. In most array languages this can be specified as an expression that takes all but the last elements of an (intermediate) array that itself is derived from the initial array by dropping the very first elements along each axis. Naïve compilation explicitly creates the intermediate array that contains all but the first elements. To avoid the associated overhead, several elaborate techniques have been developed. They reach from *drag-along and beating* [1] to WITH-LOOP-FOLDING [24].

A different source of intermediate arrays are nested operations on arrays. Often it often turns out to be convenient to consider an n-dimensional array to be an $n-m$-dimensional array of m-dimensional subarrays. Prominent examples are applications where individual array elements are arrays themselves, e.g. arrays of complex numbers or vectors of linear functions each being represented by a matrix. Further examples include operations that are to be applied to selected axes of an array only, i.e., an outer operation splits up a given array, applies an inner operation to individual subarrays, and recombines individual results into the overall result. In all these cases naïve compilation creates a temporary representation for each intermediate subarray.

This paper presents on optimization technique called WITH-LOOP-SCALAR-IZATION, which aims at avoiding this kind of intermediate arrays. It is based on a meta representation for high-level array operations called WITH-loop, as proposed in the context of the functional array programming language SAC (for Single Assignment C) [26]. The basic idea of WITH-LOOP-SCALARIZATION has been sketched out in the context of SAC's *axis control notation* [16], a WITH-loop-based technique for applying array operations to selected axes of an array. The particular contributions of this paper are

- a new optimization scheme which is based on a more flexible meta representation called multi-generator WITH-loop, rather than on ordinary WITH-loops. This allows WITH-LOOP-SCALARIZATION to interact with several other optimizations such as WITH-LOOP-FOLDING, which turns out to be mutually beneficial.
- extended auxiliary transformation schemes that further enhance the applicability of WITH-LOOP-SCALARIZATION in general.
- investigations on the performance impact of WITH-LOOP-SCALARIZATION in the current SAC compiler release.

The remainder of this paper is organized as follows. Section 2 provides a brief introduction into the basic concepts of SAC for those readers who are not yet familiar with the language. Multi-generator WITH-loops as the basis for the definition of WITH-LOOP-SCALARIZATION are sketched out in Section 3. Section 4 introduces the basic compilation scheme realizing WITH-LOOP-SCALARIZATION, while Section 5 discusses the auxiliary transformation schemes. The impact of WITH-LOOP-SCALARIZATION on runtime performance is investigated in Section 6. After covering some related work in Section 7, Section 8 concludes and outlines directions of future work.

2   SAC – A Brief Introduction

The core language of SAC is a functional subset of C, extended by n-dimensional arrays as first class objects. Despite the different semantics, a rule of thumb for SAC code is that everything that looks like C also behaves as in C. Arrays are represented by two vectors, a shape vector that specifies an array's extent wrt. each of its axes, and a data vector that contains all its elements. Array types include arrays of fixed shape, e.g. `int[3,7]`, arrays with a fixed number of dimensions, e.g. `int[.,.]`, and arrays with any number of dimensions, i.e. `int[+]`.

In contrast to other array languages SAC provides only a very small set of built-in operations on arrays. Basically, they are primitives to retrieve data pertaining to the structure and contents of arrays, e.g. an array's rank (`dim(array)`), its shape (`shape(array)`), or individual elements (`array[index-vector]`). Aggregate array operations are specified in SAC itself using powerful array comprehensions, called WITH-loops. Their (simplified) syntax is outlined in Fig. 1.

$$
\begin{array}{ll}
WithLoopExpr & \Rightarrow \text{ with } (\ Generator \ ) \ \big[\ AssignBlock \ \big] \ Operation \\
Generator & \Rightarrow Expr \ RelOp \ Id \ RelOp \ Expr \ \big[\ Filter \ \big] \\
RelOp & \Rightarrow < \ | \ <= \\
Filter & \Rightarrow \text{ step } Expr \ \big[\text{ width } Expr \ \big] \\
Operation & \Rightarrow \text{ genarray } (\ Expr \ , \ Expr \ ) \ | \ ...
\end{array}
$$

Fig. 1. Syntax of with-loop expressions.

A WITH-loop basically consists of two parts: a *generator* and an *operation*. The generator defines a set of index vectors along with an index variable representing elements of this set. Two expressions, which must evaluate to vectors of equal length, define lower and upper bounds of a rectangular index vector range. An optional filter may further restrict this selection to grids of arbitrary width. Let a, b, s, and w denote expressions that evaluate to vectors of length n, then

$$(\ a \ \text{<=} \ i\_vec \ \text{<} \ b \ \text{step } s \ \text{width } w \ )$$

defines the following set of index vectors:

$$\{i\_vec \mid \forall_{j \in \{0,...,n-1\}} : a_j \leq i\_vec_j < b_j \ \wedge \ (i\_vec_j - a_j) \bmod s_j < w_j\} \ .$$

The operation specifies the computation to be performed for each element of the index vector set defined by the generator. Let shp denote a SAC expres-

sion that evaluates to a vector, and let *expr* denote any SAC expression. Then
`genarray( `*shp*`, `*expr*`)` defines an array of shape *shp* whose elements are the
values of *expr* for all index vectors from the generator-specified set and 0 otherwise. In order to simplify specification of complex expressions, the operation
part may be preceded by a block of local variable definitions, and *expr* may be
defined in terms of these variables.

Additional types of operation parts allow definition of various map- and fold-like operations. Since they are not needed in the scope of this paper, we omit
their definition here and refer to [26], which provides a detailed introduction into
SAC. A case study on a non-trivial problem investigating both the programming
style and the resulting runtime performance is presented in [14]. Additional
information on SAC is available at `http://www.sac-home.org/`.

3   Multi-generator With-Loops

As pointed out in the introduction, WITH-LOOP-FOLDING [25], a SAC-specific
optimization technique plays a vital role in achieving high runtime performance.
Its purpose is to avoid the creation of intermediate arrays by condensing consecutive WITH-loops into a single one according to the well-known equivalence

$$(\text{map } f) \circ (\text{map } g) \quad \Longleftrightarrow \quad \text{map } (f \circ g) \quad .$$

A simple WITH-LOOP-FOLDING example is shown in Fig. 2: selection of all inner
elements of an array by a combination of `take` and `drop` For reasons of simplicity,
we use constant boundary expressions in this example and expect the argument
array `A` to be of shape `[100,100]`. While `take([99,99],A)` "takes" the first 99
rows and columns of the argument matrix `A`, the subsequent `drop([1,1],...)`
"drops" the first row and the first column of the intermediate matrix. Inlining
both `take` and `drop` yields two consecutive WITH-loops; subsequent WITH-LOOP-FOLDING transforms them into a single operation that selects all inner elements
of `A` directly, i.e. without creating an intermediate array.

The example shown in Fig. 2 represents a trivial case of WITH-LOOP-FOLDING
as the second generator defines a subset of index positions of the first generator.

```
res = drop( [1,1], take( [99,99], A));

        ⇓        FUNCTION INLINING

tmp = with ([0,0] <= iv < [99,99])
        genarray( [99,99], A[iv]);
res = with ([0,0] <= iv < [98,98])
        genarray( [98,98], tmp[iv+[1,1]]);

        ⇓        WITH-LOOP-FOLDING

res = with ([0,0] <= iv < [98,98])
        genarray( [98,98], A[iv+[1,1]]);
```

Fig. 2. WITH-LOOP-FOLDING example.

As a consequence, the entire operation can still be represented by a single generator. However, generators of subsequent WITH-loops may also define disjoint or overlapping sets of index vectors. In these cases, different elements of the target array must be computed according to different specifications, a property which is not supported by WITH-loops.

$$WithLoopExpr' \Rightarrow \text{ with } \left[\, Part \,\right]^{+} Operation$$
$$Part \qquad \Rightarrow \; Generator \left[\, AssignBlock \,\right] : \; Expr$$

Fig. 3. Pseudo syntax of multi-generator WITH-loops.

To address this problem and to create a representation that is closed under WITH-LOOP-FOLDING, user-level WITH-loops are internally embedded into a more general representation called *multi-generator* WITH-*loop* [15]. Its pseudo syntax is defined in Fig. 3. The main difference between internal multi-generator WITH-loops and user-level WITH-loops is that the former consist of an entire sequence of *parts*. Each part is made up by an individual generator, an associated goal expression, and an optional block of local declarations. Being an internal format only allows to guarantee certain regularity properties, e.g., the index variables in the various generators are all the same, and the set of generators forms a partition of the target array's index space, i.e., each element of the target array is covered by exactly one generator.

The importance of multi-generator WITH-loops lies in the fact that all array operations in SAC are internally represented in this format. Hence, any optimization technique on array operations must be defined based on this representation. For additional information on multi-generator WITH-loops see [15] or [26].

4   With-Loop Scalarization – The Base Case

A convenient way of describing complex array operations is to map the basic operations defined in the SAC standard library to arrays of higher rank by means of WITH-loops. Since the library operations are themselves implemented by WITH-loops, this layered approach to software design results in nested WITH-loops in intermediate code, an example of which is shown in Fig. 4.

```
A = with ([0] <= iv < [4]) {
    B = with ([0] <= jv < [4])
        genarray( [4], iv[0] + 2 * jv[0]);
    }
    genarray( [4], B);
```

$$A = \begin{pmatrix} 0\ 2\ 4\ 6 \\ 1\ 3\ 5\ 7 \\ 2\ 4\ 6\ 8 \\ 3\ 5\ 7\ 9 \end{pmatrix}$$

Fig. 4. Array A is defined by two nested WITH-loops.

Unfortunately naïve compilation does not translate nested WITH-loops into efficient programs. Like in the case of consecutive array operations addressed by

WITH-LOOP-FOLDING creation of temporary arrays forms the main obstacle for achieving competitive runtime performance. Even worse, the number of intermediate arrays is not proportionate to the number of consecutive operations, but to the size of the index range defined by the outer generator.

WITH-LOOP-SCALARIZATION is a high-level program transformation that approaches this problem by merging nested WITH-loops into single ones. For example, application of WITH-LOOP-SCALARIZATION to the WITH-loops in Fig. 4 would replace the nesting with the equivalent WITH-loop shown in Fig. 5.

$$
\begin{array}{ll}
\texttt{A = with ([0,0] <= iv < [4,4])} & \\
\quad \texttt{genarray([4,4], iv[0] + 2 * iv[1]);} & A = \begin{pmatrix} 0\ 2\ 4\ 6 \\ 1\ 3\ 5\ 7 \\ 2\ 4\ 6\ 8 \\ 3\ 5\ 7\ 9 \end{pmatrix}
\end{array}
$$

Fig. 5. Array A is generated by a single scalar WITH-loop.

The code transformation applied can be generalized to the compilation scheme shown in Fig. 6. For illustrative purposes we define WITH-LOOP-SCALARIZATION on ordinary WITH-loops first and extend this scheme to multi-generator WITH-loops later in this section. WITH-LOOP-SCALARIZATION replaces two nested WITH-loops with a single one, which is defined as follows:

– The new generator's boundary, step, and width vectors result from the concatenation (denoted by $++$) of the original outer WITH-loop's vectors with the corresponding vectors of the inner WITH-loop.
– The shape vector is also defined by the concatenation of the two original shape vectors.
– The body equals that of the inner WITH-loop prepended with a reconstruction of the two former index vectors. To maintain dimension invariance, these are defined by **take** and **drop** operations performed on the new index vector.

$$
\mathcal{SWLS} \left[\!\!\left[\!\!\begin{array}{l}
\texttt{with (} lb_1 \texttt{ <= } iv_1 \texttt{ < } ub_1 \texttt{ step } s_1 \texttt{ width } w_1 \texttt{) \{} \\
\quad val_{outer} = \texttt{with (} lb_2 \texttt{ <= } iv_2 \texttt{ < } ub_2 \texttt{ step } s_2 \texttt{ width } w_2 \texttt{)} \\
\quad \quad \texttt{\{} \\
\quad \quad \quad val_{inner} = expr(\ iv_1, iv_2)\texttt{;} \\
\quad \quad \texttt{\} genarray(} shape_{inner},\ val_{inner})\texttt{;} \\
\texttt{\} genarray(} shape_{outer},\ val_{outer})
\end{array}\!\!\right]\!\!\right]
$$

$$
= \begin{cases}
\texttt{with (} lb_1{+}{+}lb_2 \texttt{ <= } iv \texttt{ < } ub_1{+}{+}ub_2 \texttt{ step } s_1{+}{+}s_2 \texttt{ width } w_1{+}{+}w_2 \texttt{) \{} \\
\quad iv_1 = \texttt{take(shape(} lb_1)\texttt{, } iv \texttt{);} \\
\quad iv_2 = \texttt{drop(shape(} lb_1)\texttt{, } iv \texttt{);} \\
\quad val_{inner} = expr(\ iv_1, iv_2)\texttt{;} \\
\texttt{\} genarray(} shape_{outer}{+}{+}shape_{inner},\ val_{inner})
\end{cases}
$$

if $iv_1 \notin FV(lb_2) \wedge iv_1 \notin FV(ub_2) \wedge iv_1 \notin FV(s_2) \wedge iv_1 \notin FV(w_2)$

Fig. 6. A simplified compilation scheme for WITH-LOOP-SCALARIZATION.

– The result expression of the new WITH-loop is the same as that of the original inner WITH-loop.

This scheme can be applied to most of the cases in which the elements of an outer WITH-loop are defined by an inner WITH-loop. However, WITH-LOOP-SCALARIZATION cannot be applied if lb_2, ub_2, s_2, or w_2 depend on iv_1, since no reference must be lifted outside the binding scope of the variable it refers to.

As pointed out in Section 3, user-level WITH-loops are internally embedded into multi-generator WITH-loops. Hence, the compilation scheme illustrates the working principle of WITH-LOOP-SCALARIZATION, but further generalization is required to adapt it to multi-generator WITH-loops. To reuse elements of the simplified compilation scheme, multi-generator WITH-LOOP-SCALARIZATION is split into two consecutive phases. The first phase, called *distribution phase*, deals with multiple generators occurring in inner WITH-loops. It distributes the generator of the surrounding part over all inner parts. This is done by creating an outer part for each of the inner parts, as depicted in Fig. 7. Step and width vectors are omitted for reasons of simplicity. They are treated in the same way as boundary vectors.

The internal representation of multi-generator WITH-loops as a result of the distribution phase is characterized by overlapping generators. However, this deficiency is addressed by the subsequent *scalarization phase*, which completes WITH-LOOP-SCALARIZATION. Basically, this is achieved by mapping the simplified compilation scheme from Fig. 6 to all parts of the outer WITH-loop, as shown in Fig. 8. Finally, the composition of both compilation phases yields a scheme for multi-generator WITH-LOOP-SCALARIZATION:

$$\mathcal{WLS} = \mathcal{DIST} \circ \mathcal{SCAL} \quad .$$

It remains to be pointed out that the same restrictions apply for multi-generator WITH-LOOP-SCALARIZATION as mentioned for the simplified case. If some inner generator depends on the index vector of an outer generator, the compound operation cannot be expressed by a single multi-generator WITH-loop and, hence, there is no opportunity for WITH-LOOP-SCALARIZATION.

5   With-Loop Scalarization – Enhancing Applicability

Unfortunately, WITH-LOOP-SCALARIZATION as defined in the previous section is insufficient to handle all cases of nested array operations. The compilation scheme for multi-generator WITH-loops requires each part of an outer WITH-loop to contain exactly one nested WITH-loop. However, in many cases intermediate code which would benefit from WITH-LOOP-SCALARIZATION does not comply to this restricted format, e.g., an inner WITH-loop may be accompanied by additional code or the inner non-scalar expression may not be given as a WITH-loop at all.

This section is about making WITH-LOOP-SCALARIZATION applicable in a broader range of optimization cases. Three auxiliary transformation schemes are presented which tackle a specific code pattern each and result in nested WITH-loops, thus enabling WITH-LOOP-SCALARIZATION.

$$
\begin{aligned}
&\mathcal{DIST} \quad
\begin{bmatrix}
\texttt{with} \\
\quad \vdots \\
\quad (\; lb_l \; \texttt{<=} \; iv_1 \; \texttt{<} \; ub_l) \; \{ \\
\qquad val_l \; \texttt{=} \; \texttt{with} \; (\; lb_{l,1} \; \texttt{<=} \; iv_2 \; \texttt{<} \; ub_{l,1}) \; \{ \\
\qquad\qquad\qquad val_{l,1} \; \texttt{=} \; expr_{l,1}(\; iv_1, iv_2); \\
\qquad\qquad \} \; : \; val_{l,1} \\
\qquad\qquad \vdots \\
\qquad\qquad (\; lb_{l,k} \; \texttt{<=} \; iv_2 \; \texttt{<} \; ub_{l,k}) \; \{ \\
\qquad\qquad\qquad val_{l,k} \; \texttt{=} \; expr_{l,k}(\; iv_1, iv_2); \\
\qquad\qquad \} \; : \; val_{l,k} \\
\qquad\quad \textbf{genarray}(\; shape_{inner}); \\
\quad \} \; : \; val_l \\
\quad \vdots \\
\textbf{genarray}(\; shape_{outer}\;)
\end{bmatrix} \\[2mm]
&= \left\{
\begin{aligned}
&\texttt{with} \\
&\quad \vdots \\
&\quad (\; lb_l \; \texttt{<=} \; iv_1 \; \texttt{<} \; ub_l) \; \{ \\
&\qquad val_l \; \texttt{=} \; \texttt{with} \; (\; lb_{l,1} \; \texttt{<=} \; iv_2 \; \texttt{<} \; ub_{l,1}) \; \{ \\
&\qquad\qquad\qquad val_{l,1} \; \texttt{=} \; expr_{l,1}(\; iv_1, iv_2); \\
&\qquad\qquad \} \; : \; val_{l,1} \\
&\qquad\quad \textbf{genarray}(\; shape_{inner}); \\
&\quad \} \; : \; val_l \\
&\quad \vdots \\
&\quad (\; lb_l \; \texttt{<=} \; iv_1 \; \texttt{<} \; ub_l) \; \{ \\
&\qquad val_l \; \texttt{=} \; \texttt{with} \; (\; lb_{l,k} \; \texttt{<=} \; iv_2 \; \texttt{<} \; ub_{l,k}) \; \{ \\
&\qquad\qquad\qquad val_{l,k} \; \texttt{=} \; expr_{l,k}(\; iv_1, iv_2); \\
&\qquad\qquad \} \; : \; val_{l,k} \\
&\qquad\quad \textbf{genarray}(\; shape_{inner}); \\
&\quad \} \; : \; val_l \\
&\quad \vdots \\
&\textbf{genarray}(\; shape_{outer}\;)
\end{aligned}
\right. \\[2mm]
&\text{if } \; iv_1 \notin FV(lb_{i,j}) \; \wedge \; iv_1 \notin FV(ub_{i,j})
\end{aligned}
$$

Fig. 7. The distribution phase of multi-generator WITH-LOOP-SCALARIZATION.

5.1 Vectors

The first auxiliary transformation deals with the case of the non-scalar element of a WITH-loop being given in vector notation. As can be seen in Fig. 9, it suffices to replace the reference to the vector with a WITH-loop that contains one part for each of the vector's elements. Hence, each generator describes an index space containing exactly one element. The resulting WITH-loop nesting can then be scalarized using multi-generator WITH-LOOP-SCALARIZATION.

$$
\mathcal{SCAL}
\left[
\begin{array}{l}
\textbf{with} \\
\quad \vdots \\
\quad (\ lb_l \ \texttt{<=}\ iv_1\ \texttt{<}\ ub_l)\ \{ \\
\qquad val_l\ \texttt{=}\ \textbf{with}\ (\ lb_{l,1}\ \texttt{<=}\ iv_2\ \texttt{<}\ ub_{l,1})\ \{ \\
\qquad\qquad\qquad\qquad\quad val_{l,1}\ \texttt{=}\ expr_{l,1}(\ iv_1,iv_2)\texttt{;} \\
\qquad\qquad\qquad \}\ \texttt{:}\ val_{l,1} \\
\qquad\qquad\quad \textbf{genarray}(\ shape_{inner})\texttt{;} \\
\quad \}\ \texttt{:}\ val_l \\
\quad \vdots \\
\quad (\ lb_l \ \texttt{<=}\ iv_1\ \texttt{<}\ ub_l)\ \{ \\
\qquad val_l\ \texttt{=}\ \textbf{with}\ (\ lb_{l,k}\ \texttt{<=}\ iv_2\ \texttt{<}\ ub_{l,k})\ \{ \\
\qquad\qquad\qquad\qquad\quad val_{l,k}\ \texttt{=}\ expr_{l,k}(\ iv_1,iv_2)\texttt{;} \\
\qquad\qquad\qquad \}\ \texttt{:}\ val_{l,k} \\
\qquad\qquad\quad \textbf{genarray}(\ shape_{inner})\texttt{;} \\
\quad \}\ \texttt{:}\ val_l \\
\quad \vdots \\
\textbf{genarray}(\ shape_{outer}\ )
\end{array}
\right]
$$

$$
=
\left\{
\begin{array}{l}
\textbf{with} \\
\quad \vdots \\
\quad (\ lb_l\texttt{++}lb_{l,1}\ \texttt{<=}\ iv\ \texttt{<}\ ub_l\texttt{++}ub_{l,1})\ \{ \\
\qquad iv_1\ \texttt{=}\ \textbf{take}(\ \textbf{shape}(\ lb_l)\texttt{,}\ iv\ )\texttt{;} \\
\qquad iv_2\ \texttt{=}\ \textbf{drop}(\ \textbf{shape}(\ lb_l)\texttt{,}\ iv\ )\texttt{;} \\
\qquad val_{l,1}\ \texttt{=}\ expr_{l,1}(\ iv_1,iv_2)\texttt{;} \\
\quad \}\ \texttt{:}\ val_{l,1} \\
\quad \vdots \\
\quad (\ lb_l\texttt{++}lb_{l,k}\ \texttt{<=}\ iv\ \texttt{<}\ ub_l\texttt{++}ub_{l,k})\ \{ \\
\qquad iv_1\ \texttt{=}\ \textbf{take}(\ \textbf{shape}(\ lb_l)\texttt{,}\ iv\ )\texttt{;} \\
\qquad iv_2\ \texttt{=}\ \textbf{drop}(\ \textbf{shape}(\ lb_l)\texttt{,}\ iv\ )\texttt{;} \\
\qquad val_{l,k}\ \texttt{=}\ expr_{l,k}(\ iv_1,iv_2)\texttt{;} \\
\quad \}\ \texttt{:}\ val_{l,k} \\
\quad \vdots \\
\textbf{genarray}(\ shape_{outer}\texttt{++}shape_{inner}\ )
\end{array}
\right.
$$

Fig. 8. The scalarization phase of the multi-generator WITH-LOOP-SCALARIZATION.

5.2   Arbitrary Arrays

In general, non-scalar elements of a WITH-loop may not only be given by nested WITH-loops or by vectors, but may also result from WITH-loops defined outside of the WITH-loop or even from function applications. In these cases the arrays' contents are hidden from the view of any local optimization strategy.

As illustrated in Fig. 10, WITH-LOOP-SCALARIZATION can handle this problem by inserting an *identity* WITH-*loop* whose index space covers the entire array, and its operation is just a selection. Hence, the identity WITH-loop replaces a reference to an array with a definition of it and thereby enables WITH-LOOP-SCALARIZATION.

$$
\mathcal{VEC} \left[\!\!\left[\begin{array}{l} A \text{ = with} \\ \quad \vdots \\ \quad (\ lb_l \ \texttt{<=} \ iv_1 \ \texttt{<} \ ub_l) \ \{ \\ \qquad v \ \texttt{=} \ [v_1, ..., v_n]; \\ \quad \} \ : \ v \\ \quad \vdots \\ \quad \texttt{genarray(} \ shp \ \texttt{);} \end{array}\right]\!\!\right]
$$

$$
= \left\{ \begin{array}{l} A \text{ = with} \\ \quad \vdots \\ \quad (\ lb_l \ \texttt{<=} \ iv_1 \ \texttt{<} \ ub_l) \ \{ \\ \qquad val_l \ \texttt{= with} \ (\ \texttt{[0]} \ \texttt{<=} \ iv_2 \ \texttt{<} \ \texttt{[1]}) \ : \ v_1 \\ \qquad\qquad \vdots \\ \qquad\qquad\qquad (\ [n-1] \ \texttt{<=} \ iv_2 \ \texttt{<} \ [n]) \ : \ v_n \\ \qquad\qquad \texttt{genarray(} \ \texttt{[n]} \ \texttt{);} \\ \quad \} \ : \ val_l \\ \quad \vdots \\ \quad \texttt{genarray(} \ shp \ \texttt{);} \end{array}\right.
$$

Fig. 9. Auxiliary transformation scheme for arrays given in vector notation.

5.3   Imperfect Nestings

All optimization strategies presented so far can only be applied if WITH-loops form perfect nestings, i.e., there must be no code before inner WITH-loops. To handle imperfect nestings as well, WITH-LOOP-SCALARIZATION is accompanied by the auxiliary transformation scheme shown in Fig. 11. The scheme pushes

$$
\mathcal{ID} \left[\!\!\left[\begin{array}{l} A \text{ = } someArray; \\ B \text{ = with} \\ \quad \vdots \\ \quad (\ lb_l \ \texttt{<=} \ iv_1 \ \texttt{<} \ ub_l) \ : \ A \\ \quad \vdots \\ \quad \texttt{genarray(} \ shp \ \texttt{);} \end{array}\right]\!\!\right]
$$

$$
= \left\{ \begin{array}{l} A \text{ = } someArray; \\ B \text{ = with} \\ \quad \vdots \\ \quad (\ lb_l \ \texttt{<=} \ iv_1 \ \texttt{<} \ ub_l) \ \{ \\ \qquad val_l \ \texttt{= with} \ \texttt{(0*shape(}A\texttt{)} \ \texttt{<=}iv_2\texttt{<} \ \texttt{shape(}A\texttt{))} \ : \ A[iv_2] \\ \qquad\qquad \texttt{genarray(} \ \texttt{shape(}A\texttt{)} \ \texttt{);} \\ \quad \} \ : \ val_l \\ \quad \vdots \\ \quad \texttt{genarray(} \ shp \ \texttt{);} \end{array}\right.
$$

Fig. 10. Inserting an identity WITH-loop enables WITH-LOOP-SCALARIZATION.

```
    [[ with
          ⋮
          ( lb_l <= iv_1 < ub_l) {
             var = expr_l( iv_1);
             val_l = with
                        ⋮
                        ( lb_l,k <= iv_2 < ub_l,k) {
PD                         val_l,k = expr_l,k( iv_1,iv_2,var);
                        } : val_l,1
                        ⋮
                     genarray( shp_inner );
          } : val_l
          ⋮
       genarray( shp_outer )                                   ]]

       ⎧ with
       ⎪    ⋮
       ⎪    ( lb_l <= iv_1 < ub_l) {
       ⎪       val_l = with
       ⎪                  ⋮
       ⎪                  ( lb_l,k <= iv_2 < ub_l,k) {
  =    ⎨                     var = expr_l( iv_1);
       ⎪                     val_l,k = expr_l,k( iv_1,iv_2,var);
       ⎪                  } : val_l,k
       ⎪                  ⋮
       ⎪               genarray( shp_inner );
       ⎪    } : val_l
       ⎪    ⋮
       ⎩ genarray( shp_outer )
```

Fig. 11. Auxiliary transformation scheme for imperfect WITH-loop nestings.

down assignments into the inner WITH-loop and this way creates perfect nestings. While this transformation enables WITH-LOOP-SCALARIZATION, a serious drawback is that the moved expressions may be evaluated repeatedly. However, in many situations the performance increase achieved by WITH-LOOP-SCALARIZATION outweighs the cost of redundant code execution. Still, this transformation has speculative character and should be used carefully.

6 Performance Evaluation

This section reports on some experiments evaluating the performance impact of WITH-LOOP-SCALARIZATION. All reported tests have been made on a SUN Ultra 1 workstation using SUN Workshop 5.0 compilers for code generation. Additional experiments on an Intel Pentium III based PC running LINUX and gcc 3.2 confirmed the figures.

6.1   A Customized Benchmark

Fig. 12 shows a SAC micro benchmark tailor-made for estimating the performance impact of WITH-LOOP-SCALARIZATION. It defines a matrix in a row-wise manner, i.e. by creating one intermediate vector per matrix row. The constants SIZE and INNER allow for specific investigations on the impact of the intermediate vector's size while retaining the overall problem size.

```
A = with ([0] <= iv < [SIZE/INNER])
    {
      B = with ([0] <= jv < [INNER])
          genarray( [INNER], iv[0] + 2 * jv[0]);
    }
    genarray( [SIZE/INNER], B);
```

Fig. 12. Computational kernel of simple WITH-LOOP-SCALARIZATION test.

Fig. 13 shows program runtimes for systematic variations of the intermediate vector's size. Prior to WITH-LOOP-SCALARIZATION this manipulation has an enormous impact on overall performance due to memory management costs, loop overhead, and various cache effects. WITH-LOOP-SCALARIZATION not only accelerates program execution by between 33% and a factor of 5, it also eliminates any dependence between result matrix shape and runtime performance.

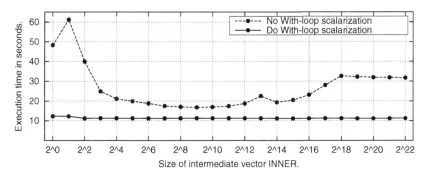

Fig. 13. Performance evaluation of simple WITH-LOOP-SCALARIZATION test.

6.2   Arithmetic on Complex Numbers

Arithmetic on arrays of complex numbers is a particularly prominent example of nested array operations and, hence, a good motivation for WITH-LOOP-SCALARIZATION. Fig. 14 shows an excerpt from the SAC standard library, which defines complex numbers as 2-element vectors and provides overloaded versions of the usual arithmetic operators. In a second step, these overloaded operators a mapped to arrays of any rank and shape. Dots as boundary expressions in

```
typedef double[2] complex;
complex (+) (complex a, complex b)
{
  return( [ a[0] + b[0], a[1] + b[1]]);
}
complex[+] (+) (complex[+] a, complex[+] b)
{
  res = with (. <= iv <= .)
        genarray( shape(a), a[iv] + b[iv]);
  return( res);
}
```

Fig. 14. Complex numbers in SAC.

WITH-loop generators are syntactic sugar referring to the least and the greatest legal index vector of the array to be created. The impact of WITH-LOOP-SCALAR-IZATION on the runtime performance achieved by this 2-level implementation is shown in Fig. 15; program execution times are given for 100 additions/multiplications of matrices of 1000 by 1000 complex numbers.

WITH-LOOP-SCALARIZATION reduces runtimes by 60% and by 50% for addition and for multiplication, respectively. To provide readers with an impression of absolute performance values achieved by SAC, Fig. 15 also presents corresponding runtimes of equivalent FORTRAN-90 and C programs. Whereas the FORTRAN-90 code benefits from built-in support for complex numbers including built-in arithmetic operators on arrays of complex numbers, straightforward C implementations do not achieve the same performance levels. In the case of multiplication SAC even outperforms C. Due to the functional semantics of SAC the compiler manages to identify multiple references to identical array elements when computing each complex product. Whereas the SAC compiler avoids these superfluous memory accesses, a C compiler must make conservative assumptions, which result in lower performance or require hand optimization.

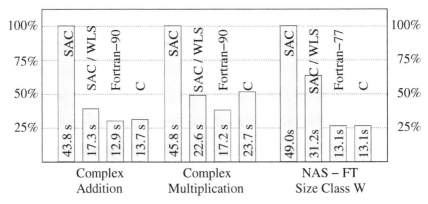

Fig. 15. Performance impact of WITH-LOOP-SCALARIZATION (WLS).

6.3   NAS Benchmark FT

To evaluate the performance impact of WITH-LOOP-SCALARIZATION on a larger application we have chosen the NAS benchmark FT [3]. It implements a solver for a class of partial differential equations by means of repeated 3-dimensional forward and inverse complex fast-Fourier transforms. This benchmark has previously been used for evaluating the suitability of functional languages for numerical computing [18]. A high-level SAC implementation is described in [17].

Fig. 15 shows that WITH-LOOP-SCALARIZATION reduces the total benchmark execution time by as much as one third. Comparing SAC runtimes with highly hand-optimized FORTRAN-77 and C implementations of the benchmark makes clear that WITH-LOOP-SCALARIZATION reduces the performance penalty of high-level programming from a factor of 4 down to less than a factor of 2.4, numbers which are significantly better than those reported in [18].

7   Related Work

In functional languages separate parts of a program are typically glued together using intermediate data structures. Their detection and elimination is crucial for achieving good runtime performance. Optimizations to this effect are generally referred to as *deforestation* or *fusion* techniques [29, 13, 11, 12, 27]. Although being similar in spirit, they completely differ from WITH-LOOP-SCALARIZATION in the concrete setting. Whereas they are based on linked lists, WITH-LOOP-SCALARIZATION acts on multidimensional arrays. Moreover, deforestation connects one producer to one consumer, whereas WITH-LOOP-SCALARIZATION combines the creation of a single array with the creation of many subarrays, one for each element position.

Since main-stream functional programming is based on algebraic data types, research on functional arrays has mostly been focused on achieving reasonable efficiency under less than optimal side conditions discussing such issues as strictness, unboxing, or the aggregate update problem [2, 28, 9]. A variant of deforestation for arrays is described in [8]; it is similar in spirit to WITH-LOOP-FOLDING [24] adapted to the context of HASKELL arrays.

A notable exception from the main-stream of functional programming that puts the emphasis on arrays rather than on lists is SISAL [22]. However, with a vector-of-vectors representation of multidimensional arrays, SISAL avoids the need for an optimization like WITH-LOOP-SCALARIZATION, but pays with inefficient array accesses in general [23, 25].

An optimization bearing some resemblance to WITH-LOOP-SCALARIZATION is the flattening transformation [6] developed in the context of NESL [5]. In contrast to SAC, arrays in NESL are irregular, e.g., each row of a matrix may have a different size. This format is particularly amenable to the representation of irregular problems or sparse data structures, but incurs substantial overhead in the case of regular arrays. The flattening operation aims at transforming a multidimensional irregular array into a flat data vector and an auxiliary vector encapsulating all structural information.

In imperative array languages, e.g. FORTRAN-90 or ZPL [10], optimizations like WITH-LOOP-SCALARIZATION have not been pursued because in their context operational aspects are decoupled from data layout aspects. Memory representations of arrays are defined through explicit declaration, not by the operations that incrementally initialize their elements. In contrast, high-level array processing, as in the case of SAC, combines memory layout definition and monolithic initialization in a single conceptual step. As memory layout generally follows the initializing operation, optimizations like WITH-LOOP-SCALARIZATION must ensure that stepwise initializations do not incur costly intermediate data layouts.

8   Conclusion and Future Work

Creation of large numbers of temporary arrays at runtime and, hence, a mediocre runtime performance is the price which typically must be paid for a high-level coding style. To make this way of programming reasonable in areas where performance matters requires powerful optimization schemes that eliminate temporary arrays by meaning-preserving code transformations. This paper discusses WITH-LOOP-SCALARIZATION, a new optimization technique based on WITH-loops. It focuses on intermediate arrays arising from nested array operations. Several experiments show that WITH-LOOP-SCALARIZATION may have a tremendous impact on the runtime performance of compiled code. It turns out to be one key technique to achieve levels of performance competitive to FORTRAN.

WITH-LOOP-SCALARIZATION requires intermediate code to follow a quite specific pattern. To improve its applicability in practice it is accompanied by auxiliary transformation schemes which rewrite intermediate code accordingly. One of these transformations intentionally moves code into the body of a nested WITH-loop. This runs counter traditional optimization strategies, which aim at removing loop-invariant code, and may lead to repeated evaluation of expressions. Experience shows that in many cases other optimizations effectively solve this problem and eliminate repeated evaluations by means beyond the scope of this paper. Nevertheless, future work is needed to gain any guarantees to this effect. Our current approach is to wait until the final code generation phase when multidimensional WITH-loops are eventually transformed into complex nestings of FOR-loops. As soon as binding levels for individual loop variables are once again discriminated, an additional backend loop invariant removal phase would solve the problem.

References

1. P.S. Abrams. An APL Machine. SLAC 114, Stanford Linear Accelerator Center, 1970.
2. S. Anderson and P. Hudak. Compilation of Haskell Array Comprehensions for Scientific Computing. In *Proceedings of the ACM SIGPLAN Conference on Programming Language Design and Implementation (PLDI'90), White Plains, New York, USA*, volume 25 of *SIGPLAN Notices*, pages 137–149. ACM Press, 1990.

3. D.H. Bailey, E. Barszcz, J.T. Barton, D.S. Browning, R.L. Carter, L. Dagum, R.A. Fatoohi, P.O. Frederickson, T.A. Lasinski, T.A. Schreiber, R.S. Simon, V. Venkatakrishnam, and S.K. Weeratunga. The NAS Parallel Benchmarks. *International Journal of Supercomputer Applications*, 5(3):63–73, 1991.

4. R. Bernecky. APEX: The APL Parallel Executor. Master's thesis, University of Toronto, Toronto, Canada, 1997.

5. G.E. Blelloch. NESL: A Nested Data-Parallel Language (Version 3.1). Technical Report CMU-CS-95-170, Carnegie Mellon University, Pittsburgh, Pennsylvania, USA, 1995.

6. G.E. Blelloch and G.W. Sabot. Compiling Collection-Oriented Languages onto Massively Parallel Computers. *Journal of Parallel and Distributed Computing*, 8(2):119–134, 1990.

7. T. Budd. *An APL Compiler*. Springer-Verlag, Berlin, Germany, 1988.

8. M.M.T. Chakravarty and G. Keller. Functional Array Fusion. In *Proceedings of the 6th ACM SIGPLAN International Conference on Functional Programming (ICFP'01), Florence, Italy*, pages 205–216. ACM Press, 2001.

9. M.M.T. Chakravarty and G. Keller. An Approach to Fast Arrays in Haskell. In J. Jeuring and S. Peyton Jones, editors, *Summer School and Workshop on Advanced Functional Programming, Oxford, England, UK, 2002*, volume 2638 of *Lecture Notes in Computer Science*, pages 27–58. Springer-Verlag, Berlin, Germany, 2003.

10. B.L. Chamberlain, S.-E. Choi, C. Lewis, L. Snyder, W.D. Weathersby, and C. Lin. The Case for High-Level Parallel Programming in ZPL. *IEEE Computational Science and Engineering*, 5(3), 1998.

11. W.N. Chin. Safe Fusion of Functional Expressions II: Further Improvements. *Journal of Functional Programming*, 4(4):515–550, 1994.

12. A. Gill. *Cheap Deforestation for Non-strict Functional Languages*. PhD thesis, Glasgow University, Glasgow, Scotland, UK, 1996.

13. A. Gill, J. Launchbury, and S.L. Peyton Jones. A Short Cut to Deforestation. In *Proceedings of the Conference on Functional Programming Languages and Computer Architecture (FPCA'93), Copenhagen, Denmark*, pages 223–232. ACM Press, 1993.

14. C. Grelck. Implementing the NAS Benchmark MG in SAC. In *Proceedings of the 16th International Parallel and Distributed Processing Symposium (IPDPS'02), Fort Lauderdale, Florida, USA*. IEEE Computer Society Press, 2002.

15. C. Grelck, D. Kreye, and S.-B. Scholz. On Code Generation for Multi-Generator WITH-Loops in SAC. In P. Koopman and C. Clack, editors, *Proceedings of the 11th International Workshop on Implementation of Functional Languages (IFL'99), Lochem, The Netherlands, selected papers*, volume 1868 of *Lecture Notes in Computer Science*, pages 77–94. Springer-Verlag, Berlin, Germany, 2000.

16. C. Grelck and S.-B. Scholz. Axis Control in SAC. In R. Peña and T. Arts, editors, *Proceedings of the 14th International Workshop on Implementation of Functional Languages (IFL'02), Madrid, Spain, selected papers*, volume 2670 of *Lecture Notes in Computer Science*, pages 182–198. Springer-Verlag, Berlin, Germany, 2003.

17. C. Grelck and S.-B. Scholz. Towards an Efficient Functional Implementation of the NAS Benchmark FT. In V. Malyshkin, editor, *Proceedings of the 7th International Conference on Parallel Computing Technologies (PaCT'03), Nizhni Novgorod, Russia*, volume 2763 of *Lecture Notes in Computer Science*, pages 230–235. Springer-Verlag, Berlin, Germany, 2003.

18. J. Hammes, S. Sur, and W. Böhm. On the Effectiveness of Functional Language Features: NAS Benchmark FT. *Journal of Functional Programming*, 7(1):103–123, 1997.

19. International Standards Organization. Programming Language APL, Extended. ISO N93.03, ISO, 1993.

20. K.E. Iverson. *J Introduction and Dictionary*. Iverson Software Inc., Toronto, Canada, 1995.

21. M.A. Jenkins and W.H. Jenkins. *The Q'Nial Language and Reference Manual*. Nial Systems Ltd., Ottawa, Canada, 1993.

22. J.R. McGraw, S.K. Skedzielewski, S.J. Allan, R.R. Oldehoeft, et al. Sisal: Streams and Iteration in a Single Assignment Language: Reference Manual Version 1.2. M 146, Lawrence Livermore National Laboratory, Livermore, California, USA, 1985.

23. R.R. Oldehoeft. Implementing Arrays in SISAL 2.0. In *Proceedings of the 2nd SISAL Users Conference, San Diego, California, USA*, pages 209–222. Lawrence Livermore National Laboratory, 1992.

24. S.-B. Scholz. With-loop-folding in SAC — Condensing Consecutive Array Operations. In C. Clack, T. Davie, and K. Hammond, editors, *Proceedings of the 9th International Workshop on Implementation of Functional Languages (IFL'97), St. Andrews, Scotland, UK, selected papers*, volume 1467 of *Lecture Notes in Computer Science*, pages 72–92. Springer-Verlag, Berlin, Germany, 1998.

25. S.-B. Scholz. A Case Study: Effects of WITH-Loop Folding on the NAS Benchmark MG in SAC. In K. Hammond, T. Davie, and C. Clack, editors, *Proceedings of the 10th International Workshop on Implementation of Functional Languages (IFL'98), London, UK, selected papers*, volume 1595 of *Lecture Notes in Computer Science*, pages 216–228. Springer-Verlag, Berlin, Germany, 1999.

26. S.-B. Scholz. Single Assignment C — Efficient Support for High-Level Array Operations in a Functional Setting. *Journal of Functional Programming*, 13(6):1005–1059, 2003.

27. D. van Arkel, J. van Groningen, and S. Smetsers. Fusion in Practice. In R. Peña and T. Arts, editors, *Proceedings of the 14th International Workshop on Implementation of Functional Languages (IFL'02), Madrid, Spain, selected papers*, volume 2670 of *Lecture Notes in Computer Science*, pages 51–67. Springer-Verlag, Berlin, Germany, 2003.

28. J. van Groningen. The Implementation and Efficiency of Arrays in Clean 1.1. In W. Kluge, editor, *Proceedings of the 8th International Workshop on Implementation of Functional Languages (IFL'96), Bonn, Germany, selected papers*, volume 1268 of *Lecture Notes in Computer Science*, pages 105–124. Springer-Verlag, Berlin, Germany, 1997.

29. P. Wadler. Deforestation: Transforming Programs to Eliminate Trees. *Theoretical Computer Science*, 73(2):231–248, 1990.

Building an Interface Between Eden and Maple: A Way of Parallelizing Computer Algebra Algorithms*

Rafael Martínez and Ricardo Peña

Departamento de Sistemas Informáticos y Programación
Universidad Complutense de Madrid, Spain
rmartine@fdi.ucm.es, ricardo@sip.ucm.es

Abstract. Eden is a parallel functional language extending Haskell with processes. This paper describes the implementation of an interface between the Eden language and the Maple system. The aim of this effort is to parallelize Maple programs by using Eden as coordination language. The idea is to leave in Maple the computational intensive functions of the (sequential) algorithm and to use Eden skeletons to set up the parallel process topology in the available parallel machine. A Maple system is instantiated in each processor. Eden processes are responsible for invoking Maple functions with appropriate parameters and of getting back the results, as well as of performing all the data communication between processes.

The interface provides the following services: instantiating and terminating a Maple system in each processor, performing data conversion between Maple and Haskell objects, invoking Maple functions from Eden, and ensuring mutual exclusion in the access to Maple from different concurrent threads in the local processor.

A parallel version of Buchberger's algorithm to compute Gröbner bases is presented to illustrate the use of the interface.

Keywords: Functional parallel programming, skeletons, computer algebra algorithms, foreign language interfaces.

1 Introduction

Computer algebra algorithms, usually programmed in specialized systems such as Maple [8], are known to need much computer time. Many of these algorithms run for hours, days and even weeks.

Eden is a parallel functional language extending Haskell with processes [2]. It runs on most Unix-like platforms supporting the PVM (*Parallel Virtual Machine*) library [14]. It has been shown that building parallel algorithms in Eden is a rather easy task [7]. Moreover, Eden provides now a wide library of predefined *skeletons* fitting most of the typical parallel applications [6, 7]. Doing parallel programming with skeletons is as convenient as doing functional programming with higher-order functions.

---

* Work partially supported by the Spanish project TIC 2000-0738.

P. Trinder, G. Michaelson, and R. Peña (Eds.): IFL 2003, LNCS 3145, pp. 135–151, 2004.

To try to bring together the advantages of both systems, Maple and Eden, is a worthwhile effort. On the one hand, computer algebra specialists might continue to use one of their favorite tools while getting the speedups of a parallel implementation. With an appropriate parallel machine, they could easily cut the running time of their algorithms. On the other hand, they would not have to deal with complex parallel libraries such as PVM and the like to explicitly program the parallel versions. In other words, they would not be forced to pay the effort of an explicit parallel implementation. Instead, if Eden provides the appropriate skeleton, only a few simple Haskell functions would have to be provided, as it will be shown in the example of Section 5.

The idea is simple: to leave in Maple the complex algebraic computations and to give to Eden the task of creating and communicating processes. The idea of having a coordination language on top of a computation language is by no means new (e.g., see [4, 9]) but this is the first time that the combination Eden-Maple has been tried. Then, what is needed is an interface through which Eden programs may invoke Maple functions. This paper explains in detail the implementation of such an interface and its use in the development of a complex hybrid Eden-Maple parallel algorithm.

The structure of the paper is as follows: In Section 2 we present previous work, an interface Haskell-Maple, on which we have based our own interface. Section 3 gives a quick introduction to Eden and explains the parallel structure of hybrid Eden-Maple algorithms. In Section 4, we give an account of the concurrency problems which may arise in every single processor and of how we have solved them. Section 5 presents the application example: computing the Gröbner basis of a set of polynomials. Once the problem is introduced, we develop a new Eden skeleton fitting the parallel structure of the algorithm. Then, the skeleton is instantiated with problem dependent functions, so solving in parallel the Gröbner basis problem. It is in some of these problem dependent functions where Maple functions are invoked by using the Eden-Maple interface. Finally, Section 6 draws some conclusions and future work.

2   The Sequential Interface

The starting point for our work has been an interface between GHC [11] and Maple written by Wolfgang Schreiner and Hans-Wolgang Loidl [12] in order to invoke Maple functions from Haskell. The versions used at that time were GHC-4.08.1 and Maple 5.1, both running under Unix-like operating systems. They tried also to build a parallel version to be able to interface *Glasgow Parallel Haskell* programs [15] to Maple but, to our knowledge, this version was never completed.

The main idea of the interface, which we have preserved in our version, is to run Maple 'as it is' in a separate Unix process. All the interface to Maple is done through the standard input and the standard output of this process, i.e. the Haskell process simulates a user terminal for the Maple process. Additionally, a small interpreter was written in the Maple side in such a way that, by using a simple protocol through the standard input/ouput, Haskell could ask the interpreter to invoke any Maple function and to translate data objects from external format to Maple internal format and the other way around. The idea was to convert the initial data of a complex computer algebra algorithm to Maple internal format; then, to invoke Maple functions by delivering their parameters and recovering their results in internal format; and lastly, to convert the final results of the algorithm to external, character oriented, format. In this way, the total number of format conversions were minimized.

This separation of Haskell and Maple in different processes simplifies many problems concerning the memory management and the merging of both runtime systems, problems that would have arisen in an alternative approach consisting of running both systems as a single Unix process.

The sequential interface consists of a Haskell fragment and a C fragment. The C part is mainly devoted to invoke Posix services. They are needed to initiate the Maple process, to establish the pipe connections with it, and to send commands to or to receive results from this process. The C part also provides static memory to store Unix objects that must be preserved between calls. These are the file descriptors of the pipes, the process identity of the Maple process, and some buffers and global variables.

The Haskell part provides the interface functions to user programs and implements the communication protocol with the Maple process. It invokes the C functions by using the plain _ccall_ facility of GHC. The main functions a Haskell programmer may use are the following ones:

```
mapleEval       :: String -> [MapleObject] -> MapleObject
mapleEvalN      :: String -> [MapleObject] -> [MapleObject]
string2MapleExpr :: String -> MapleObject
mapleExpr2String :: MapleObject -> String
```

The first two allows Haskell programs to invoke any Maple function just by giving the name and the list of its parameters as Maple objects. The second version must be used to invoke Maple functions returning more than one object. The other two provide conversion of Maple objects from external format to internal one and the other way around. In addition, the Haskell program must make an initial _ccall_ to function **mapleInit**, and a final _ccall_ to function **mapleTerm**.

A Maple object is returned by (must be sent to) Maple as a sequence of bytes. From the interface point of view, type **MapleObject** is defined as a Haskell **ByteArray**, a type now deprecated but available in GHC-4.08. Other deprecated Haskell types used by the interface were **Addr** and **MutableArray**. The type **MapleObject** is exported to user programs as an abstract type.

We acknowledge the big effort and the good ideas contained in this interface. But, from our point of view, this is only half of the way we have to go. Despite the fact that a hybrid Haskell-Maple algorithm is executed by two Unix processes, it is obvious that they will never be concurrently computing in the sense that, while the Maple process is involved in a call, the Haskell process must wait for the result before resuming it own computation, and while the Haskell process is computing, the Maple process must also wait for the next command to arrive. From this perspective, it is not dangerous to call Unix primitives such as `sleep`, `fwrite`, `fgets` or `select` that completely block the calling process.

As we will see in the next sections, a hybrid Eden-Maple algorithm is more complex. In principle, several computers (in what follows we will refer to them as PEs, or *processing elements*) may participate in the computation and so a Maple process should be available in each computer needing to access Maple. Also, several concurrent Eden processes may be instantiated in the same PE. Some of them may need to access Maple and some other not. As we will explain, Eden processes, and Eden threads within a process, are *lightweight*, i.e. they do not correspond to Unix processes. All Eden threads running in the same PE are scheduled from inside a single Unix process. From this point of view, it is not admissible to block the entire Unix process just because a thread is accessing Maple. This will block the rest of the threads, what may lead the whole algorithm to a deadlock.

3   The Parallel Structure of Eden-Maple Algorithms

3.1   Eden

The parallel-functional language Eden extends the lazy functional language Haskell by constructs to explicitly define and communicate processes. The three main new concepts are *process abstractions*, *process instantiations* and the non-deterministic process abstraction `merge`.

A *process abstraction* expression of type `Process a b` defines the behaviour of a process having as input a formal parameter of type `a` and returning as output a result of type `b`. Process abstractions are created by the predefined function `process :: (a -> b) -> Process a b` which converts a function into a process. A process instantiation is achieved by using the predefined infix operator `(#)` :: `Process a b -> a -> b`. The main difference between a process and a function is that the former, when instantiated, is executed in parallel with the rest of the computation.

The evaluation of an expression `e1 # e2` leads to the dynamic creation of a process together with its interconnecting communication channels. The instantiating or *parent process* is responsible for evaluating and sending `e2` via an implicitly generated channel, while the new *child process* first evaluates the expression `e1` until a process abstraction `process (\x -> e)` is obtained and then the application `(\x -> e) e2`, returning the result via another implicitly generated channel. For input tuples, independent concurrent threads are created in the parent to evaluate each component. Also, if the output is a tuple, an independent thread is created in the child to evaluate each component. Once a process is running, only fully evaluated data objects (or lambda abstractions) are communicated. The only exceptions are lists, which are transmitted in a *stream*-like fashion, i.e. element by element. Each list element is first evaluated to full normal form and then transmitted. Concurrent threads trying to access input which is not available yet, are temporarily suspended.

Lazy evaluation is changed to eager evaluation in two cases: Processes are eagerly instantiated, and instantiated processes produce their output even if it is not demanded. These modifications aim at increasing the parallelism degree and at speeding up the distribution of the computation. The rest of the language is as lazy as Haskell.

Non-determinism is introduced in Eden by means of a predefined process abstraction `merge :: Process [[a]] [a]` which *fairly* interleaves a set of input lists, to produce a single non-deterministic list. Its implementation immediately copies to the output list any value appearing at any of the input lists. So, `merge` can profitably be used to quickly react to requests coming in an unpredictable order from a set of processes. This feature is essential in reactive systems and very useful in some deterministic parallel algorithms (see skeleton in Section 5.2).

A last feature are *dynamic reply channels*. The predefined function `new ::` `(ChanName a -> a -> b) -> b` creates a channel of type `a` whose name of type `ChanName a` can be sent to a remote process, and then executes an expression of type `b`. The creating process can receive data from the remote one by trying to evaluate the created channel. The remote one can send a value of type `a` through the channel by using its name and the predefined function `parfill ::` `ChanName a -> a -> c -> c`. This function creates a concurrent thread to send an expression of type `a` through the dynamic channel of type `ChanName a` and then executes an expression of type `c`. As an example, consider the following program where process `one` receives an integer from the remote process `two` by using the dynamic channel `c` of name `cn`:

```
one :: Process Int Int
one = process (\x -> new (\cn c -> let nothing = two # cn in x + c))

two :: Process (ChanName Int) ()
two = process (\cn -> parfill cn 3 ())
```

The Eden runtime system runs on top of the parallel library PVM [14]. This creates a parallel virtual machine by instantiating, previously to run time, a number of PVM processes. A PVM process corresponds to a Unix process and, ideally, only a PVM process should be instantiated in each PE (otherwise the virtual machine would be concurrent rather than parallel). The correspondence between Eden processes and PVM processes is as follows: all PVM processes of the parallel virtual machine contains a copy of the Eden code. Initially, only PVM process 0 has activity by executing the main Eden expression called `main`. The rest of the PVM processes are in a quiescent state. Each time a new Eden process is instantiated by the operator #, their threads are created in a different PVM process which abandons its quiescent state. When/if the number of instantiated Eden processes becomes bigger that the number of PVM processes, then one or more PVM processes will be overloaded with new Eden processes. The threads of all processes within a PVM process are managed by the Eden runtime system. We call this runtime system a *Dream* (*Distributed Eden Abstract Machine*). Summarizing, there is a bijective correspondence between PVM processes and Dreams, a many-to-one correspondence between Eden processes and

Dreams, and a many-to-one correspondence between threads and Eden processes. All threads within a Dream share the same heap but each one has its own stack.

Eden has been successfully used to implement many parallel algorithms using machines with several dozens of processors. Good speedups have been obtained and satisfactory comparisons with other parallel functional languages have been established [5]. A number of skeletons [3] have been defined in Eden to fit most of parallel algorithms [7]. Examples of useful skeletons are: *parallel map, parallel divide and conquer, parallel branch and bound, parallel iterate until, torus and ring topologies, etc.*. A distinguishing feature of Eden is that it gives programmers the possibility to define their own skeletons or to adapt the existing ones to their needs given that skeletons are just Eden programs.

3.2   Algorithms Eden-Maple

As it has been said in the introduction, the idea to parallelize computer algebra algorithms is to use Eden as the coordination language and Maple as the computing language. Eden would be responsible for instantiating processes, communicating them and controlling the global load balancing of the parallel algorithm. Ideally, this should be done in a problem independent way by using or creating a polymorphic higher-order skeleton.

Maple functions would be responsible for doing the intensive algebraic computations. All the problem specific aspects (data types, sequential algorithms, etc.) should be coded into simple Haskell functions calling Maple functions through the interface. These Haskell functions would be used to fit the parameters of the polymorphic skeleton. We believe that this separation of concerns leads to a low-effort parallelization of computer algebra algorithms. In Section 5 we illustrate the methodology with a typical computer algebra problem.

So, in the worst case, a Maple process is needed in each PE. It makes no sense to have several Maple processes in the same PE as only one of them would be computing at a given time. So, we establish a bijective correspondence between PVM processes needing Maple and Maple processes. We will call the Maple process the *companion* process of the corresponding Dream. Two unidirectional pipes will connect each Dream to its companion as in the sequential interface described in Section 2. Figure 1 shows the process topology.

The interface will create the companion process and establish the pipes the first time an Eden thread calls the initialization function, called now `mapleInitPE`. Accordingly, it will kill the companion process when the last thread using Maple calls the termination function, called now `mapleTermPE`.

In order to upgrade the interface to this new environment, the first important change has been to replace the intermediate C functions calling Unix by calls to the Posix package supported by GHC. The following functions are called:

```
forkProcess    :: IO (Maybe ProcessId)
createPipe     :: IO (Fd, Fd)
dupTo          :: Fd -> Fd -> IO ()
executeFile    :: FilePath->Bool->[String]->Maybe [(String,String)]-> IO ()
signalProcess  :: Signal -> ProcessId -> IO ()
```

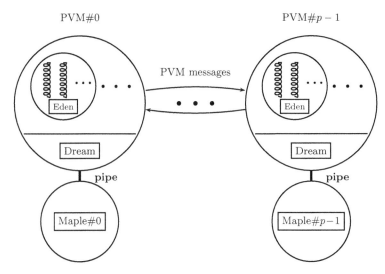

Fig. 1. Process topology of a hybrid Eden-Maple program.

They are responsible for instantiating the companion, establishing the pipe connections, instructing the OS to initialize the companion with a Maple executable, and killing the companion when Maple is no longer needed. However, we refuse to use functions used by the sequential interface such as `fdRead, fdWrite` and `fdClose` which block the calling Unix process. Instead, we lift Unix objects such as `Fd` (file descriptor of a pipe) to Haskell's world by using the conversion

```
fdToHandle :: Fd -> IO Handle
```

and then calling the standard Haskell I/O functions `hGetLine, hPutStrLn` and `hClose` which use a `Handle` as parameter. It must be said that the protocol with the Maple process is line-oriented, although a 'line' may as long a needed. These functions have been designed for a concurrent runtime system and only block the calling thread. Fortunately, the Eden runtime system is an extension of the Concurrent Haskell one [10] and these primitives still work with Eden.

For the same reason, we have replaced calls to Unix `sleep :: Int -> IO ()` by calls to Concurrent Haskell `threadDelay :: Int -> IO ()`.

Altogether, these changes have allowed us to eliminate most of the _ccall_ and a big portion of the C part (the number of C pages has decreased from 11 to only 2 in the new interface), achieving a more compact and legible code.

4   Concurrency Issues Within a Processor

The next group of changes deals with providing mutual exclusion in the access to Maple from different Eden threads. We have established the following protocol for an Eden process `p` to access Maple functionality:

```
p :: Process a b
p = process (\x -> unsafePerformIO $
            do mapleInitPE
               let y = ··· compute result from x using Maple ···
               mapleTermPE 'demanding' rnf y
               return y)
```

The function `rnf` reduces result y to normal form. This one and the `demanding` function are defined in module `Strategies` developed by the creators of GpH (see [16] for details). They are needed to ensure that no calls to Maple are made after the call to `mapleTermPE`, as it would be the case if we allowed the result y to be lazily evaluated.

At runtime, there may be many Eden processes in the same PE following this protocol. So, the first problem to be solved is to initialize the companion Maple process only once, namely when the first call to `mapleInitPE` is received. The rest of the calls to `mapleInitPE` are just counted in order to know how many Eden threads are concurrently using Maple. When calls to `mapleTermPE` are received, the counter is decreased. Only when the counter becomes 0 (meaning that no more threads are using the interface) should the companion process be killed.

To this aim, the interface provides a global variable in C static memory counting the number of threads allowed to use the Maple interface. The same variable is also used to provide a primitive form of mutual exclusion during the transient state in which the first thread is creating the companion process but it is not still available. This may take a noticeable time during which the interface must not allow the remaining threads to proceed.

Once the interface is stable, the second problem is to make calls to Maple functions atomic, i.e. a critical region should be created from the call to the interface up to the returning of results to the user program. We remind the reader that Maple may need a noticeable time to reply to a call because Maple functions are assumed to perform the computation intensive parts of the algorithm.

To solve this problem we rely on Eden dynamic reply channels (see Section 3.1). For each Eden thread calling Maple when the interface is busy, the latter creates a reply channel by using Eden function `new` and blocks the thread on it. When the interface becomes idle again, the first waiting thread is awaked by sending a value through its corresponding channel using the Eden function `parfill`. These synchronizations create the desired critical region around each call. Reply channels must be stored somewhere between calls to the interface, so they are kept in C static memory. Conversions between Haskell objects and C data types are done through the facilities of GHC's `Ptr` library:

```
newStablePtr   :: a -> IO (StablePtr a)
deRefStablePtr :: StablePtr a -> IO a
freeStablePtr  :: StablePtr a -> IO ()
```

We have also developed an alternative mutual exclusion mechanism by using the Concurrent Haskell `MVar` [10]. A nonempty `MVar` is created by the interface at initialization time by using the function `newMVar`. Critical regions are created by executing `takeMvar` at the beginning of each Maple call, and `putMVar` at the end. This is transparent to the programmer: the MVar is created by the interface and stored in static memory between calls; calls to takeMvar and putMVar are done from inside the interface. Concurrent Haskell MVar works properly with Eden runtime system. The interface version with MVar could of course be used by Concurrent Haskell programs.

The part of the interface devoted to the proper shyncronization of the concurrent calls has been the more involved, and is responsible for half of the code.

5   Case Study: Gröbner Bases

5.1   The Sequential Algorithm

Gröbner bases computation is a very well-known algorithm for computer algebra researchers. Gröbner bases have plenty of applications in commutative algebra, geometry and systems theory. The problem can be explained in the following terms: Given a finite set of polynomials $F = \{f_1, \ldots, f_s\}$ in n indeterminates $x_1, \ldots, x_n$, a Gröbner basis is another finite set of polynomials $G = \{g_1, \ldots, g_t\}$ determining the same ideal and satisfying an additional canonical property.

The ideal I determined by a set S of polynomials, denoted $I = \langle S \rangle$ is the smallest set containing S and closed under polynomial addition and product:

$$\langle S \rangle \stackrel{\text{def}}{=} \{ \sum_{f_i \in S} u_i f_i \mid u_i \in P[x_1, \ldots, x_n] \}$$

being $P[x_1, \ldots, x_n]$ the set of all polynomials in n indeterminates.

Given an ideal I determined by a finite set F of polynomials, there exists an algorithm due to B. Buchberger [1] which computes a Gröbner basis G for I starting from F. It is shown in Figure 2. It makes intensive use of two elementary steps: computing to so called called S-polynomial of two polynomials f and g, denoted $S(f, g)$, and the *reduction* of a polynomial r to normal form h with respect to a set G of polynomials, denoted $r \xrightarrow{G} * h$ If G is finite, being s its

```
function Buchberger (F = {f₁,...,fₛ}) return G
    G := F;  P := {(fᵢ, fⱼ) | fᵢ, fⱼ ∈ F, i ≠ j};
    while P ≠ ∅ do
        (f, g) ← chooseAPair (P);  P := P − {(f, g)}
        S(f, g) ─G→ * h such that h is reduced w.r.t. G
        if h ≠ 0 then
            P := P ∪ {(u, h) | u ∈ G};
            G := G ∪ {h}
        end if
    end while
    return G
end function
```

Fig. 2. Buchberger's sequential algorithm computing a Gröbner basis.

cardinality, the algorithm for computing $r \xrightarrow{G} * h$ is quadratic. More precisely, it belongs to $O(ms)$ in the worst case, being m the length of the maximum strictly decreasing chain of power products that can be constructed starting with the leading term of f. This, in turn, is related to the degree of f and the number n of indeterminates. The cost of computing $S(f, g)$ is in $O(n)$.

It has been proved that the algorithm always terminates and that its cost is in $O(msp)$, where m, s are as before – now, they are considered to be worst case values for the polynomials and the cardinality of G –, and p is the number of pairs in the final G. The value of p is *a priori* unknown and depends on the form of the initial polynomials in F. In the worst case, p can be exponential on the cardinality of F.

Maple systems usually provide a sub-library to compute Gröbner bases. But they also provide the elementary steps of the algorithm as individual functions. In particular, there exists a function called `spoly` computing the S-polynomial of two given polynomials, and a function called `normalf` computing the reduction of a polynomial to normal form with respect to a set of polynomials.

5.2   The Stateful Replicated Workers Skeleton

As we (as Eden programmers) are not interested in doing polynomial crunching in Haskell, the idea for the parallel version of Buchberger's algorithm is to leave in Maple the computation of $S(f, g) \xrightarrow{G} * h$ and to compute this reduction to normal form in parallel for different pairs (f, g). The order in which such pairs are chosen is not important for the correctness and the termination of the algorithm, so they can safely be done in parallel. The granularity of such computation is large enough to justify the communication of the polynomials f and g. So, the strategy chosen is to have a *manager* process communicating pairs (f, g) to a fixed set of *worker* processes, and getting back the results h of such reductions. If the result is 0, the manager just moves to the next pair. If it is different from 0, the manager computes additional pairs which are joined to the list of pending pairs.

In Eden we have developed several versions of a skeleton called *replicated workers* [6], which fits this idea of a manager process distributing work to a fixed number of workers. The main interesting property of the skeleton is that it achieves a very good load balancing as work is distributed to workers on demand: as soon as a worker finishes a task, it is fed with a new one, if there is one available. So, it may be the case that a worker solves a few big granularity tasks, while another one solves many small granularity tasks.

We have adapted one version of the replicated workers skeleton to fulfill the following new needs:

1. Worker processes must maintain an internal state. Notice that workers must reduce a pair (f, g) with respect to a polynomial set G which is changing along time.
2. There must be provisions to update from time to time workers' internal state.

```
strw  :: (Trans tsk, Trans act, Trans res, Trans wl) =>
        Int ->                                -- no. of PE
        Int ->                                -- buffer size
        (inp -> Int -> ([wl],[tsk],ml)) ->    -- split function
        (wl -> tsk -> [act] -> (res,wl)) ->   -- worker function
        (ml -> res -> Int -> ([[act]],[tsk],ml)) -> -- combine function
        (ml -> result) ->                     -- result function
        inp ->                                -- skeleton input
        result                                -- skeleton result

strw np prefetch split wf combine rf inp =  r
 where
  (iniwls,iniTasks,iniml)   = split inp np
  outss                     = [process (worker i wf) #  (wl,actsks) |
                               (i,wl,actsks)<-zip3 [0..np-1] iniwls actskss]
                               'using' spine
  unorderedResults          = merge # outss
  (moreReqs,results)        = unzip unorderedResults
  (moreTks,asss,moreGns,r)  = manager np combine rf iniml results
  iniReqs                   = concat (replicate prefetch [0..np-1])
  iniGens                   = concat (replicate prefetch (replicate np 0))
  tasks                     = iniTasks ++ moreTks
  actskss                   = distribute np 0 (length iniTasks)
                               (replicate np 0) tasks asss
                               (zip iniReqs (repeat 0)++zip moreReqs [1..])
                               (iniGens ++ moreGns)
```

Fig. 3. The Eden skeleton `strw` of *Stateful Replicated Workers.*

3. The manager has also an internal state updatable as a consequence of a worker result.
4. The algorithm output depends on the final state reached to by the manager.

We call the resulting skeleton *stateful replicated workers*, abbreviated `strw`. This insistence in developing first a problem independent skeleton and then instantiating it with problem dependent parameters is just a separation of concerns strategy common to all areas of software development. In doing so, we concentrate first on the parallel nature of the problem, i.e. on the process topology and the load balancing issues of the algorithm and then, as a separate activity, on problem specific issues. There are also advantages in the testing phase: first we test the skeleton with a toy problem and, once the skeleton is properly working, we feed it with the (more complex) Gröbner basis computation problem.

Figure 3 shows the type and the implementation of `strw` in Eden. We begin by explaining the type. Eden type class `Trans` includes all types which can be transmitted in messages. Essentially, they are those for which a normal form can be computed. The first two parameters are the number of workers to be created by the skeleton and the size of the prefetch buffer. We usually create a worker per PE and leave the manager process to share a PE with one of the workers.

The load on the manager is low and it does not justify a complete PE for it. The worker sharing its PE with the manager will do less work than the others, but this is not important as PE loads are dynamically balanced by the manager. The prefecth buffer size is the number of tasks initially assigned to each worker. We usually choose this parameter to be 2 so that, when a worker finishes the current task asking for a new one, and while this one arrives, it may work on the task in the buffer. As a consequence, workers idle times are minimized.

The next four parameters are the problem dependent functions delivered to the skeleton. The `split` function is initially called by the skeleton to get the initial state of each worker, the initial set of tasks and the initial state of the manager. It receives as parameters the input data `inp` of the skeleton, and the number `np` of workers. The worker function `wf` is called by the skeleton to solve each individual task. It receives as parameters the current state of the worker, the task to be solved, and a list of pending updates. It delivers a result and an updated internal state. The manager is responsible for accumulating the pending updates for each individual worker. The updates are generated as a consequence of results received from other workers in the meantime while the worker is solving a task. The `combine` function receives the manager internal state, a worker's result and the number `np` of workers, and computes three results: a list of updates, one for each worker, a list of new tasks, and a new internal state for the manager. The internal list in the type `[[act]]` is used as a `Maybe` type: an empty list means no update; otherwise, the list contains a single update for the worker. The `combine` function is called by the skeleton each time a worker's result is received. Finally, the result function `rf` is called at the end of skeleton's execution to compute the output of the algorithm from the final internal state of the manager.

The implementation of `strw` presents the aspect of a set of mutually recursive definitions. These are needed to establish a circular communication topology between the manager and the workers. The communication channels are essentially lists: a worker receives a list of tuples, each one containing a list of pending updates and a task, while the manager receives a list of unordered results coming from the workers. The results are received in the temporal order in which they are produced. To achieve this goal, it is essential the application of the reactive process `merge` to the list of lists `outss` of outputs produced by the workers. Strategy `spine` is used to eagerly instantiate the worker processes.

Perhaps the most important auxiliary function of the skeleton is `distribute` whose details are shown in Figure 4. Its purposes are:

1. To detect when a worker has finished a task and to assign it a new one.
2. To compute the list of pending updates for each individual worker and to include it together with the new assigned task.
3. To detect the termination of the skeleton. To this aim, it controls the number `ngen` of tasks generated by the skeleton, the number `ndis` of tasks distributed to workers, and the number `nrec` of results received from workers. The termination condition is `ngen == ndis && ndis == nrec`.

```
distribute :: Int -> Int -> Int -> [Int] -> [tsk] -> [[[act]]] ->
              [(Int,Int)] -> [Int] -> [[([act],tsk)]]
distribute np ndis ngen cs ts asss ((i,nrec):is) (n:ns)
 |ngen' == ndis && ndis == nrec = replicate np []
 |ngen' == ndis && ndis > nrec = distribute np ndis ngen' cs ts asss is ns
 where ngen' = ngen + n
distribute np ndis ngen cs (t:ts) asss ((i,nrec):is) (n:ns) =
 insert i (as,t) (distribute np (ndis+1) (ngen+n) cs' ts asss' is ns)
 where ndif                 = nrec - cs !! i
       (ass1,ass2)          = splitAt ndif (asss !! i)
       as                   = concat ass1
       cs'                  = replace i nrec cs
       asss'                = replace i ass2 asss
       replace 0     e ~(x:xs) = e : xs
       replace (n+1) e ~(x:xs) = x : replace n e xs
       insert 0 e ~(x:xs)      = (e:x) : xs
       insert (n+1) e ~(x:xs ) = x : insert n e xs
```

Fig. 4. Distribution function of skeleton `strw`.

5.3 The Problem Dependent Functions

First, we instantiate the polymorphic types of the skeleton for our problem:

$$
\begin{aligned}
\text{inp} &\overset{\text{def}}{=} \{f_1, \ldots, f_s\} \subseteq P[x_1, \ldots, x_n] \\
\text{wl} &\overset{\text{def}}{=} G \subseteq P[x_1, \ldots, x_n] \\
\text{tsk} &\overset{\text{def}}{=} (f, g) \in P[x_1, \ldots, x_n] \times P[x_1, \ldots, x_n] \\
\text{ml} &\overset{\text{def}}{=} G \subseteq P[x_1, \ldots, x_n] \\
\text{res} &\overset{\text{def}}{=} [\,], [h] \in List\ (P[x_1, \ldots, x_n]) \\
\text{act} &\overset{\text{def}}{=} h \in P[x_1, \ldots, x_n] \\
\text{result} &\overset{\text{def}}{=} G \subseteq P[x_1, \ldots, x_n]
\end{aligned}
$$

By looking at the sequential algorithm of Figure 2, it is straightforward to define the four problem dependent functions. We give them in a schematic way as the coded version would exhibit more (non essential) details:

$$
\text{split}\ F\ np \overset{\text{def}}{=} (\overbrace{[F, \ldots, F]}^{np}, [(f_i, f_j) \mid f_i, f_j \in F, i \neq j], F)
$$

$$
\text{wf}\ G\ (f, g)\ [h_1, \ldots, h_r] \overset{\text{def}}{=} (\text{res}, G') \quad \text{where}
$$

$$
G' = G \cup \{h_1, \ldots, h_r\}
$$

$$
\text{res} = \begin{cases} [\,] & \text{, if } S(f, g) \xrightarrow{G'}* 0 \\ [h] & \text{, if } S(f, g) \xrightarrow{G'}* h \neq 0 \end{cases}
$$

$$\text{combine } G \text{ res np} \stackrel{\text{def}}{=} (\overbrace{[\text{res}, \ldots, \text{res}]}^{\text{np}}, \text{tsks}, G') \quad \text{where}$$

$$(\text{tsks}, G') = \begin{cases} ([\,], G) & , \text{if res} = [\,] \\ ([(u, h) \mid u \in G], G \cup \{h\}) & , \text{if res} = [h] \end{cases}$$

$$\text{result } G \qquad \stackrel{\text{def}}{=} G$$

The worker function $\texttt{wf}$ does its work by delegating to Maple the computation of $S(f, g) \xrightarrow{G'} * h$. To this aim, it calls through the interface the Maple functions $\texttt{spoly}$ and $\texttt{normalf}$, respectively computing the S-polynomial of f and g and its reduction to normal form with respect to the updated set of polynomials G'.

In order to initialize and to finalize the interface, skeleton $\texttt{strw}$ has been slightly modified. On the one hand, the predefined function $\texttt{process}$ called in line 4 of $\texttt{strw}$ definition in Figure 3, has been replaced by function $\texttt{mapleProcess}$ defined as follows:

```
mapleProcess :: (Trans a, Trans b) => (a -> b) -> Process a b
mapleProcess f = process (\x -> unsafePerformIO $
                 do mapleInitPE
                    let res = f x
                    return res)
```

On the other hand, the first line of the definition of function $\texttt{worker}$, which represents the termination of the worker process, has been replaced by the following fragment:

```
worker i wf (local,[]) = unsafePerformIO $ do mapleTermPE
                                              return []
```

These modifications do not exactly match the process scheme at the beginning of Section 4. The reason has to do with preserving the laziness of the lists produced by the workers. Should we add to $\texttt{mapleProcess}$ a line $\texttt{mapleTermPE}$ 'demanding' $\texttt{rnf res}$ before $\texttt{return res}$, the entire skeleton would become blocked (in fact, we have 'seen' this deadlock while debugging the skeleton). The interface must be closed when worker's output list has been completely produced.

5.4   Performance Results

We have run all the pieces together – the skeleton, the problem dependent functions and the Eden-Maple interface – in a home-made Beowulf cluster with five processors at 233 Mhz CPU and 64 Mb RAM, running *i386-mandrake 7.2-linux*, Eden compiler *mec-5.02.3*, *Maple 7*, and *PVM 3.4*. The final Gröbner basis had 33 polynomials with a worst case of 4 indeterminates and a leading term of degree 8. A total of 528 tasks were generated and the absolute sequential time of the pure Maple algorithm was 212 sec. The speedups obtained can be seen in Figure 5. We have got an absolute speedup of 3.72 with 5 processors with respect to the pure Maple sequential version, and a rather good relative speedup of 4.91 with respect to the parallel version running on one processor. This one is already

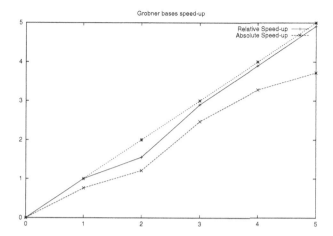

Fig. 5. Absolute and relative speedups for Grobner basis using `strw`.

32% slower than the reference Maple version, so better absolute speedups cannot be expected. This 32% overhead is due to having two Unix processes communicated by pipes, to the format conversions and to the Eden runtime system. All this machinery is absent in the Maple version.

So, we do not claim that parallelizing Maple using Eden is optimal compared to other approaches. In [13] a survey of many other strategies to parallelizing Maple programs can be found. All of them require some extra programming effort for splitting the work into parallel tasks, assigning tasks to processors or/and sending explicit messages between tasks. Perhaps [13] is one of the most implicit programming models we have found but, nevertheless, it requires new Maple primitives for launching remote tasks and for waiting for results. Our claim is that parallelizing with Eden is *easier* compared to more explicit approaches and, however that, *acceptable* speedups (as opposed to optimal ones) can be obtained.

The scalability of the replicated workers skeleton is good up to around 20 processors, depending on the concrete problem (see [7]). For a bigger number of processors the manager process becomes a bottleneck and the speedup decreases. We plan to do more complete masurements in the near future.

6   Conclusions

The first contribution of the paper is the engineering effort of developing the interface. In doing this work, we have put into action many different technologies. Firstly, we have achieved that two systems so distant from each other such as Maple and Eden may work together in a single problem. Also, while building the interface, we have made use of GHC libraries such as Posix, Ptr, Concurrent Haskell functions and Glasgow Parallel Haskell Strategies. Standard Haskell input/output with handles has also found its place in the interface. Finally, we have needed some knowledge of Unix functions, on how to interface Haskell to C, and on how to set up PVM.

With respect to the original sequential interface, the changes has been of three types: a) eliminating the old types and libraries in order to port the code to the new version of GHC; b) replacing primitives blocking the Unix process by primitives blocking only the current thread; and c) introducing several kinds of locks and synchronization primitives in order to cope with concurrent calls to the interface. As a whole, less than 10% of the original code remains.

The second contribution has been the parallelization of a non trivial computer algebra algorithm and showing that all the pieces, Eden, Maple and the interface, fit together. Now that the interface is running, we hope to reinforce our links with the computer algebra department of our university and to be able to parallelize some of their interesting algorithms. The proposed strategy is the cooperation between functional and computer algebra groups. Functional people would be responsible for understanding the sequential algorithm and for providing the appropriate Eden skeleton, while algebra people would implement the problem dependent functions of the skeleton and the Maple side of the algorithm.

Acknowledgments

We appreciate again the work made by Wolfgang Schreiner and Hans-Wolgang Loidl in their sequential interface. We are also grateful to our Marburg colleagues Rita Loogen, Jost Berthold and Nils Weskcamp for upgrading the Eden compiler to GHC 5.02 and for answering our numerous questions.

References

1. W. W. Adams and P. Loustaunau. *An Introduction to Gröbner Bases*. American Mathematical Society, 1994.
2. S. Breitinger, R. Loogen, Y. Ortega-Mallén, and R. Peña. Eden: Language Definition and Operational Semantics. Technical Report, Bericht 96-10. Revised version 1.998, Philipps-Universität Marburg, Germany, 1998.
3. M. Cole. *Algorithmic Skeletons: Structured Management of Parallel Computation*. Research monographs in parallel and distributed computing. Pitman, 1989.
4. J. Darlington, Y. K Guo, H. W. To, and J. Yang. Functional Skeletons for Parallel Coordination. In *Proceedings of Europar*, volume 996, pages 55–69. Springer-Varlag, 1995.
5. W. Loidl H, F. Rubio, N. Scaife, K. Hammond, S. Horiguchi, U. Klusik, R. Loogen, G. J. Michaelson, R. Peña, A. J. Rebón Portillo, S. Priebe, and P. Trinder. Comparing Parallel Functional Languages: Programming and Performance. *Higher-Order and Symbolic Computation*, 16(3):203–251, 2003.
6. U. Klusik, R. Peña, and F. Rubio. Replicated Workers in Eden. In *Constructive Methods for Parallel Programming (CMPP'2000)*. Nova Science, 2002.
7. R. Loogen, Y. Ortega-Mallén, R. Peña, S. Priebe, and F. Rubio. *Patterns and Skeletons for Parallel and Distributed Computing*. F. Rabhi and S. Gorlatch (eds.), chapter *Parallelism Abstractions in Eden*, pages 95–128. Springer-Verlag, 2002.

8. R. Nicolaides and N. Walkington. *MAPLE, A Comprehensive Introduction.* Cambridge University Press, 1996.
9. S. Pelagatti. *Structured Development of Parallel Programs.* Taylor and Francis, 1998.
10. S. L. Peyton Jones, A. Gordon, and S. Finne. Concurrent Haskell. In *ACM Symp. on Principles of Prog. Lang. POPL'96.* ACM Press, 1996.
11. S. L. Peyton Jones, C. V. Hall, K. Hammond, W. D. Partain, and P. L. Wadler. The Glasgow Haskell Compiler: A Technical Overview. In *Joint Framework for Inf. Technology, Keele*, pages 249–257, 1993.
12. W. Schreiner and H.-W. Loidl. GHC-Maple Interface, version 0.1. Available at http://www.risc.uni-linz.ac.at/software/ghc-maple/, 2000.
13. W. Schreiner, C. Mittermaier, and K. Bosa. Distributed Maple: Parallel Computer Algebra in Networked Environments. Preprint submitted to the Journal of Symbolic Computation, 2002.
14. V. S. Sunderam. PVM: A framework for parallel distributed computing. *Concurrency: practice and experience*, 2(4):315–339, 1990.
15. P. W. Trinder, K. Hammond, J. S. Mattson Jr., and A. S. Partridge. GUM: a Portable Parallel Implementation of Haskell. In *ACM SIGPLAN PLDI, Philadelphia, USA.* ACM Press, May 1996.
16. P. W. Trinder, K. Hammond, H. W. Loidl, and S. L. Peyton Jones. Algorithm + Strategy = Parallelism. *Journal of Functional Programming*, 8(1), 1998.

Generic Graphical User Interfaces

Peter Achten, Marko van Eekelen, and Rinus Plasmeijer

Department of Software Technology, University of Nijmegen, The Netherlands
{peter88,marko,rinus}@cs.kun.nl

Abstract. It is important to be able to program GUI applications in a
fast and easy manner. Current GUI tools for creating visually attractive
applications offer limited functionality. In this paper we introduce a new,
easy to use method to program GUI applications in a pure functional
language such as Clean or Generic Haskell. The method we use is a refined
version of the model-view paradigm.
The basic component in our approach is the Graphical Editor Component
(GEC_τ) that can contain *any* value of *any* flat data type τ and that can
be freely used to display and edit its value. GEC_τs can depend on others,
but also on themselves. They can even be mutually dependent. With
these components we can construct a flexible, reusable and customizable
editor. For the realization of the components we had to invent a new
generic implementation technique for interactive applications.

1 Introduction

Making an attractive Graphical User Interface (GUI) for an application is not
an easy task. One can of course use the GUI library offered by the operating
system (Windows, Mac, Linux). These GUI libraries are powerful (they determine
what is possible on a particular OS), but the offered level of abstraction is in
general rather low. Therefore, most people will prefer to use a visual editor as
offered by many commercial programming environments. Such tools are very
user friendly at the expense of offering limited functionality. One still has to
combine the graphical elements made with the visual editor with the program
code for handling the actual GUI events. Inherently, graphical representations
that depend on run-time data cannot be drawn in advance. Summarizing, a
visual editor is a good tool for certain simple GUI applications, but for more
complicated ones one still has to struggle with low level programming code.

For dealing with more complicated applications in a simpler way, we want to
define GUIs on a higher level of abstraction. Modern, pure functional programming languages enable the definition and construction of high abstraction levels.
The Object I/O library [1] is probably the largest GUI library available for pure
functional languages. GUI applications can be defined in Object I/O in a platform independent way. The Object I/O library has been defined in Clean and is
currently available for Windows and MacOSX. A subset has been ported to Linux
[11]. Object I/O has been ported to Haskell by Peter Achten and Simon Peyton
Jones [2] and Krasimir Angelov [4]. Recently, it has become possible to combine

P. Trinder, G. Michaelson, and R. Peña (Eds.): IFL 2003, LNCS 3145, pp. 152–167, 2004.
© Springer-Verlag Berlin Heidelberg 2004

Haskell programs with Clean programs [12, 10]. Hence, in various ways Object I/O is nowadays available for a large community of pure functional programmers.

In Clean, impressive GUI applications have been made using Object I/O: e.g. the Clean IDE (including a text editor and a project manager), 2D-platform games, and the proof assistant Sparkle. The latter application in particular demonstrates the expressive power of Object I/O.

We have experienced that GUI elements such as dialogs, menus, and simple windows are relatively easy to define on a high level of abstraction. An application like the proof assistant Sparkle requires much more knowledge of the Object I/O primitives. In Sparkle [9], an action in one window (e.g. the completion of the proof of a theorem) has many consequences for the information displayed in the other windows (e.g. the list of completed theorems). Sparkle in this respect resembles the behavior of applications that are made with the well-known *model-view* paradigm [18]. The message passing primitives of Object I/O can handle such a complicated information flow. However, the learning curve to program such complicated mutual influences is rather steep.

Clearly, we need better tools to construct GUI applications on a high level of abstraction. However, we require that these tools are not as restrictive as standard GUI builders. Furthermore, we want to be able to create GUI applications in a versatile way. On the one hand it must be easy to combine standard components and on the other hand these components should be easily customized to adapt to our wishes.

In this paper we fulfill this need by introducing a new way for constructing GUI elements that respond to the change of other GUI elements. Proper customization requires a rigid separation of value versus visualization, and has lead to a refined version of the model-view paradigm (but note that at this moment only one view is supported). The basic idea is the concept of a Graphical Editor Component (a GEC_τ) with which one can display and edit values of *any* flat[1] type τ. Any change in a value is directly passed to all other GECs that depend on the changed value. Using generic programming techniques, a GEC_τ for a concrete (user defined) type τ can be generated automatically. Apart from defining the data type and customization definitions almost no additional programming effort is needed. For applications in which the particular *look* is less of an issue, it is even sufficient to provide only the data type. This makes it an excellent tool for *rapid prototyping*. All low level communication that is required to accomplish the information flow between the graphical elements, is taken care of by the system. The proposed technique is *universal, customizable* and *compositional*. Moreover, it is a novel application of generic programming [13, 8].

In Sect. 2 we present the basic idea of a GEC_τ. Sect. 3 shows how these GEC_τs can be combined to construct more complicated GUIs. In Sect. 4 we reveal how a GEC_τ is implemented using generic programming techniques. Sect. 5 explains how a GEC_τ can be customized to display its components in an alternative way. Thereafter, we will discuss related work. Finally, we draw conclusions and point out future work.

---

[1] A *flat* type is a type that does not contain any function types.

2   The Concept of a Graphical Editor Component

We want to be able to make complicated GUI applications with minimal programming effort. The basic building block of our method is a customizable Graphical Editor Component (GEC_τ), which we can generate automatically for any flat type τ. More precisely, a GEC_τ is a generated function that contains a value of type τ and creates a visual component that:

1. can be used by a programmer to automatically display *any* value of type τ;
2. can be used by the application user to view and edit a value of type τ;
3. can be customized by a programmer such that its elements can be displayed in an alternative way;
4. can communicate any value change made by the user or by the program to any other component that depends on that change.

It is important to note that a GEC_τ is a very general component: in languages such as Clean and Haskell, every expression represents a value of a certain type. Since a GEC_τ can display any value of type τ, it can also be used to display any object (expression) of that type. Each GEC_τ is completely tailored to its type τ. It guarantees that each value edited is well-typed.

2.1   Interactive Functional Programming

Before continuing, we have to make a few remarks for people unfamiliar with functions that perform I/O in Clean. (Generic programming in Clean is explained in Sect. 4.1.) Object I/O uses an explicit environment passing style [1] supported by the uniqueness type system [5] of Clean. Consequently, any function that does something with I/O (like mkGEC in Sect. 2.2) is an explicit state transition function working on a program state (PSt st) returning at least a new program state. (In this paper the identifier env will be a value of this type.) The uniqueness type system of Clean will ensure single threaded use of such a state. In the Haskell variant of Object I/O, a state monad is used instead. Uniqueness type attributes that actually appear in the type signatures are not shown in this paper, in order to simplify the presentation.

2.2   Creating GEC_τs

In this section we explain in general terms what the generic function to create GEC_τs, mkGEC, does. In the next section we will show how mkGEC can be used to connect different GEC_τs.

In order to create a GEC_τ one only has to apply the generic function mkGEC which has the following type:

```
generic mkGEC t :: [GECAttribute] t (CallBackFunction t (PSt ps)) (PSt ps)
                                    ->² (GEC t (PSt ps), PSt ps)

:: CallBackFunction t env :== t -> env -> env
```

---

² The Clean type a b -> c is equivalent to the Haskell type a -> b -> c.

Hence, in order to call mkGEC the following arguments have to be provided:

- a GECAttribute list controlling behavioral aspects. In this paper we restrict it to two data constructors: OutputOnly and BelowPrev,
- an initial value of type t,
- a call-back function defined by the programmer that will be called automatically each time the value of type t is edited by the user or by the program,
- the current unique state of the program.

The function mkGEC returns

- a record (GEC) containing methods that can be used to handle the newly created GEC_t component for type t, and
- the new unique program state (as usual for I/O handling functions in Clean).

```
:: GEC t env = { gecGetValue :: env -> (t,env)
              , gecSetValue :: t -> env -> env
              }
```

The GEC record that is returned contains several other useful methods for a program that are not shown above. These are methods to open and close the created GEC_τ or to show or hide its appearance. For application programmers the methods gecGetValue and gecSetValue are the most interesting. The method gecGetValue can be used to obtain from the GEC_τ component the currently stored value of type τ. The method gecSetValue can be used to *set* a *new* value in the corresponding GEC_τ.

When the user of the application changes the content of a GEC_τ, the corresponding call-back function will be automatically called with the new value. This call-back function can be used to store new values in other GEC_τs using the gecSetValue method of these GEC_τs as will be demonstrated in Sect. 3.

The appearance of a standard GEC_τ is illustrated by the following example. Assume that the programmer has defined the type Tree a as shown below and consider the following application of mkGEC:

```
:: Tree a = Node (Tree a) a (Tree a) | Leaf
```

```
mkGEC [] (Node Leaf 1 Leaf) identity³ env
```

This defines a window containing the $GEC_{\texttt{Tree Int}}$ displaying the indicated initial value (see Fig. 1). The application user can edit this initial value in any desired order thus producing new values of type Tree Int. Each time a new value is created, the call-back function identity is called automatically. In this example this has no effect (but see Sect. 3). The shape and lay-out of the tree being displayed adjusts itself automatically. Default values are made up by the editor when needed.

Notice that a GEC_τ is strongly typed. Only well-typed values of type τ can be created with a GEC_τ. Therefore, with a $GEC_{\texttt{Tree Int}}$ the user can only create

---

[3] In several examples identity will be used as a synonym for const id.

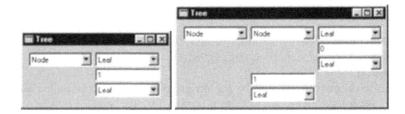

Fig. 1. The initial Graphical Editor Component for a tree of integers (Left) and a changed one (Right: with the pull-down menu the upper `Leaf` is changed into a `Node`).

values of type `Tree Int`. If the user makes a mistake, for instance by typing an arbitrary string into the integer box, the previous displayed integer value is restored. Any created editor also includes many other features for free, such as: automatic scroll facilities, an automatic hint box showing the type of any displayed item, and the option to hide and show any part of a data structure. All of this is generated completely given a type τ.

3   Combining Graphical Editor Components

In this section we will give some small examples how GEC_τs can be combined. A simple combination scheme is the following. If one GEC_τ B depends on a change made in a GEC_σ A, then one can pass GEC_τ B to the call-back function of A. Each time A is changed, its call-back function is called automatically and as a reaction it can set a new value in B by applying a function of type $\sigma \rightarrow \tau$. Below, conform this scheme, two such GEC_τs are created in the function `apply2GECs` such that the call-back function of GEC_A employs GEC_B.

```
apply2GECs :: (a -> b) a (PSt ps) -> (PSt ps)
apply2GECs f va env
    #⁴ (GEC_B, env) = mkGEC []                        (f va)  identity    env
    #  (GEC_A, env) = mkGEC [OutputOnly,BelowPrev]  va      (set GEC_B f) env
    = env

set⁵ :: (GEC b (PSt ps)) (a -> b) a (PSt ps) -> (PSt ps)
set gec f nva env = gec.gecSetValue (f nva) env
```

With these definitions, `apply2GECs toBalancedTree [1,5,2,8,3,9]` env, results in two GEC_τs. One for a `[Int]`, and one for a `Tree Int`. Assuming that `toBalancedTree` is a function that transforms a list into a balanced tree, any change made by the user to the displayed list[6] will automatically result

---

[4] The `#`-notation of Clean has a special scope rule such that the same variable name can be used for subsequent non-recursive `#`-definitions.

[5] This function `set` will also be used in other examples.

[6] A Clean list is internally represented with the constructors _Nil and _Cons.

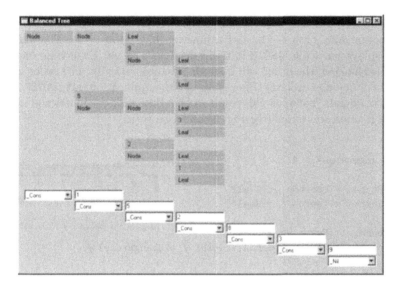

Fig. 2. A window that contains a non-editable $GEC_{\text{Tree Int}}$ which shows the effect of applying the function `toBalancedTree` after any user editing performed on $GEC_{[\text{Int}]}$.

into a corresponding re-balanced tree being displayed (see Fig. 2). In order to emphasize the functional dependency of the tree editor, it can not be edited by the user (controlled by the `GECAttribute OutputOnly`.)

As this example demonstrates, combining GEC_τs is very easy. One GEC_τ can have an effect on arbitrary many GEC_τs including itself! Consider:

```
selfGEC :: (a -> a) a (PSt ps) -> (PSt ps)
selfGEC f va env = new_env
where⁷ (thisGEC,new_env) = mkGEC [] (f va) (set thisGEC f) env
```

Initially, this function displays the effect of applying a given function `f` to a given value `va` of type `a`. Any change a user makes using the editor automatically causes a re-evaluation of `f` to the new value thus created. Consequently, `f` has to be a function of type $a \to a$. For example, one can use `selfGEC` to display and edit a balanced tree. Now, each time the tree is edited, it will re-balance *itself*. Notice that, due to the explicit environment passing style, it is trivial in Clean to connect a GEC_τ to itself. In Haskell's monadic I/O one needs to tie the knot with `fixIO`.

In a similar way one can define mutually dependent GEC_τs. Take the following definition of `mutualGEC`.

```
mutualGEC :: a (a -> b) (b -> a) (PSt ps) -> (PSt ps)
mutualGEC va a2b b2a env = env2
where (GEC_B,env1) = mkGEC []          (a2b va) (set GEC_A b2a) env
      (GEC_A,env2) = mkGEC [BelowPrev]     va   (set GEC_B a2b) env1
```

---

⁷ The #-notation can not be used here since the definition of `selfGEC` is recursive.

This function displays two GEC_τs. It is given an initial value va of type a, a function a2b :: a → b, and a function b2a :: b → a. The GEC A initially displays va, while GEC B initially displays a2b va. Each time one of the GEC_τs is changed, the other will be updated automatically. The order in which changes are made is irrelevant. For example, the application mutualGEC {euros = 3.5} toPounds toEuros will result in an editor that calculates the exchange between pounds and euros (see Fig. 3) and vice versa.

```
exchangerate = 1.4

:: Pounds = {pounds :: Real}
:: Euros  = {euros  :: Real}

toPounds :: Euros -> Pounds
toPounds {euros} = {pounds = euros / exchangerate}

toEuros :: Pounds -> Euros
toEuros {pounds} = {euros = pounds * exchangerate}
```

Fig. 3. Mutually dependent GEC_{Pounds} and GEC_{Euros} in one window.

The example of Fig. 3 may look a bit like a tiny spreadsheet, but it is essentially different since standard spreadsheets don't allow mutual dependencies between cells. Notice also the separation of concerns: the way GEC_τs are coupled is defined completely separate from the actual functionality.

4   Implementation Design of GEC_τs

Although the implementation of the system is not very big (1800 loc for the implementation modules, including comments and tracing statements) it is not possible to describe all relevant implementation aspects in this paper. We restrict ourselves to the key aspects of the design.

4.1   Generic Functions

Recently, generic functions have been added to Clean [3]. A generic function is an ultimate reusable function that allows reflection on the structure of any data in a type safe way. It is not a single function, but actually a special kind of overloaded function. One might be tempted by the idea to design some suitable universal type, and define generic functions on values of this type, and convert the changed value back to the actual type. However, it is a fundamental property of the language that (without some kind of reflection) there cannot exist a single universal type with which values of any type can be represented.

Instead, the types used by generic function definitions approximate the universal type idea. They do not constitute a single type but a *family of types*. Each concrete user defined type is represented by a different combination of members of this generic type family. Such a particular representation by itself has a type that depends on the combination of values of the generic types that is used.

Hence, to define a generic function, instances have to be defined for a finite number of types, the *generic types*, out of which any value of any type in the language can be constructed.

```
:: Unit        = Unit
:: Either a b = Left a | Right b
:: Pair a b    = Pair a b
:: TypeCons a = TypeCons InfoT a
:: DataCons a = DataCons InfoC a
```

The generic types consist of the basic types (`Bool`, `Int`, `Real`, ..., which are used to represent themselves), `Unit` (to represent a zero arity data constructor), `Pair` (product type, used to combine arguments of data constructors), and `Either` (the sum type to indicate which data constructor of a certain type is used). Furthermore, there are two special additional types `TypeCons` and `DataCons`. They contain additional information (in `InfoT` and `InfoC`) about the name and arity of the original type and data constructors. This is useful for making generic functions that can parse or print. We will need them to display the values in our graphical editor.

With a collection of generic types, values of any user-defined type can be represented, e.g. `[1]::[Int]` is represented by `TypeCons _List (Left (DataCons _Cons (Pair 1 (TypeCons _List Right (DataCons _Nil Unit)))))`, see also Fig. 4 on page 161.

Once defined by the programmer, a generic function can be applied to values of any concrete (user defined) type. The compiler will automatically add conversion functions (*bimaps*) that will transform the concrete type to the corresponding combination of generic types. Furthermore, the generic types returned by the generic function are converted back again to the actual type demanded.

In order to be able to deal with (mutual) recursive types, it is *vital* that these transformations are done in a lazy way (see [14] and [3]).

Generic functions are very useful for defining work of a general nature. Because generic functions can be specialized for any specific concrete type as well, they can also be customized easily. So far, the technique has been successfully used to define functions like equality, map, foldr, as well as for the construction of various parsers and pretty printers. Also, generic programming techniques play an important role in the implementation of automatic test systems [17]. The use of generic programming techniques for the creation of GUI applications has to our knowledge never been done before.

4.2   Creating a GEC_τ with Generic Functions

A GEC_τ component basically is an interactive editor for data of type τ, which can be edited in any order. A special property of such an editor is that all data elements have to be visualized and still have to be modifiable *as well*.

For our kind of interactive programs generic functions cannot be used in the standard way (in which a user type is converted lazily to the generic representation after which the generic function is applied and the result is converted back again). We need a variant in which the generic representation is not discarded but persists somehow, such that interactions (and corresponding conversions to the user types) can take place.

Consequently, we have to create a family of objects of different types to accommodate the generic representation. One solution might be to create a family of functional heaps (like Haskell MVars [19]). This family of heaps should then be used to create the required communication infrastructure. Instead we have used *receiver objects* [1], a facility of Object I/O. A receiver object (or, in short, *receiver*) has an internal state in the same way as functional heaps do, but they are more flexible because one can attach an arbitrary number of methods to them that also have access to the world environment. In this way, receivers enable an object-oriented style of programming. With these methods we have implemented the communication infrastructure.

The methods of a receiver that 'manages' a t value are invoked via Object I/O message passing functions. These require an identification value of abstract type (GECId t). These are generated with the function openGECId :: (PSt ps) → (GECId t,PSt ps). For the earlier mentioned gecGetValue and gecSetValue methods of the GEC record corresponding functions have been defined that handle the details of message passing. These are gecGetValue‘ :: (GECId t) (PSt ps) → (t,PSt ps) and gecSetValue‘ :: (GECId t) t (PSt ps) → (PSt ps) respectively. The GEC record methods are simply curried applications of these message passing functions.

Using receivers, we can create a family of objects that store the corresponding values of the generic type family, that communicate with their children using their typed identifiers, and that communicate with their parent using the callback interface. The topology of the receiver objects is similar to the generic representation.

In Fig. 4 we show the objects that are created to represent the value [1] generically. Notice the similarity between the generic representation and the topology of the receiver objects created. For this particular value, 11 receiver objects are initially created. The figure reveals that, compared to the generic representation, two additional (inactive) receivers (indicated by dark grey boxes, one marked Nil :: and one marked Cons ::) have been created. The reason is that in order to allow a user to change a constructor to another one, the infrastructure to handle that other constructor must already be available.

In general, a lot of communication takes place when the application user operates the editor. For instance, when a leaf value in the tree of receivers is changed, all spine receiver objects that depend on it will be informed. The required underlying communication infrastructure is far from trivial, but we only have to define it once. Each receiver object of a certain (generic) type furthermore requires a view to display and edit a value of that type. How this view can be adapted, is explained in Sect. 5.

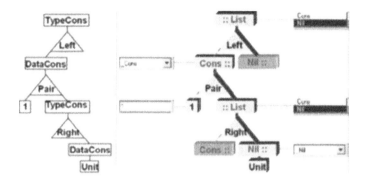

Fig. 4. The representation of [1] using generic types (Left), and the topology of the created receiver objects (see page 160) representing the same expression (Right).

Once the editor is created for a certain type and the corresponding views have been created, the application user can use the views to edit the value. For the implementation this means that receivers have to be created dynamically as well. If the application user makes a larger structure (e.g. [1,2]) out of a smaller one (e.g. [1]), we have to increase the number of receivers accordingly. It is possible that a receiver is not needed anymore because the user has chosen some other value. Receivers are only deleted when the whole editor is closed. Until then we mark unused receivers as inactive but remember their values. We simply close the views of these inactive receivers and reopen them when the user regrets his decision. In this way the application user can quickly switch from one value to another and backwards without being forced to retype information.

When a user switches from one data constructor to another, we have to create default values. For instance, if a Nil is changed into a Cons using an editor for a list of integers, we will generate a default integer (0) and a default list of integers (Nil). We use a generic function to make up such a default value. A programmer can easily change this by specializing this generic default function for a particular type.

5   Customizing Graphical Editor Components

5.1   The Counter Example

No paper about GUIs is complete without the counter example. To make such a counter we need an integer value and an up-down button. The counter has to be increased or decreased each time the corresponding button is pressed. Notice that our editors only react to changes made in the displayed data structure. Consequently, if the application user chooses Up two times in a row, the second Up will only be noticed if its value was not Up before. Therefore, we need a three state button with a neutral position (Neutral) that can be changed to either Up or Down. After being pressed it has to be reset to the neutral position

```
:: UpDown      = Up | Down | Neutral
:: Counter    :== (Int,UpDown)

updCntr :: Counter -> Counter
updCntr (n,Up)   = (n+1,Neutral)
updCntr (n,Down) = (n-1,Neutral)
updCntr any      = any
```

Fig. 5. Two $GEC_{Counter}$s. The standard one (on top) and a customized one.

again. The counter can be created automatically by applying `selfGEC updCntr`
(0,Neutral), using the concise definitions in Fig. 5.

The definition of the counter, the model, is intuitive and straightforward. The
generated $GEC_{Counter}$ works as intended, and we get it for free. Unfortunately,
its view is a counterexample of a good-looking counter (bottom window in Fig.
5). In this case we want to hide the tuple data constructor editor, and place the
integer box next to the button editor. And finally we prefer to display ⊟ instead
of ⊡ that we generate as default editor for values of the type UpDown.

5.2   Full Customization

One of the goals in this project was to obtain fully customizable GUI editors.
Here, we explain how this can be done.

Each receiver object that is generically created by the instances of `mkGEC`
requires a graphical editor definition that will tell how a value of that type can
be displayed and edited. This is done by a set of 'mirror' functions that takes
two additional parameters. These are a fresh receiver identification value, and a
view definition function. Below this is shown for the generic `Pair` case, the other
generic cases proceed analogously:

```
generic mkGEC t :: [GECAttribute] t (CallBackFunction t (PSt ps)) (PSt ps)
                                      -> (GEC t (PSt ps),  PSt ps)
mkGEC{|Pair|} gx gy as v f env
   # (pairId,env) = openGECId env
   = pairGEC pairId (pairGUI pairId) gx gy as v f env
```

The view definition function is of type (PSt ps) $\rightarrow$ (GECGUI t (PSt ps),
PSt ps): an environment based function in order to allow it to allocate the
necessary resources. Hence, the view of a GEC_t is defined by a GECGUI$_t$. A
GECGUI$_t$ on an environment env is a record with the following functions:

1. `guiLocs` reserves GUI screen space for the subcomponents of t. It is a function that returns a list of GUI locations[8], given its own location. For this
   reason it has type Location $\rightarrow$ [Location].

---

[8] The number of elements is actually dependent on the kind: zero for $\star$, one for $\star \rightarrow \star$,
two for $\star \rightarrow \star \rightarrow \star$ etc.

2. `guiOpen` creates the view and the reserved GUI screen estate, given its own location. Hence, it must be an action. It has type `Location` → env → env.

3. `guiUpdate` defines how a new value set from the outside[9] has to be displayed. It has the obvious type `t` → env → env.

4. `guiClose` closes the view (usually a trivial Object I/O close action, which is the inverse operation of 2 above). It has the action type env → env.

For each instance of the generic family one such 'mirror' function and corresponding view definition has been predefined. For any (user defined) type, an editor is constructed automatically by combining these generic editors. The specialization mechanism of Clean can be used to change any part of a GEC_τ since a specialized definition for a certain type overrules the default editor for that type. Therefore, to create a good-looking counter one only has to redefine the editor for `(,)` and `UpDown`. Because the `UpDown` editor behaves as a basic value editor, its definition uses the mirror function for basic types, which is `basicGEC`:

```
mkGEC{|UpDown|} as v f env
  # (updownId,env) = openGECId env
  = basicGEC updownId (updownGUI (gecSetValue' updownId)) as v f env
```

The actual definition of `updownGUI` is 50 loc. Half of the code is 'ordinary' Object I/O code to implement the `guiOpen` function. The other functions are one-liners (this is typical).

To show the effect of the customized representation, we construct a slightly more complicated example. Below, in the record structure `DoubleCounter` we store two counters and an integer value, which will always display the sum of the two counters. Notice that the programmer can specify the wanted behavior just by applying `updCntr` on each of the counters. The sum is calculated by taking the sum of the resulting counter values. One obtains a very clear specification without any worry about the graphical representation or edit functionality. All one has to do is to apply `selfGEC updDoubleCntr` to the initial value {counter1 = (0,Neutral), counter2 = (0,Neutral), sum = 0}.

For large data structures it may be infeasible to display the complete data structure. Customization can be used to define a GEC_τ that creates a view on a finite subset of such a large data structure with buttons to browse through the rest of the data structure. This same technique can also be used to create GEC_τs for lazy infinite data structures. For these infinite data structures customization is a must since clearly they can never be fully displayed.

6 Related Work

The system described in this paper is a refined version of the well-known *model-view* paradigm [18], introduced by Trygve Reenskaug in the language Smalltalk (then named as the *model-view-controller* paradigm).

---

[9] Note that the other direction is simply a parameter of the editor component.

```
:: DoubleCounter = { counter1 :: Counter
                   , counter2 :: Counter
                   , sum      :: Int
                   }

updDoubleCntr::DoubleCounter -> DoubleCounter
updDoubleCntr cntr
    = { counter1 = newcounter1
      , counter2 = newcounter2
      , sum      = fst newcounter1 + fst newcounter2
      }
where newcounter1 = updCntr cntr.counter1
      newcounter2 = updCntr cntr.counter2
```

Fig. 6. An editor with two counters and a resulting sum.

In our approach the data type plays the *model* role, and the *views* are derived automatically from the generic decomposition of values of that type. The *controller* role is dealt with by both the automatically derived communication infrastructure and the views (as they need to handle user actions). Because views are derived automatically, a programmer in our system does not need to explicitly 'register' nor program views. Views can be customized via overruling instance declarations of arbitrary types.

A distinguishing feature of our approach is the distributed nature of both the model and the views. The model is distributed using the generic decomposition of the model value. The subvalues are stored in the receivers. This implies that it should be relatively easy to distribute this framework over a collection of distributed interactive processes. The view is distributed as well, as each view of a generic component is responsible for showing that particular generic instance only. Its further responsibility is to define GUI space for the subcomponents.

Frameworks for the model-view paradigm in a functional language use a similar value-based approach as we do (Claessen *et al* [7]), or an event-based version [15]. In both cases, the programmer needs to explicitly handle view registration and manipulation. In our framework, the information-flow follows the structure that is derived by the generic decomposition of the model value. This suggests that we could have used a stream-based solution such as FUDGETS [6]. However, stream based approaches are known to impose a much to rigid coupling between the stream based communication and the GUI structure resulting in a severe loss of flexibility and maintainability. For this reason, we have chosen to use a call-back mechanism as the interface of our GEC_τ components.

The Vital project [16] has similar goals as our project. Vital is an interactive graphical environment for direct manipulation of Haskell-like scripts. Shared goals are: direct manipulation of functional expressions (Haskell expressions vs. flat values), manipulation of custom types, views that depend on the data type (*data type styles*), *guarded* data types (we use selfGEC), and the ability to work with infinite data structures. Differences are that our system is completely implemented in Clean, while the Vital system has been implemented in Java. This implies that our system can handle, by construction, all flat Clean values, and all values are obviously well-typed. In addition, the purpose of a GEC_τ is to edit values of type τ, while the purpose of a Vital session is to edit Haskell scripts.

7   Conclusions and Future Work

Graphical Editor Components are built on top of the Object I/O GUI library. The Object I/O library offers a lot of functionality (e.g. one can define menus, draw objects, make timers, etcetera) and it is also very flexible, but at the expense of a steep learning curve. Graphical Editor Components offer a more limited functionality: a customizable view and editor for any type. The customization abilities make it possible to incorporate the functionality of Object I/O. It does not exclude Object I/O; it is fully integrated with it. One can still use windows, dialogs, menus, timers, and so on. The abstraction layer offered by the Graphical Editor Components is much higher. The learning curve is short and flat because one basically has to learn only the mkGEC function instead of approximately 500 Object I/O functions. The arguments of mkGEC are similar to most Object I/O functions. The most important advantages are:

- for any value of any flat type one gets an editor for free;
- the editor can be used to give type safe input to the application;
- any output or intermediate result can be displayed;
- visualization is separated from the value infrastructure and is customizable by redefining the components that need to be displayed differently;
- editors can be combined including mutually dependent editors.

The presented method offers a good separation of concerns. The specification of the wanted functionality of a component is completely separated from the specification of its graphical representation. One even obtains a default graphical representation for free. This makes it an excellent tool for rapid prototyping. Also one can abstract from the way components are connected. As a result, complicated interactive applications can be created without a lot of understanding of graphical I/O handling.

Editors can be used for programming GUI objects, from simple dialogs to complicated spreadsheets. They can also be used for tracing and debugging.

The automatic generation of components was only possible thanks to the generic programming facilities of Clean. The interactive nature of the components caused some interesting implementation problems. We had to store the generic representation in special objects (Object I/O receivers). We also hit on a disturbing limitation of the current implementation in Clean: one cannot overload generic functions in their generic type. For this reason we introduced the 'mirror' functions in Sect. 5. We intend to solve this.

We plan to extend the system with support for non-flat types. This will require the ability to deal with function types. An interesting direction of research seems to be to use the Esther shell of the experimental operating system

Famke, which deals with creating and composing functions in an interactive and dynamically typed way. This shell is written in Clean as well [20].

Furthermore, we will investigate the expressive power of our graphical editor components by conducting experiments and case studies.

Acknowledgements

The authors would like to thank Arjen van Weelden, Pieter Koopman, Ronny Wichers Schreur and the anonymous referees for their valuable comments.

References

1. P. Achten and R. Plasmeijer. Interactive Functional Objects in Clean. In Clack, Hammond, and Davie, editors, *The 9th International Workshop on the Implementation of Functional Languages, IFL 1997, Selected Papers*, volume 1467 of *LNCS*, pages 304–321. St.Andrews, UK, Springer, 1998.
2. Achten, Peter and Peyton Jones, Simon. Porting the Clean Object I/O Library to Haskell. In M. Mohnen and P. Koopman, editors, *The 12th International Workshop on the Implementation of Functional Languages, IFL 2000, Selected Papers*, volume 2011 of *LNCS*, pages 194–213. Aachen, Germany, Springer, 2001.
3. A. Alimarine and R. Plasmeijer. A Generic Programming Extension for Clean. In T. Arts and M. Mohnen, editors, *The 13th International workshop on the Implementation of Functional Languages, IFL'01, Selected Papers*, pages 168–186. Älvsjö, Sweden, Sept. 2002.
4. Angelov, Krasimir Andreev. ObjectIO for Haskell. Description and Sources at www.haskell.org/ObjectIO/, Applications at /free.top.bg/ka2_mail/, 2003.
5. E. Barendsen and S. Smetsers. *Handbook of Graph Grammars and Computing by Graph Transformation*, chapter 2, Graph Rewriting Aspects of Functional Programming, pages 63–102. World Scientific, 1999.
6. M. Carlsson and T. Hallgren. FUDGETS - a graphical user interface in a lazy functional language. In *Proceedings of the ACM Conference on Functional Programming and Computer Architecture, FPCA '93*, Kopenhagen, Denmark, 1993.
7. K. Claessen, T. Vullinghs, and E. Meijer. Structuring Graphical Paradigms in TkGofer. In *Proceedings of the 1997 ACM SIGPLAN International Conference on Functional Programming (ICFP '97)*, volume 32(8), pages 251–262, Amsterdam, The Netherlands, 9-11 June 1997. ACM Press.
8. D. Clarke and A. Löh. Generic Haskell, Specifically. In J. Gibbons and J. Jeuring, editors, *Generic Programming. Proceedings of the IFIP TC2 Working Conference on Generic Programming*, pages 21–48, Schloss Dagstuhl, July 2003. Kluwer Academic Publishers. ISBN 1-4020-7374-7.
9. M. de Mol, M. van Eekelen, and R. Plasmeijer. Theorem proving for functional programmers - Sparkle: A functional theorem prover. In T. Arts and M. Mohnen, editors, *Selected Papers from the 13th International Workshop on Implementation of Functional Languages, IFL 2001*, volume 2312 of *LNCS*, pages 55–72, Stockholm, Sweden, 2001. Springer.
10. Diviánszky P. Haskell - Clean Compiler. ELTE, Budapest, 2003. Software at aszt.inf.elte.hu/~fun_ver/2003/software/HsCleanAll2.0.2.zip.

11. Fulgham, Brent. The Clean ObjectIO Library under Linux (Gtk+). Description at people.debian.org/~bfulgham/clean_examples, May 2003. Sources at people.debian.org/~bfulgham/clean/objectio-linux.tar.gz.

12. Hegedus H. Haskell to Clean Front End. Master's thesis, ELTE, Budapest, Hungary, 2001.

13. Hinze, Ralf. A new approach to generic functional programming. In *The 27th Annual ACM SIGPLAN-SIGACT Symposium on Principles of Programming Languages*, pages 119–132. Boston, Massachusetts, January 2000.

14. Hinze, Ralf and Peyton Jones, Simon. Derivable Type Classes. In G. Hutton, editor, *2000 ACM SIGPLAN Haskell Workshop*, volume 41(1) of *ENTCS*. Montreal, Canada, Elsevier Science, 2001.

15. W. Karlsen, Einar and S. Westmeier. Using Concurrent Haskell to Develop Views over an Active Repository. In *Implementation of Functional Languages, Selected Papers*, volume 1467 of *LNCS*, pages 285–303, St.Andrews, Scotland, 1997. Springer.

16. Keith Hanna. Interactive Visual Functional Programming. In S. P. Jones, editor, *Proc. Intnl Conf. on Functional Programming*, pages 100–112. ACM, October 2002.

17. P. Koopman, A. Alimarine, J. Tretmans, and R. Plasmeijer. Gast: Generic Automated Software Testing. In R. Peña and T. Arts, editors, *The 14th International Workshop on the Implementation of Functional Languages, IFL'02, Selected Papers*, volume 2670 of *LNCS*, pages 84–100. Springer, 2003.

18. G. Krasner and S. Pope. A cookbook for using the Model-View-Controller user interface paradigm in Smalltalk-80. *Journal of Object-Oriented Programming*, 1(3):26–49, August 1988.

19. S. Peyton Jones, A. Gordon, and S. Finne. Concurrent Haskell. In *23rd ACM Symposium on Principles of Programming Languages (POPL'96)*, pages 295–308, St.Petersburg Beach, Florida, 1996. ACM.

20. A. van Weelden and R. Plasmeijer. Towards a strongly typed functional operating system. In R. Peña and T. Arts, editors, *The 14th International Workshop on the Implementation of Functional Languages, IFL'02, Selected Papers*, volume 2670 of *LNCS*, pages 215–231. Springer, Sept. 2002.

Polytypic Programming in Haskell

Ulf Norell and Patrik Jansson

Computing Science, Chalmers University of Technology, Sweden
{ulfn,patrikj}@cs.chalmers.se
http://www.cs.chalmers.se/~{ulfn,patrikj}/

Abstract. A polytypic (or generic) program captures a common pattern of computation over different datatypes by abstracting over the structure of the datatype. Examples of algorithms that can be defined polytypically are equality tests, mapping functions and pretty printers.
A commonly used technique to implement polytypic programming is specialization, where a specialized version of a polytypic function is generated for every datatype it is used at. In this paper we describe an alternative technique that allows polytypic functions to be defined using Haskell's class system (extended with multi-parameter type classes and functional dependencies). This technique brings the power of polytypic programming inside Haskell allowing us to define a Haskell library of polytypic functions. It also increases our flexibility, reducing the dependency on a polytypic language compiler.

1   Introduction

Functional programming draws great power from the ability to define polymorphic, higher order functions that can capture the structure of an algorithm while abstracting away from the details. A polymorphic function is parameterized over one or more types and thus abstracting away from the specifics of these types. The same is true for a polytypic (or generic) function, but while all instances of a polymorphic function share the same definition, the instances of a polytypic function definition also depend on a type.

By parameterizing the function definition by a type one can capture common patterns of computation over different datatypes. Examples of functions that can be defined polytypically include the map function that maps a function over a datatype but also more complex algorithms like unification and term rewriting.

Even if an algorithm will only be used at a single datatype it may still be a good idea to implement it as a polytypic function. First of all, since a polytypic function abstracts away from the details of the datatype, we cannot make any datatype specific mistakes in the definition and secondly, if the datatype changes, there is no need to change the polytypic function.

A common technique to implement polytypic programming is to specialize the polytypic functions to the datatypes at which they are used. In other words the polytypic compiler generates a separate function for each polytypic function-datatype pair. Unfortunately this implementation technique requires global access to the program using the polytypic functions. In this paper we describe an

P. Trinder, G. Michaelson, and R. Peña (Eds.): IFL 2003, LNCS 3145, pp. 168–184, 2004.
© Springer-Verlag Berlin Heidelberg 2004

alternative technique to implement polytypic programs using the Haskell class system. The polytypic programs that can be defined are restricted to operate on regular, single parameter datatypes. That is, datatypes that are not mutually recursive and where the recursive calls all have the same form as the left hand side of the datatype definition. Note that datatypes are allowed to contain function spaces. This technique has been implemented as a Haskell library and as a modification of the PolyP [8] compiler (PolyP version 2). The implementation of PolyP 2 is available from the polytypic programming home page [7]. In the following text we normally omit the version number — PolyP will stand for the improved language and its (new) compiler.

1.1   Overview

The rest of this paper is structured as follows. Section 2 describes how polytypic programs can be expressed inside Haskell. The structure of regular datatypes is captured by pattern functors (expressed using datatype combinators) and the relation between a regular datatype and its pattern functor is captured by a two parameter type class (with a functional dependency). In this setting a polytypic definition is represented by a class with instances for the different datatype combinators. Section 3 shows how the implementation of PolyP has been extended to translate PolyP code to Haskell classes and instances. Section 4 discusses briefly the structure of a polytypic language. Section 5 describes related work and section 6 concludes.

2   Polytypism in Haskell

In this section we show how polytypic programs can be embedded in Haskell[1]. The embedding uses datatype constructors to model the top level structure of datatypes, and the two-parameter type class FunctorOf to relate datatypes to their structures.

The embedding closely mimics the features of the language PolyP [8], an extension to (a subset of) Haskell that allows definitions of polytypic functions over regular, unary datatypes. This section gives a brief overview of the embedding and compares it to PolyP.

2.1   Datatypes and Pattern Functors

As mentioned earlier we allow definition of polytypic functions over regular datatypes of kind $\star \to \star$. A datatype is regular if it is not mutually recursive with another type and if the argument to the type constructor is the same in the left-hand side and the right-hand side of the definition.

We describe the structure of a regular datatype by its *pattern functor*. A pattern functor is a two-argument type constructor built up using the combinators

---

[1] The code for this paper works with current (January 2004) versions of ghc and hugs, and can be obtained from the polytypic programming home page [7].

```
data (g :+: h) p r     = InL (g p r)  |  InR (h p r)
data (g :*: h) p r     = g p r :*: h p r
data Empty p r         = Empty
newtype Par p r        = Par{unPar :: p}
newtype Rec p r        = Rec{unRec :: r}
newtype (d :@: g) p r = Comp{unComp :: d (g p r)}
newtype Const t p r  = Const{unConst :: t}
newtype (g :→: h) p r = Fun{unFun :: g p r → h p r}
```

Fig. 1. Pattern functor combinators.

shown in figure 1. The infix combinators are right associative and their order of precedence is, from lower to higher: (:+:), (:*:), (:→:), (:@:). We use records purely for convenience, to get the *un*-functions for free. In Haskell, a datatype with records can be treated as any other datatype. For the datatype List a we can use these combinators to define the pattern functor ListF as follows:

```
data List a = Nil | Cons a (List a)
type ListF  = Empty :+: Par :*: Rec
```

An element of ListF p r can take either the form InL Empty, corresponding to Nil or the form InR (Par x :*: Rec xs), corresponding to Cons x xs.

The pattern functor d :@: g represents the composition of the regular datatype constructor d and the pattern functor g, allowing us to describe the structure of datatypes like Rose:

```
data Rose a = Fork a (List (Rose a))
type RoseF  = Par :*: List :@: Rec
```

A constant type in a datatype definition is modeled by the pattern functor Const t. For instance, the pattern functor of a binary tree storing height information in the nodes can be expressed as

```
data HTree a = Leaf a | Branch Int (HTree a) (HTree a)
type HTreeF  = Par :+: Const Int :*: Rec :*: Rec
```

The pattern functor (:→:) is used to model datatypes with function spaces. Only a few polytypic functions are possible to define for such datatypes. We include the combinator (:→:) here because our system can handle it, but for the rest of the paper we assume regular datatypes *without* function spaces.

In general we write Φ_D for the pattern functor of the datatype D a, so for example Φ_{List} = ListF. To convert between a datatype and its pattern functor we use the methods *inn* and *out* in the multi-parameter type class FunctorOf:

```
class FunctorOf f d | d → f where
    inn :: f a (d a) → d a
    out :: d a → f a (d a)
```

The functions *inn* and *out* realize the isomorphism $d\ a \cong \Phi_d\ a\ (d\ a)$, that holds for every regular datatype. (We can view a regular datatype $d\ a$ as the least fixed point of the corresponding functor $\Phi_d\ a$.)

In our list example we have

```
instance FunctorOf (Empty :+: Par :*: Rec) List where
    inn (InL Empty)            = Nil
    inn (InR (Par x :*: Rec xs)) = Cons x xs
    out Nil                    = InL Empty
    out (Cons x xs)            = InR (Par x :*: Rec xs)
```

Note that *inn* (*out*) only folds (unfolds) the top level structure and it is therefore normally a constant time operation.

The functional dependency $d \rightarrow f$ in the FunctorOf-class means that the set of instances defines a type level function from datatypes to their pattern functors. Several different datatypes can map to the same pattern functor if they share the same structure, but one datatype can not have more than one associated pattern functor. For an example where we use the fact the several datatypes can have the same structure see the function *coerce* in section 2.6. The functional dependency allows the Haskell compiler to infer unambiguous types of most generic functions — without the dependency, disambiguating type annotations are often required.

2.2 Pattern Functor Classes

In addition to the class FunctorOf, used to relate datatypes to pattern functors, we also use one *pattern functor class* P_name for each (group of related) polytypic definition(s) *name*. A pattern functor class is just a constructor class with one parameter of kind $\star \rightarrow \star \rightarrow \star$ with one (or more) polytypic definitions as methods. The set of instances for a class P_name defines for which pattern functors the polytypic definition(s) *name* is meaningful.

An example is a generalization of the standard Haskell Prelude class Functor to the pattern functor class P_fmap2:

```
class Functor f where
    fmap :: (a → b) → (f a → f b)
class P_fmap2 f where
    fmap2 :: (a → c) → (b → d) → (f a b → f c d)
```

All pattern functors except (:→:) are instances of the class P_fmap2. Pattern functor classes and their instances are discussed in more detail in section 3.

2.3 PolyLib in Haskell

PolyLib [9] is a library of polytypic definitions including generalized versions of well-known functions such as *map*, *zip* and *sum*, as well as powerful recursion combinators such as *cata*, *ana* and *hylo*. All these library functions have been converted to work with our new framework, so that PolyLib is now available as a normal Haskell library. The library functions can be used on all datatypes which are instances of the FunctorOf class and if the user provides the FunctorOf-instances, no tool support is needed. Alternatively, for all regular datatypes, these instances can be generated automatically by the new PolyP compiler (or by DrIFT or Template Haskell).

Using *fmap2* from the P_fmap2-class and *inn* and *out* from the FunctorOf class we can already define quite a few polytypic functions from the Haskell version of PolyLib. For instance

$$
\begin{aligned}
pmap &\ ::\ (\mathsf{FunctorOf}\ f\ d, \mathsf{P\_fmap2}\ f) \Rightarrow (a \to b) \to (d\ a \to d\ b) \\
cata &\ ::\ (\mathsf{FunctorOf}\ f\ d, \mathsf{P\_fmap2}\ f) \Rightarrow (f\ a\ b \to b) \to (d\ a \to b) \\
ana &\ ::\ (\mathsf{FunctorOf}\ f\ d, \mathsf{P\_fmap2}\ f) \Rightarrow (b \to f\ a\ b) \to (b \to d\ a)
\end{aligned}
$$

$$
\begin{aligned}
pmap\ f &= inn \circ fmap2\ f\ (pmap\ f) \circ out \\
cata\ \varphi &= \varphi \circ fmap2\ id\ (cata\ \varphi) \circ out \\
ana\ \psi &= inn \circ fmap2\ id\ (ana\ \psi) \circ \psi
\end{aligned}
$$

We can use the functions above to define other polytypic functions. For instance, we can use *cata* to define a generalization of *sum* :: Num $a \Rightarrow [a] \to a$ which works for all regular datatypes. Suppose we have a pattern functor class P_fsum with the method *fsum*:

$$fsum\ ::\ \mathsf{Num}\ a \Rightarrow f\ a\ a \to a$$

(Method *fsum* takes care of summing the top-level, provided that the recursive occurrences have already been summed.) Then we can sum the elements of a regular datatype by defining

$$
\begin{aligned}
psum &\ ::\ (\mathsf{FunctorOf}\ f\ d, \mathsf{P\_fmap2}\ f, \mathsf{P\_fsum}\ f, \mathsf{Num}\ a) \Rightarrow d\ a \to a \\
psum &= cata\ fsum
\end{aligned}
$$

We return to the function *fsum* in section 3.1 when we discuss how the pattern functor classes are defined. In the type of *psum* we can see an indication of a problem that arises when combining polytypic functions without instantiating them to concrete types: we get large class constraints. Fortunately we can let the Haskell compiler infer the type for us in most cases, but our setting is certainly one which would benefit from extending Haskell type constraint syntax with wildcards, allowing us to write the type signature as *psum* :: _ $\Rightarrow d\ a \to a$.

2.4   Perfect Binary Trees

A benefit of using the class system to do polytypic programming is that it allows us to treat (some) non-regular datatypes as regular, thus providing a *regular view* of the datatype. For instance, take the nested datatype of perfect binary trees, defined by

data Bin a = Single a | Fork (Bin (a, a))

$$
\begin{array}{l}
\textbf{instance}\ \texttt{FunctorOf}\ (\texttt{Par :+: Rec :*: Rec})\ \texttt{Bin}\ \textbf{where} \\
\quad inn\ (\texttt{InL}\ (\texttt{Par}\ x)) = \texttt{Single}\ x \\
\quad inn\ (\texttt{InR}\ (\texttt{Rec}\ l\ \texttt{:*:}\ \texttt{Rec}\ r)) = \texttt{Fork}\ (join\ (l, r)) \\
\quad out\ (\texttt{Single}\ x) = \texttt{InL}\ (\texttt{Par}\ x) \\
\quad out\ (\texttt{Fork}\ t) = \texttt{InR}\ (\texttt{Rec}\ l\ \texttt{:*:}\ \texttt{Rec}\ r) \\
\qquad \textbf{where}\ (l, r) = split\ t
\end{array}
$$

$$
\begin{array}{l}
join :: (\texttt{Bin}\ a, \texttt{Bin}\ a) \rightarrow \texttt{Bin}\ (a, a) \\
join\ (\texttt{Single}\ x, \texttt{Single}\ y) = \texttt{Single}\ (x, y) \\
join\ (\texttt{Fork}\ l, \texttt{Fork}\ r) = \texttt{Fork}\ (join\ (l, r))
\end{array}
$$

$$
\begin{array}{l}
split :: \texttt{Bin}\ (a, a) \rightarrow (\texttt{Bin}\ a, \texttt{Bin}\ a) \\
split\ (\texttt{Single}\ (x, y)) = (\texttt{Single}\ x, \texttt{Single}\ y) \\
split\ (\texttt{Fork}\ t) = (\texttt{Fork}\ l,\ \texttt{Fork}\ r) \\
\quad \textbf{where}\ (l, r) = split\ t
\end{array}
$$

Fig. 2. A FunctorOf instance for perfect binary trees.

This type can be viewed as having the pattern functor Par :+: Rec :*: Rec, i.e. the same as the ordinary binary tree.

$$\textbf{data}\ \mathsf{Tree}\ a = \mathsf{Leaf}\ a \mid \mathsf{Branch}\ (\mathsf{Tree}\ a)\ (\mathsf{Tree}\ a)$$

By defining an instance of the FunctorOf class for Bin (see Fig. 2) we can then use all the PolyLib functions on perfect binary trees. For instance we can use an anamorphism to generate a full binary tree of a given height as follows.

$$
\begin{array}{l}
full :: a \rightarrow \mathsf{Int} \rightarrow \mathsf{Bin}\ a \\
full\ x = ana\ (step\ x) \\
\quad \textbf{where}\ step\ x\ 0 = \mathsf{InL}\ (\mathsf{Par}\ x) \\
\qquad\qquad step\ x\ (n+1) = \mathsf{InR}\ (\mathsf{Rec}\ n)\ (\mathsf{Rec}\ n)
\end{array}
$$

By forcing the perfect binary trees into the regular framework we (naturally) loose some type information. Had we, for instance, made a mistake in the definition of *full* so that it didn't generate a full tree, we would get a run-time error (pattern match failure in *join*) instead of a type error.

2.5 Abstract Datatypes

In the previous example we provided a regular view on a non-regular datatype. We can do the same thing for (some) abstract datatypes. Suppose we have an abstract datatype Stack, with methods

$$
\begin{array}{l}
push :: a \rightarrow \mathsf{Stack}\ a \rightarrow \mathsf{Stack}\ a \\
pop :: \mathsf{Stack}\ a \rightarrow \mathsf{Maybe}\ (a,\ \mathsf{Stack}\ a) \\
empty :: \mathsf{Stack}\ a
\end{array}
$$

By giving the following instance, we provide a view of the stack as a regular datatype with the pattern functor Empty :+: Par :*: Rec.

```
instance FunctorOf (Empty :+: Par :*: Rec) Stack where
    inn (InL Empty)         = empty
    inn (InR (Par x :*: Rec s)) = push x s

    out s = case pop s of
        Nothing    → InL Empty
        Just (x, s') → InR (Par x :*: Rec s')
```

As in the previous example, this instance allows us to use polytypic functions on stacks, for instance applying the function *psum* to a stack of integers or using *pmap* to apply a function to all the elements on a stack.

2.6   Polytypic Functions in Haskell

We have seen how to make different kinds of datatypes fit the polytypic framework, thus enabling us to use the polytypic functions from PolyLib on them, but we can also use the PolyLib functions to create new polytypic functions. One interesting function that we can define is the function *coerce*

```
coerce :: (FunctorOf f d, FunctorOf f e, P_fmap2 f) ⇒ d a → e a
coerce = cata inn
```

that converts between two regular datatypes with the same pattern functor. For instance we could convert a perfect binary tree from section 2.4 to a normal binary tree or convert a list to an element of the abstract stack type from section 2.5.

Another use of polytypic functions in Haskell is to define default instances of the standard type classes. For instance we can define

```
instance (FunctorOf f d, P_fmap2 f) ⇒ Functor d where
    fmap = pmap
```

Since this is an instance for a type variable, we need the Haskell extensions (available in ghc and hugs) for overlapping and undecidable instances.

Using the polytypic library we can also define more complex functions such as the *transpose* function that transposes two regular datatypes. For instance, converting a list of trees to a tree of lists. To define *transpose* we first define the function *listTranspose* for the special case of transposing the list type constructor with another regular type constructor. We omit the class constraints in the types for brevity.

```
listTranspose :: _ ⇒ [d a] → d [a]
listTranspose (x : []) = pmap singleton x
listTranspose (x : xs) = pzipWith (:) x (listTranspose xs)
```

The function *pzipWith* (from PolyLib [9]) is the polytypic version of the Haskell prelude function *zipWith* and has type _ ⇒ (a → b → c) → d a → d b → d c. If the structures of the arguments to *pzipWith* differ the function fails. Using *listTranspose* we can define *transpose* as follows:

$transpose :: \_ \Rightarrow d\ (e\ a) \rightarrow e\ (d\ a)$
$transpose\ x = pmap\ (combine\ s)\ (listTranspose\ l)$
    where $(s, l) = separate\ x$

The idea is to separate the structure and the contents of the argument to
$transpose$ using the function $separate :: \_ \Rightarrow d\ a \rightarrow (d\ (), [a])$. The unstruc-
tured representation is then transposed using $listTranspose$ and the structure is
re-applied using $combine :: \_ \Rightarrow d\ () \rightarrow [a] \rightarrow d\ a$. Again $combine$ might fail if
the length of the list doesn't match the number of holes in the structure. It is
easy to modify $transpose$ to use the Maybe monad to catch the potential failures.

3   Translating PolyP into Haskell

So far we have seen how we can use the polytypic functions defined in PolyLib
directly in our Haskell program, either applying them to specific datatypes or
using them to define other polytypic functions. In section 3.1 below, we describe
how to define polytypic functions from scratch using a slightly modified version of
the PolyP language [8]. The polytypic definitions in PolyP *can* also be expressed
in Haskell (as described in section 2), but the syntax of the language extension is
more convenient than writing the classes and the instances by hand. Sections 3.2
to 3.6 discuss how the PolyP definitions are compiled into Haskell.

3.1   The Polytypic Construct

In section 2.1 we introduced the pattern functor Φ_d of a regular datatype $d\ a$.
In PolyP we define polytypic functions by recursion over this pattern functor,
using a type case construct that allows us to pattern match on pattern functors.
This type case construct is translated by the compiler into a pattern functor
class and instances corresponding to the branches.
    To facilitate the definition of polytypic functions we define a few useful func-
tions to manipulate the pattern functors.

$(f \triangledown g)\ (\mathsf{InL}\ x) = f\ x$
$(f \triangledown g)\ (\mathsf{InR}\ y) = g\ y$
$f \mathrel{+\!\!\!+} g \qquad = (\mathsf{InL} \circ f) \triangledown (\mathsf{InR} \circ g)$

The operators $(\triangledown)$ and $(+\!\!\!+)$ are the elimination and map functions for sums.
The types of these functions are a little more complex than one would like, since
they operate on binary functors. For this reason we have chosen to omit them
in this presentation.
    Using the type case construct and the functions above, in Fig. 3 we define
the function $fsum$ from section 2.3 that operates on pattern functors applied to
some numeric type. This function takes an element of type $f\ a\ a$ where a is in
Num and f is a pattern functor. The first a means that the parameter positions
contain numbers and the second a means that all the substructures have been
replaced by numbers (sums of the corresponding substructures). The result of

polytypic *fsum* :: Num $a \Rightarrow f \, a \, a \rightarrow a$
= **case** f **of**
$\quad g :+: h \rightarrow fsum \, \triangledown \, fsum$
$\quad g :*: h \rightarrow \lambda(x :*: y) \rightarrow fsum \, x + fsum \, y$
$\quad \mathsf{Empty} \rightarrow const \, 0$
$\quad \mathsf{Par} \quad\;\; \rightarrow unPar$
$\quad \mathsf{Rec} \quad\;\; \rightarrow unRec$
$\quad d :@: g \rightarrow psum \circ pmap \, fsum \circ unComp$
$\quad \mathsf{Const} \, t \rightarrow const \, 0$

Fig. 3. Defining *fsum* using the **polytypic** construct.

fsum is the sum of the numbers in the top level structure. To sum the elements of something of a sum type we just apply *fsum* recursively regardless of if we are in the left or right summand. If we have something of a product type we sum the components and add the results together. The sum of Empty or a constant type is zero and when we get one Par and Rec they already contain a number so we just return it. If the pattern functor is a regular datatype $d \, a$ composed with a pattern functor g we map *fsum* over d and use the function *psum* to sum the result.

In general a **polytypic** definition has the form

polytypic $p :: \tau$
$= \lambda x_1 \, \ldots \, x_m \rightarrow$ **case** f **of**
$$\varphi_1 \rightarrow e_1$$
$$\vdots$$
$$\varphi_n \rightarrow e_n$$

where f is the pattern functor (occurring somewhere in τ) and φ_i is an arbitrary pattern matching a pattern functor. The lambda abstraction before the type case is optional and a short hand for splicing in the same abstraction in each of the branches. The type of the branch body depends on the branch pattern; more specifically we have $(\lambda x_1 \, \ldots \, x_m \rightarrow e_i) :: \tau[\varphi_i/f]$.

A **polytypic** definition operates on the pattern functor level, but what we are really interested in are functions on the datatype level. We have already seen how to define these functions in Haskell and the only difference when defining them in PolyP is that the class constraints are simpler. Take for instance the datatype level function *psum* which can be defined as the catamorphism of *fsum*:

$psum :: (\mathsf{Regular} \, d, \mathsf{Num} \, a) \Rightarrow d \, a \rightarrow a$
$psum = cata \, fsum$

The class constraint Regular d is translated by the PolyP compiler to a constraint FunctorOf $\Phi_d \, d$ and constraints for any suitable pattern functor classes on Φ_d.

In summary, the **polytypic** construct allows us to write polytypic functions over pattern functors by recursion over the structure of the pattern functor. We can then use these functions together with the functions *inn* and *out* to define functions that work on all regular datatypes.

3.2   Compilation: From PolyP to Haskell

Given a PolyP program we want to generate Haskell code that can be fed into a standard Haskell compiler. Our approach differs from the standard one in that we achieve polytypism by taking advantage of the Haskell class system, instead of specializing polytypic functions to the datatypes on which they are used. The compilation of a PolyP program consists of three phases each of which is described in the following subsections. In the first phase, described in section 3.3, the pattern functor of each regular datatype is computed and an instance of the class FunctorOf is generated, relating the datatype to its functor. The second phase (section 3.4) deals with the **polytypic** definitions. For every polytypic function a type class is generated and each branch in the type case is translated to an instance of this class. The third phase is described in section 3.5 and consists of inferring the class constraints introduced by our new classes. Section 3.6 describes how the module interfaces are handled by the compiler. Worth mentioning here is that we do not need to compile ordinary function definitions (i.e. functions that have not been defined using the **polytypic** keyword) even when they use polytypic functions. So for instance the definition of the function *psum* from section 3.1 is the same in the generated Haskell code as in the PolyP code. The type on the other hand does change, but this is handled by phase three.

3.3   From Datatypes to Instances

When compiling a PolyP program into Haskell we have to generate an instance of the class FunctorOf for each regular datatype. How to do this is described in the rest of this section. First we observe that we can divide the pattern functor combinators into two categories: *structure* combinators that describe the datatype structure and *content* combinators that describe the contents of the datatype. The structure combinators, $(:+:)$, $(:*:)$ and Empty, tell you how many constructors the datatype has and their arities, while the content combinators, Par, Rec, Const and $(:@:)$ represent the arguments of the constructors. For a content pattern functor g we define the *meaning* of g, denoted by $\hat{g}$, as

$$
\begin{aligned}
\widehat{\text{Par } p\ r} &= p \\
\widehat{\text{Rec } p\ r} &= r \\
\widehat{\text{Const } t\ p\ r} &= t \\
\widehat{d :@:\ g}\ p\ r &= d\ (\hat{g}\ p\ r)
\end{aligned}
$$

Using this notation we can write the general form of a regular datatype as

$$
\begin{aligned}
\textbf{data } D\ a = &\ C_1\ (\widehat{g_{11}}\ a\ (D\ a)) \ \ldots\ (\widehat{g_{1m_1}}\ a\ (D\ a)) \\
&\ \vdots \\
&\ |\ C_n\ (\widehat{g_{n1}}\ a\ (D\ a)) \ \ldots\ (\widehat{g_{nm_n}}\ a\ (D\ a))
\end{aligned}
$$

The corresponding pattern functor Φ_D is

$$
\Phi_D = (g_{11} :*: \cdots :*: g_{1m_1}) :+: \cdots :+: (g_{n1} :*: \cdots :*: g_{nm_n})
$$

where we represent a nullary product by Empty. When defining the functions inn and out for $D\ a$ we need to convert between g_{ij} and $\widehat{g}_{ij}$. To do this we associate with each content pattern functor g two functions to_g and $from_g$ such that

$$
\begin{array}{llll}
to_g & :: \widehat{g}\ p\ r \to g\ p\ r & — & to_g \circ from_g = id \\
from_g & :: g\ p\ r \to \widehat{g}\ p\ r & — & from_g \circ to_g = id
\end{array}
$$

For the pattern functors Par, Rec and Const, to and $from$ are defined simply as adding and removing the constructor. In the case of the pattern functor $d :@: g$ we also have to map the conversion function for g over the regular datatype $d\ a$, as shown below.

$to_{\mathsf{Par}}\quad = \mathsf{Par}$	$from_{\mathsf{Par}}\quad = unPar$
$to_{\mathsf{Rec}}\quad = \mathsf{Rec}$	$from_{\mathsf{Rec}}\quad = unRec$
$to_{\mathsf{Const}\ t} = \mathsf{Const}$	$from_{\mathsf{Const}\ t} = unConst$
$to_{d\,@\,g}\quad = \mathsf{Comp} \circ pmap\ to_g$	$from_{d\,@\,g}\quad = pmap\ from_g \circ unComp$

Now define ι_m^n to be the sequence of InL and InR's corresponding to the mth constructor out of n, as follows

$$
\iota_m^n\ x = \begin{cases}
x & \text{if } n = m = 1 \\
\mathsf{InL}\ x & \text{if } m = 1 \wedge n > 1 \\
\mathsf{InR}\ (\iota_{m-1}^{n-1}\ x) & \text{if } m, n > 1
\end{cases}
$$

For instance the second constructor out of three is $\iota_2^3\ x = \mathsf{InR}\ (\mathsf{InL}\ x)$.

Finally an instance FunctorOf $\Phi_D\ D$ for the general form of a regular datatype $D\ a$ can be defined as follows:

instance FunctorOf $\Phi_D\ D$ **where**
$$
\begin{array}{ll}
inn\ (\iota_k^n\ (x_1 :*: \ldots :*: x_{m_k})) = & C_k\ (to_{g_{k1}}\ x_1) \ \ldots\ (to_{g_{km_k}}\ x_{m_k}) \\
out\ (C_k\ x_1\ \ldots\ x_{m_k}) \quad = & \iota_k^n\ (from_{g_{k1}}\ x_1 :*: \ldots :*: from_{g_{km_k}}\ x_{m_k})
\end{array}
$$

3.4   From Polytypic Definitions to Classes

The second phase of the code generation deals with the translation of the **polytypic** construct. This translation is purely syntactic and translates each polytypic function into a pattern functor class with one method (the polytypic function) and an instance of this class for each branch in the type case. More formally, given a polytypic function definition like the left side in Fig. 4 the translation produces the result on the right.

However, the instances generated by this phase are not complete. To make them pass the Haskell type checker we have to fill in the appropriate class constraints ρ_i. For example, in the definition of $fsum$ from section 3.1, the instance P_fsum $(g :+: h)$ needs instances of P_fsum for g and for h. How to infer these constraints is the topic of the next section.

$$
\left.\begin{array}{l}
\textbf{polytypic } p \ :: \ \tau \\
\quad = \textbf{ case } f \textbf{ of} \\
\qquad \varphi_1 \ \rightarrow \ e_1 \\
\qquad \vdots \\
\qquad \varphi_n \ \rightarrow \ e_n
\end{array}\right\}
\quad \Longrightarrow \quad
\left\{\begin{array}{l}
\textbf{class} \qquad\qquad \textsf{P\_p} f \ \textbf{ where } p \ :: \ \tau \\
\textbf{instance } \rho_1 \ \Rightarrow \textsf{P\_p} \varphi_1 \textbf{ where } p \ = \ e_1 \\
\vdots \\
\textbf{instance } \rho_n \ \Rightarrow \textsf{P\_p} \varphi_n \textbf{ where } p \ = \ e_n
\end{array}\right.
$$

Fig. 4. Translation of a polytypic construct to a class and instances.

3.5 Inferring Class Constraints

When we introduce a new class for every polytypic function we automatically introduce a class constraint everywhere this function is used. Ideally the Haskell compiler should be able to infer these constraints for us, allowing us to simply leave out the types in the generated Haskell code. This is indeed the case most of the time, but there are a few exceptions that require us to take a more rigorous approach. For example, class constraints must be explicitly stated in instance declarations. In other cases the Haskell compiler can infer the type of a function, but it might not be the type we want. For instance, the inferred type of the (translation of) function $pmap$ is

$$pmap \ :: \ (\textsf{FunctorOf } f \ d, \ \textsf{FunctorOf } f \ e, \ \textsf{P\_fmap2 } f) \Rightarrow (a \rightarrow b) \rightarrow d \ a \rightarrow e \ b$$

which is a little too general to be practical. For instance, in the expression $psum \ (pmap \ (1+) \ [1, 2, 3])$, the compiler wouldn't be able to infer the return type of $pmap$. To get the type we want the inferred type is unified with the type stated in the PolyP code. When doing this we have to replace the constraint $\textsf{Regular } d$ in the PolyP type, by the corresponding Haskell constraint $\textsf{FunctorOf } f \ d$ for a free type variable f. Subsequently we replace all occurrences of Φ_d in the type body with f. We also add a new type constraint variable to the given type, that can be unified with the set of new constraints inferred in the type inference. In the case of $pmap$ we would unify the inferred type from above with the modified version of the type stated in the PolyP code:

$$(\textsf{FunctorOf } f \ d, \ \rho) \Rightarrow (a \rightarrow b) \rightarrow d \ a \rightarrow d \ b$$

Here e would be identified with d and ρ would be unified with $\{\textsf{P\_fmap2 } f\}$, yielding the type we want.

The instance declarations can be treated in much the same way. That is, we infer the type of the method body and unify this type with the expected type of the method. We take the definition of $fsum$ in Fig. 3 as an example. This definition is translated to a class and instance declarations for each branch:

```
class           P_fsum f         where fsum :: Num a => f a a -> a
instance ρ+ => P_fsum (g :+: h) where fsum  =  fsum ▽ fsum
    ⋮
```

In the instance for the pattern functor $g :+: h$, the PolyP compiler infers the following type for *fsum*

$$(\mathsf{Num}\ a, \mathsf{P\_fsum}\ g,\ \mathsf{P\_fsum}\ h) \Rightarrow (g :+: h)\ a\ a \to a$$

This type is then unified with the type of *fsum* extended with the constraint set variable ρ_+ serving as a place holder for the extra class constraints:

$$(\mathsf{Num}\ a, \rho_+) \Rightarrow f\ a\ a \to a$$

In this case the result of the unification would be

$$
\begin{aligned}
f &\mapsto g :+: h \\
\rho_+ &\mapsto \{\mathsf{P\_fsum}\ g, \mathsf{P\_fsum}\ h\}
\end{aligned}
$$

The part of the substitution that we are interested in is the assignment of ρ_+, i.e. the class constraints that are in the instance declaration but not in the class declaration. We obtain the following final instance of $\mathsf{P\_fsum}\ (g :+: h)$:

> **instance** $(\mathsf{P\_fsum}\ g,\ \mathsf{P\_fsum}\ h) \Rightarrow \mathsf{P\_fsum}\ (g :+: h)$ **where**
>   *fsum* $=$ *fsum* $\triangledown$ *fsum*

3.6 Modules: Transforming the Interface

The old PolyP compiler used the cut-and-paste approach to modules, treating import statements as C-style includes, effectively ignoring explicit import and export lists. Since we claim that embedding polytypic programs in Haskell's class system alleviates separate compilation, we, naturally, have to do better than the cut-and-paste approach.

To be able to compile a PolyP module without knowledge of the source code of all imported modules, we generate an interface file for each module, containing the type signatures for all exported functions as well as the definitions of all exported datatypes in the module. The types of polytypic functions are given in Haskell form (that is using FunctorOf and P_name, not Regular), since we need to know the class constraints when inferring the constraints for functions in the module we are compiling.

A slightly trickier issue is the handling of explicit import and export lists in PolyP modules. Fortunately, the compilation does not change the function names, so we do not have to change which functions are imported and exported. However, we do have to import and export the generated pattern functor classes. This is done by looking at the types of the functions in the import/export list and collecting all the pattern functor classes occurring in their constraints. So given the following PolyP module

> **module** Sum $(psum)$ **where**
> **import** Base $(cata)$

polytypic *fsum* :: ...
psum = *cata fsum*

we would generate a Haskell module looking like this:

module Sum (*psum*, P_fmap2, P_fsum) **where**
import Base (*cata*, P_fmap2)
⋮

The P_fmap2 in the import declaration comes from the type of *cata*, which is looked up in the interface file for the module Base, and the two exported classes come from the inferred type of *psum*. The interface files are generated by the compiler when it compiles a PolyP module. At the moment there is no automated support for generating interface files for normal Haskell modules, though this should be possible to add.

4   Discussion

One of the benefits of using the class system is that we do not need to rely on a polytypic compiler to the same extent as when using a specializing approach. To make this more precise we identify a few disjoint sublanguages within a polytypic language:

– Base   The base language (no polytypic functions) — Haskell

– PolyCore Polytypic definitions (syntactic extension)

– PolyUse   Polytypic definitions in terms of definitions in PolyCore

– PolyInst Instantiating polytypic definitions on specific types

– Regular   Definitions of regular datatypes (a subset of Base)

Using a specializing compiler translating into Base we have to compile at least PolyCore, PolyUse, PolyInst and Regular. With the new PolyP we only need to compile PolyCore (and may choose to compile Regular), thus making it possible to write a library of polytypic functions, compile it into Haskell and use it just like any library of regular Haskell functions.

5   Related Work

A number of languages and tools for polytypic programming with Haskell have been described in the last few years:

– The old PolyP [8] allows user-defined polytypic definitions over regular data-types. The language for defining polytypic functions is more or less the same as in our work, however, the expressiveness of old PolyP is hampered by the fact that the specialization needs access to the entire program. Neither the old nor the new PolyP compiler supports full Haskell 98, something that severely limits the usefulness of the old version, while in the new version it is merely a minor inconvenience.

- Generic Haskell [2,5] allows polytypic definitions over Haskell datatypes of arbitrary kinds. The Generic Haskell compiler uses specialization to compile polytypic programs into Haskell, which means that it suffers from the drawbacks mentioned above, namely that we have to apply the compiler to any code that mentions polytypic functions or contains datatype definitions. This is not as serious in Generic Haskell as it is in old PolyP however, since Generic Haskell supports full Haskell 98 and has reasonably good support for separate compilation. A more significant shortcoming of Generic Haskell is that it does not allow direct access to the substructures in a datatype, so we cannot define, for instance, the function *children* :: $t \rightarrow [t]$ that takes an element of a datatype and returns the list of its immediate children. Generic Haskell only allows definitions of polytypic functions over arbitrary kinds, even if a function is only intended for a single kind. This sometimes makes it rather difficult to come up with the right definition for a polytypic function.
- Derivable type classes [6] is an extension of the Glasgow Haskell Compiler (ghc) which allows limited polytypic definitions. The user can define polytypic default methods for a class by giving cases for sums, products and the singleton type. To make a datatype an instance of a class with polytypic default methods it suffices to give an empty instance declaration. Nevertheless this requires the user to write an empty instance declaration for each polytypic function-datatype pair while we only require a FunctorOf-instance for each datatype. Furthermore the derivable type classes extension only allows a limited form of polytypic functions over kind $\star$, as opposed to kind $\star \rightarrow \star$ in PolyP. Only allowing polytypic functions over datatypes of kind $\star$ excludes many interesting functions, such as *pmap*, and since a datatype of kind $\star$ can always be transformed into a datatype of kind $\star \rightarrow \star$ (by adding a dummy argument) we argue that our approach is preferable. A similar extension to derivable type classes, exists also for Clean [1].
- The DrIFT preprocessor for deriving non-standard Haskell classes has been used together with the Strafunski library [12] to provide generic programming in Haskell. The library defines combinators for defining generic traversal and generic queries on datatypes of kind $\star$. A generic traversal is a function of type $t \rightarrow m\ t$ for some monad m and a generic query on t has type $t \rightarrow a$. The library does not support functions of any other form, such as unfolds or polytypic equality.
  The Strafunski implementation relies on a universal term representation, and generic functions are expressed as normal Haskell functions over this representation. This means that only the Regular sublanguage has to be compiled (suitable instances to convert to and from the term representation have to be generated). This is done by the DrIFT preprocessor.
- Recently Lämmel and Peyton-Jones [11] have incorporated a version of Strafunski in ghc providing compiler support for defining generic functions. This implementation has the advantage that the appropriate instances can be derived by the compiler, only requiring the user to write a deriving-clause for each of her datatypes. Support has been added for unfolds and so called twin

transformations (of type $t \to t \to m\ t$) which enables for instance, polytypic read, equality and zip functions. Still, only datatypes of kind $\star$ is handled, so we cannot get access to the parameters of a datatype.

- Sheard [15] describes how to use two-level types to implement efficient generic unification. His ideas, to separate the structure of a datatype (the pattern functor) from the actual recursion, are quite similar to those used in PolyP, although he lacks the automated support provided by the PolyP compiler. In fact, the functions that Sheard requires over the structure of a datatype can all be defined in PolyP.

Other implementations of functional polytypism include Charity [3], FISh [10] and G'Caml [4] but in this paper we focus on the Haskell-based languages.

6 Conclusions

In this paper we have shown how to bring polytypic programming inside Haskell, by taking advantage of the class system. To accomplish this we introduced datatype constructors for modeling the top level structure of a datatype, together with a multi-parameter type class FunctorOf relating datatypes to their top level structure.

Using this framework we have been able to rephrase the PolyLib library [9] as a Haskell library as well as define new polytypic functions such as *coerce* that converts between two datatypes of the same shape and the *transpose* function that commutes a composition of two datatypes, converting, for instance, a list of trees to a tree of lists.

To aid in the definition of polytypic functions we have a compiler that translates custom polytypic definitions to Haskell classes and instances. The same compiler can generate instances of FunctorOf for regular datatypes, but the framework also allows the programmer to provide tailor made FunctorOf instances, thus extending the applicability of the polytypic functions to datatypes that are not necessarily regular.

One area of future work that we have started exploring, is to use Template Haskell [16] to internalize the PolyP compiler as a ghc extension. Other research directions are to extend our approach to more datatypes (partially explored in [14]), or to explore in more detail which polytypic functions are expressible in this setting. It would also be interesting to measure the efficiency of the polytypic functions in this approach compared to the specialized code of previous methods.

References

1. A. Alimarine and R. Plasmeijer. A generic programming extension for Clean. In T. Arts and M. Mohnen, editors, *Proceedings of the 13th International Workshop on the Implementation of Functional Languages, IFL 2001*, volume 2312 of *LNCS*, pages 168–185. Springer-Verlag, 2001.

2. D. Clarke and A. Löh. Generic haskell, specifically. In J. Gibbons and J. Jeuring, editors, *Proceedings of the IFIP TC2 Working Conference on Generic Programming*, pages 21–48. Kluwer, 2003.

3. R. Cockett and T. Fukushima. About Charity. Yellow Series Report No. 92/480/18, Dep. of Computer Science, Univ. of Calgary, 1992.

4. J. Furuse. Generic polymorphism in ML. In *Journées Francophones des Langages Applicatifs*, 2001.

5. R. Hinze and J. Jeuring. Generic Haskell: practice and theory. In *Generic Programming, Advanced Lectures*, volume 2793 of *LNCS*, pages 1–56. Springer-Verlag, 2003.

6. R. Hinze and S. Peyton Jones. Derivable type classes. In G. Hutton, editor, *Proceedings of the 2000 ACM SIGPLAN Haskell Workshop*, volume 41.1 of Electronic Notes in Theoretical Computer Science. Elsevier Science, 2001.

7. P. Jansson. The WWW home page for polytypic programming. Available from `http://www.cs.chalmers.se/~patrikj/poly/`, 2003.

8. P. Jansson and J. Jeuring. PolyP — a polytypic programming language extension. In *POPL'97*, pages 470–482. ACM Press, 1997.

9. P. Jansson and J. Jeuring. PolyLib – a polytypic function library. Workshop on Generic Programming, Marstrand, June 1998. Available from the Polytypic programming WWW page [7].

10. C. Jay and P. Steckler. The functional imperative: shape! In C. Hankin, editor, *Programming languages and systems: 7th European Symposium on Programming, ESOP'98*, volume 1381 of *LNCS*, pages 139–53. Springer-Verlag, 1998.

11. R. Lämmel and S. Peyton Jones. Scrap your boilerplate: a practical design pattern for generic programming. *SIGPLAN Not.*, 38(3):26–37, 2003.

12. R. Lämmel and J. Visser. Typed Combinators for Generic Traversal. In *Proc. Practical Aspects of Declarative Programming PADL 2002*, volume 2257 of *LNCS*, pages 137–154. Springer-Verlag, Jan. 2002.

13. R. Lämmel and J. Visser. Typed Combinators for Generic Traversal. In Proc. Practical Aspects of Declarative Programming PADL 2002, volume 2257 of LNCS, pages 137–154. Springer-Verlag, Jan. 2002.

14. U. Norell. Functional generic programming and type theory. Master's thesis, Computing Science, Chalmers University of Technology, 2002. Available from `http://www.cs.chalmers.se/~ulfn`.

15. T. Sheard. Generic unification via Two-Level types and parameterized modules. In *ICFP'01*, pages 86–97, 2001.

16. T. Sheard and S. P. Jones. Template meta-programming for Haskell. In *Proceedings of the Haskell workshop*, pages 1–16. ACM Press, 2002.

Author Index

Achten, Peter   152

Berthold, Jost   102

Chakravarty, Manuel M.T.   20
Chitil, Olaf   1
Choppella, Venkatesh   53

Grelck, Clemens   118

Hammond, Kevin   86

Jansson, Patrik   168

Martínez, Rafael   135
McNeill, Dan   1

Norell, Ulf   168

Pang, André T.H.   20
Peña, Ricardo   69, 135
Plasmeijer, Rinus   36, 152

Runciman, Colin   1

Scholz, Sven-Bodo   118
Segura, Clara   69

Trojahner, Kai   118

van Eekelen, Marko   152
van Weelden, Arjen   36
Vasconcelos, Pedro B.   86

Lecture Notes in Computer Science

For information about Vols. 1–3198

please contact your bookseller or Springer

Vol. 3305: P.M.A. Sloot, B. Chopard, A.G. Hoekstra (Eds.), Cellular Automata. XV, 883 pages. 2004.

Vol. 3302: W.-N. Chin (Ed.), Programming Languages and Systems. XIII, 453 pages. 2004.

Vol. 3299: F. Wang (Ed.), Automated Technology for Verification and Analysis. XII, 506 pages. 2004.

Vol. 3294: C.N. Dean, R.T. Boute (Eds.), Teaching Formal Methods. X, 249 pages. 2004.

Vol. 3293: C.-H. Chi, M. van Steen, C. Wills (Eds.), Web Content Caching and Distribution. IX, 283 pages. 2004.

Vol. 3292: R. Meersman, Z. Tari, A. Corsaro (Eds.), On the Move to Meaningful Internet Systems 2004: OTM 2004 Workshops. XXIII, 885 pages. 2004.

Vol. 3291: R. Meersman, Z. Tari (Eds.), On the Move to Meaningful Internet Systems 2004: CoopIS, DOA, and ODBASE. XXV, 824 pages. 2004.

Vol. 3290: R. Meersman, Z. Tari (Eds.), On the Move to Meaningful Internet Systems 2004: CoopIS, DOA, and ODBASE. XXV, 823 pages. 2004.

Vol. 3289: S. Wang, K. Tanaka, S. Zhou, T.W. Ling, J. Guan, D. Yang, F. Grandi, E. Mangina, I.-Y. Song, H.C. Mayr (Eds.), Conceptual Modeling for Advanced Application Domains. XXII, 692 pages. 2004.

Vol. 3288: P. Atzeni, W. Chu, H. Lu, S. Zhou, T.W. Ling (Eds.), Conceptual Modeling – ER 2004. XXI, 869 pages. 2004.

Vol. 3287: A. Sanfeliu, J.F.M. Trinidad, J.A. Carrasco Ochoa (Eds.), Progress in Pattern Recognition, Image Analysis and Applications. XVII, 703 pages. 2004.

Vol. 3286: G. Karsai, E. Visser (Eds.), Generative Programming and Component Engineering. XIII, 491 pages. 2004.

Vol. 3284: A. Karmouch, L. Korba, E.R.M. Madeira (Eds.), Mobility Aware Technologies and Applications. XII, 382 pages. 2004.

Vol. 3281: T. Dingsøyr (Ed.), Software Process Improvement. X, 207 pages. 2004.

Vol. 3280: C. Aykanat, T. Dayar, İ. Körpeoğlu (Eds.), Computer and Information Sciences - ISCIS 2004. XVIII, 1009 pages. 2004.

Vol. 3278: A. Sahai, F. Wu (Eds.), Utility Computing. XI, 272 pages. 2004.

Vol. 3274: R. Guerraoui (Ed.), Distributed Computing. XIII, 465 pages. 2004.

Vol. 3273: T. Baar, A. Strohmeier, A. Moreira, S.J. Mellor (Eds.), <<UML>> 2004 - The Unified Modelling Language. XIII, 454 pages. 2004.

Vol. 3271: J. Vicente, D. Hutchison (Eds.), Management of Multimedia Networks and Services. XIII, 335 pages. 2004.

Vol. 3270: M. Jeckle, R. Kowalczyk, P. Braun (Eds.), Grid Services Engineering and Management. X, 165 pages. 2004.

Vol. 3269: J. Lopez, S. Qing, E. Okamoto (Eds.), Information and Communications Security. XI, 564 pages. 2004.

Vol. 3266: J. Solé-Pareta, M. Smirnov, P.V. Mieghem, J. Domingo-Pascual, E. Monteiro, P. Reichl, B. Stiller, R.J. Gibbens (Eds.), Quality of Service in the Emerging Networking Panorama. XVI, 390 pages. 2004.

Vol. 3265: R.E. Frederking, K.B. Taylor (Eds.), Machine Translation: From Real Users to Research. XI, 392 pages. 2004. (Subseries LNAI).

Vol. 3264: G. Paliouras, Y. Sakakibara (Eds.), Grammatical Inference: Algorithms and Applications. XI, 291 pages. 2004. (Subseries LNAI).

Vol. 3263: M. Weske, P. Liggesmeyer (Eds.), Object-Oriented and Internet-Based Technologies. XII, 239 pages. 2004.

Vol. 3262: M.M. Freire, P. Chemouil, P. Lorenz, A. Gravey (Eds.), Universal Multiservice Networks. XIII, 556 pages. 2004.

Vol. 3261: T. Yakhno (Ed.), Advances in Information Systems. XIV, 617 pages. 2004.

Vol. 3260: I.G.M.M. Niemegeers, S.H. de Groot (Eds.), Personal Wireless Communications. XIV, 478 pages. 2004.

Vol. 3258: M. Wallace (Ed.), Principles and Practice of Constraint Programming – CP 2004. XVII, 822 pages. 2004.

Vol. 3257: E. Motta, N.R. Shadbolt, A. Stutt, N. Gibbins (Eds.), Engineering Knowledge in the Age of the Semantic Web. XVII, 517 pages. 2004. (Subseries LNAI).

Vol. 3256: H. Ehrig, G. Engels, F. Parisi-Presicce, G. Rozenberg (Eds.), Graph Transformations. XII, 451 pages. 2004.

Vol. 3255: A. Benczúr, J. Demetrovics, G. Gottlob (Eds.), Advances in Databases and Information Systems. XI, 423 pages. 2004.

Vol. 3254: E. Macii, V. Paliouras, O. Koufopavlou (Eds.), Integrated Circuit and System Design. XVI, 910 pages. 2004.

Vol. 3253: Y. Lakhnech, S. Yovine (Eds.), Formal Techniques, Modelling and Analysis of Timed and Fault-Tolerant Systems. X, 397 pages. 2004.

Vol. 3252: H. Jin, Y. Pan, N. Xiao, J. Sun (Eds.), Grid and Cooperative Computing - GCC 2004 Workshops. XVIII, 785 pages. 2004.

Vol. 3251: H. Jin, Y. Pan, N. Xiao, J. Sun (Eds.), Grid and Cooperative Computing - GCC 2004. XXII, 1025 pages. 2004.

Vol. 3250: L.-J. (LJ) Zhang, M. Jeckle (Eds.), Web Services. X, 301 pages. 2004.

Vol. 3249: B. Buchberger, J.A. Campbell (Eds.), Artificial Intelligence and Symbolic Computation. X, 285 pages. 2004. (Subseries LNAI).

Vol. 3246: A. Apostolico, M. Melucci (Eds.), String Processing and Information Retrieval. XIV, 332 pages. 2004.

Vol. 3245: E. Suzuki, S. Arikawa (Eds.), Discovery Science. XIV, 430 pages. 2004. (Subseries LNAI).

Vol. 3244: S. Ben-David, J. Case, A. Maruoka (Eds.), Algorithmic Learning Theory. XIV, 505 pages. 2004. (Subseries LNAI).

Vol. 3243: S. Leonardi (Ed.), Algorithms and Models for the Web-Graph. VIII, 189 pages. 2004.

Vol. 3242: X. Yao, E. Burke, J.A. Lozano, J. Smith, J.J. Merelo-Guervós, J.A. Bullinaria, J. Rowe, P. Tiño, A. Kabán, H.-P. Schwefel (Eds.), Parallel Problem Solving from Nature - PPSN VIII. XX, 1185 pages. 2004.

Vol. 3241: D. Kranzlmüller, P. Kacsuk, J.J. Dongarra (Eds.), Recent Advances in Parallel Virtual Machine and Message Passing Interface. XIII, 452 pages. 2004.

Vol. 3240: I. Jonassen, J. Kim (Eds.), Algorithms in Bioinformatics. IX, 476 pages. 2004. (Subseries LNBI).

Vol. 3239: G. Nicosia, V. Cutello, P.J. Bentley, J. Timmis (Eds.), Artificial Immune Systems. XII, 444 pages. 2004.

Vol. 3238: S. Biundo, T. Frühwirth, G. Palm (Eds.), KI 2004: Advances in Artificial Intelligence. XI, 467 pages. 2004. (Subseries LNAI).

Vol. 3236: M. Núñez, Z. Maamar, F.L. Pelayo, K. Pousttchi, F. Rubio (Eds.), Applying Formal Methods: Testing, Performance, and M/E-Commerce. XI, 381 pages. 2004.

Vol. 3235: D. de Frutos-Escrig, M. Nunez (Eds.), Formal Techniques for Networked and Distributed Systems – FORTE 2004. X, 377 pages. 2004.

Vol. 3234: M.J. Egenhofer, C. Freksa, H.J. Miller (Eds.), Geographic Information Science. VIII, 345 pages. 2004.

Vol. 3232: R. Heery, L. Lyon (Eds.), Research and Advanced Technology for Digital Libraries. XV, 528 pages. 2004.

Vol. 3231: H.-A. Jacobsen (Ed.), Middleware 2004. XV, 514 pages. 2004.

Vol. 3230: J.L. Vicedo, P. Martínez-Barco, R. Muñoz, M. Saiz Noeda (Eds.), Advances in Natural Language Processing. XII, 488 pages. 2004. (Subseries LNAI).

Vol. 3229: J.J. Alferes, J. Leite (Eds.), Logics in Artificial Intelligence. XIV, 744 pages. 2004. (Subseries LNAI).

Vol. 3226: M. Bouzeghoub, C. Goble, V. Kashyap, S. Spaccapietra (Eds.), Semantics of a Networked World. XIII, 326 pages. 2004.

Vol. 3225: K. Zhang, Y. Zheng (Eds.), Information Security. XII, 442 pages. 2004.

Vol. 3224: E. Jonsson, A. Valdes, M. Almgren (Eds.), Recent Advances in Intrusion Detection. XII, 315 pages. 2004.

Vol. 3223: K. Slind, A. Bunker, G. Gopalakrishnan (Eds.), Theorem Proving in Higher Order Logics. VIII, 337 pages. 2004.

Vol. 3222: H. Jin, G.R. Gao, Z. Xu, H. Chen (Eds.), Network and Parallel Computing. XX, 694 pages. 2004.

Vol. 3221: S. Albers, T. Radzik (Eds.), Algorithms – ESA 2004. XVIII, 836 pages. 2004.

Vol. 3220: J.C. Lester, R.M. Vicari, F. Paraguaçu (Eds.), Intelligent Tutoring Systems. XXI, 920 pages. 2004.

Vol. 3219: M. Heisel, P. Liggesmeyer, S. Wittmann (Eds.), Computer Safety, Reliability, and Security. XI, 339 pages. 2004.

Vol. 3217: C. Barillot, D.R. Haynor, P. Hellier (Eds.), Medical Image Computing and Computer-Assisted Intervention – MICCAI 2004. XXXVIII, 1114 pages. 2004.

Vol. 3216: C. Barillot, D.R. Haynor, P. Hellier (Eds.), Medical Image Computing and Computer-Assisted Intervention – MICCAI 2004. XXXVIII, 930 pages. 2004.

Vol. 3215: M.G.. Negoita, R.J. Howlett, L.C. Jain (Eds.), Knowledge-Based Intelligent Information and Engineering Systems. LVII, 906 pages. 2004. (Subseries LNAI).

Vol. 3214: M.G.. Negoita, R.J. Howlett, L.C. Jain (Eds.), Knowledge-Based Intelligent Information and Engineering Systems. LVIII, 1302 pages. 2004. (Subseries LNAI).

Vol. 3213: M.G.. Negoita, R.J. Howlett, L.C. Jain (Eds.), Knowledge-Based Intelligent Information and Engineering Systems. LVIII, 1280 pages. 2004. (Subseries LNAI).

Vol. 3212: A. Campilho, M. Kamel (Eds.), Image Analysis and Recognition. XXIX, 862 pages. 2004.

Vol. 3211: A. Campilho, M. Kamel (Eds.), Image Analysis and Recognition. XXIX, 880 pages. 2004.

Vol. 3210: J. Marcinkowski, A. Tarlecki (Eds.), Computer Science Logic. XI, 520 pages. 2004.

Vol. 3209: B. Berendt, A. Hotho, D. Mladenic, M. van Someren, M. Spiliopoulou, G. Stumme (Eds.), Web Mining: From Web to Semantic Web. IX, 201 pages. 2004. (Subseries LNAI).

Vol. 3208: H.J. Ohlbach, S. Schaffert (Eds.), Principles and Practice of Semantic Web Reasoning. VII, 165 pages. 2004.

Vol. 3207: L.T. Yang, M. Guo, G.R. Gao, N.K. Jha (Eds.), Embedded and Ubiquitous Computing. XX, 1116 pages. 2004.

Vol. 3206: P. Sojka, I. Kopecek, K. Pala (Eds.), Text, Speech and Dialogue. XIII, 667 pages. 2004. (Subseries LNAI).

Vol. 3205: N. Davies, E. Mynatt, I. Siio (Eds.), UbiComp 2004: Ubiquitous Computing. XVI, 452 pages. 2004.

Vol. 3204: C.A. Peña Reyes, Coevolutionary Fuzzy Modeling. XIII, 129 pages. 2004.

Vol. 3203: J. Becker, M. Platzner, S. Vernalde (Eds.), Field Programmable Logic and Application. XXX, 1198 pages. 2004.

Vol. 3202: J.-F. Boulicaut, F. Esposito, F. Giannotti, D. Pedreschi (Eds.), Knowledge Discovery in Databases: PKDD 2004. XIX, 560 pages. 2004. (Subseries LNAI).

Vol. 3201: J.-F. Boulicaut, F. Esposito, F. Giannotti, D. Pedreschi (Eds.), Machine Learning: ECML 2004. XVIII, 580 pages. 2004. (Subseries LNAI).

Vol. 3199: H. Schepers (Ed.), Software and Compilers for Embedded Systems. X, 259 pages. 2004.